Eastern Left, Western Left

Eastern Left, Western Left

Totalitarianism, Freedom and Democracy

Ferenc Fehér and Agnes Heller

HUMANITIES PRESS INTERNATIONAL, INC.
Atlantic Highlands, NJ

First published in 1987 in the United States of America by
HUMANITIES PRESS INTERNATIONAL, INC., Atlantic Highlands, NJ 07716

© Ferenc Fehér and Agnes Heller, 1987

Library of Congress Cataloging-in-Publication Data
Fehér, Ferenc, 1933–
Eastern left, western left.

   1. Communist state.   2. Communist countries—
Politics and government.   3. Soviet Union—Politics
and government—1917– . 4. Europe, Eastern—
Politics and government—1945– . I. Heller,
Agnes. II. Title.
JC474.F44   1987   320.9171'7   86-20045
ISBN 0-391-03492-8   *R00582 79572*

JC
474
.F44
1987

Printed in Great Britain

Contents

1

Introduction

Ferenc Fehér and Agnes Heller

The present study has a double objective. Firstly, and most importantly, it intends to answer the questions which are inherent in its title,
within the context mainly of North America, Western and Eastern
Europe and the USSR since World War Two. These questions read as
follows: what kind of relationship exists, if any at all, between the
political forces in the 'West' and the 'East' that can be called, and call
themselves, leftist? Is there a dialogue, or even an alliance, between
them? Is this relationship characterized by a reciprocal solidarity or, on
the contrary, a lack of comprehension for each other's respective
values, interests and strategies? Does it have a political importance of
any kind that such a dialogue should exist? The replies to all these
questions seem all too easily to be self-evident. One of our primary goals
is then to show that this is by no means the case. Moreover, it is our
conviction, a conviction that shapes the method of the present study,
that there is no general answer to these questions. Both the way in
which they are raised and the answers supplied vary from period to
period in a hectic postwar history.

However, there is a deeper level at which such investigation has to be
carried out. The categories 'Left' and 'Right' with which academic
scholarship, political rhetoric and media journalism operate in 'the
West' stem, in the main, from the liberal political tradition. This very
dichotomy came about at a certain critical juncture in the history of this
tradition: at a particular period of the great French Revolution in which
a group of radical intellectuals and politicians turned deliberately
against the liberal tradition and created the Jacobin dictatorship. Ever
since, almost everyone across the political diapason uses these terms
without further consideration and critical reconsideration, with the
false presumption that they are applicable to each and every situation.
Such an extension of categories of limited content and explanatory

scope reaches an almost parodic level in certain neo-Marxist analyses – we find the labels 'Left' and 'Right' attached to African tribal wars and Middle Eastern and Asian religious conflicts. In turn, it has become political practice in these countries that indigenous political forces describe their own tendencies with the same misleading terminology in the service of correctly, and shrewdly, perceived strategic interests. It is our intention here to query this misuse and uncritical extension of certain political categories, and to show that both 'Left and 'Right' as denominations of political trends and forces change, and sometimes lose, their meaning while retaining the potential to regain and re-formulate their traditional meaning in such a way as to recover their validity as political terms.

I THE POSTWAR ENTHUSIASM AND ITS GREAT EXPECTATIONS: 1945–6

For the purposes of the present study we shall give an approximate working definition of what we mean by the term 'Left'. We believe that no unified and homogeneous definition of the term exists, for the 'Left' is the conflicting ensemble of three dimensions. The first dimension can be loosely and tentatively called the anticapitalist dimension. The formulation will become less vague if put in a negative way: there is no leftism which consciously embraces an overall capitalist organization of the economy (and wider social fields). However, the formulation necessarily becomes much more vague once it is phrased positively. For if we extend the anticapitalist dimension to the Soviet societies, we immediately face the dilemma, central to our whole analysis, that they are neither capitalist nor socialist. Therefore the anticapitalist dimension *per se* does not make sense in the context of these societies. And yet, if we analyse such substantive issues as fighting inequalities of income distribution, questioning the whole character of the techno-logical process and the command structure within the productive unit, formulating postulates of a self-management system and the like, we will find extensive similarities in the objectives of both the Western and Eastern actors of social contestation. And this remains true even if the aspirations of the latter cannot be subsumed under the heading of an 'anticapitalist dimension' pure and simple.

A second constituent is the republican dimension. The term does not refer to a simple integration of liberal principles into a leftist context.

Marx's idea of a schism between the citizen and the 'bourgeois' (in a wider sense, the egotistic private person) found surprisingly receptive partisans in theorists otherwise extremely critical of Marx. Hannah Arendt regarded the victory of the egoistic and competitive private person over the citizen as the single major catastrophe that had happened to Political Man (and Woman) in the nineteenth century. She located the roots of totalitarianism within the European political context in precisely this collapse. According to this view, the re-publican dimension of the Left is tantamount to the priority (but not the Jacobin tyranny) of free and public political activity over other types of human action. It is therefore the only basis on which a genuinely free society can be based. This definition of free activity is formal but it does not exclude, it rather invites, an anticapitalist option as well as a stance against all oppressive power structures, forms of domination, economic and political exploitation and social inequali-ties. Finally, there is a cultural dimension of the Left which cannot be defined once and for all because it changes historically, but which is, in a given context, always clearly definable. The three dimensions of the Left do not move simultaneously, nor do they necessarily create a harmonious whole. Sometimes one particular dimension, sometimes another is missing from the acts of a historical actor in the East or in the West whom observers are inclined to term 'leftist'. However, we hope that the heterogeneity of this working definition of the Left will make it possible to approach the East–West relationship more realistically than has happened up until now.

If one accepts our 'working definition', one finds in the immediate aftermath of the war a tremendous upsurge of leftist parties and mass movements in the whole of Europe up to the newly created Soviet borders, the only significant exception being the Iberian peninsula with its two surviving semi-Fascist dictatorships. The upsurge of leftist politics displayed quite unusual types of expectation among the huge masses of its following. Traditional (doctrinaire and strategic) differ-ences between its various contingents never did entirely vanish; more-over, they very soon gained the upper hand over what turned out to be a naive postwar optimism. But for a historical moment there seemed to be no difference between the ultimate ends of leftists. Hitlerism was such an 'existential shock', such a cataclysmic experience for all the feuding factions of the European Left (members of which literally became bedfellows in concentration camps) that the consciousness of a common suffering, from which common lessons should be drawn, seemed to be the overriding feeling in their ranks. In the immediate postwar enthusiasm, even the habitual 'East–West' differentiation seemed to evaporate. And there was a very good reason for this senti-ment of unity. Modern Europe had, up until Hitler, literally never lived the dark experience of being 'unified in horror' nor, for that matter, of being unified at all. Not even Napoleon's empire (which, of course, was simply not comparable to the Third Reich) had had the geographical extension of Hitler's rule, including satellites and dependent allies, between 1939 and 1942. Czechs suffered in much the same fashion, and at the hands of the same enemy, as French people did. Why should there be, then, many a leftist asked, any fundamental differences for them between newly created free institutions to guarantee to all of them that past horrors would never reappear?

In this delirium of an illusory East–West merger, important terms of European politics, above all the category of 'Central Europe', with its specific traditions, disappeared, although the disappearance of this term deprives the interpreter of a major explanatory instrument. For it seems to be clear that in a particular region within a seemingly homogeneous Soviet Empire (in Czechoslovakia, Poland and Hungary, without mentioning East Germany, which in any case needs special treatment), there are marked similarities between countries. These similarities bring them close to one another (and create a certain affinity with aspects of the Austrian situation), and at the same time, sharply distinguish them from other countries like Rumania, Bulgaria, Albania, not to mention the USSR. Briefly, these elements consist of a shared cultural tradition (despite many national diversities), an incomparably more developed civil society than can be found in any of the Eastern countries *sensu stricto*, a greater proximity to the West, and so on.

The overarching category of this projected, or rather wishfully conceived, merger of Eastern and Western Left was an apparently ultimate and irrevocable rejection of 'tyranny'. Hitlerism became identical with tyranny as such in leftist rhetoric, and since the whole of the Left had been victimized by this tyranny, for a moment it seemed inconceivable that leftists of any sort would embrace regimes with tyrannical institutions. An equally common, and equally emotional, rejection of the external violation of other nations' sovereignty, 'foreign domination' or 'conquest' of any kind also seemed to reign supreme in this atmosphere of universal fraternity. The catharsis caused by the first all-European empire contributed tremendously to a rapidly growing anti-colonialist stance among the European left. As a further feature of the postwar 'great expectations', a vague condemnation of capitalism (or 'big business') emerged, going far beyond leftist circles in the strict sense. It is extremely arguable, and seemed so to many even then, whether Hitler's predatory regime was indeed the 'supreme form of monopoly capitalism', as the famous Comintern formula put forward by Dimitrov had suggested. However, it was beyond any doubt that looting, ravaging and butchering whole countries and human groups was indeed big business (for the Nazi bosses and for German industrial and financial capital) as well as representing at least a material advantage for the German populace (in exchange, of course, for the lives of a generation of young Germans). This vague but emotional and emphatic condemnation of capitalism or 'big business' as literally sucking the blood of millions seemed to unify factions of the Left which had indulged in internecine strife for decades. Tenets of past doctrine seemed suddenly faded and irrelevant when compared to the realities of Hitler's rule.

All those who were politically active in the postwar period or who study this period in retrospect are free to point out endless numbers of facts in the period under consideration which would expose all these great expectations as so much infantile daydreaming. And yet, to dismiss these hopes as simple pipe-dreams is not only an inexcusable misreading of the cataclysmic 'Hitler experience', it also implies a total lack of comprehension of two fundamental trends of the postwar situation. True enough, both have been discarded by 'History' (or superpower empire-building) but they were then undeniably present on the political arena. The first trend was an aspiration for a 'new democracy'.[1] 'New democracy' as a political slogan was in many ways a continuation of the honest expectations characterizing the Popular Front strategy (basically, a 'Trojan horse' strategy for seizing power) but it relied on the new hopes we have delineated above. The theorists who put it forward sincerely nurtured the hope that humanity, in contrast to what Hegel's cynical wisdom suggests, could learn from 'History' and that it would indeed draw some practical conclusions from the fact that its worst nightmares had come true. The terms in which the conception of a 'new democracy' was interpreted were, indeed, inadmissibly vague. And yet, the aspiration and the political will to realize it were genuine across 'Eastern' and 'Western' Left. In addition, this same political will aimed at a rearrangement of international affairs in a manner totally different from the spirit of the Yalta–Potsdam system. It can once again be reasonably argued that

---

[1] To our knowledge, the clearest, and therefore the most transparently naive, formulation of this conception can be found in the writings of G. Lukács in 1945–6. But typically, much more sceptical democrats of non-doctrinaire leanings, such as István Bibó in Hungary, at the time used much the same terminology and expressed very similar aspirations with a nearly identical number of illusions.

people should have shown more common sense concerning the nature of agreements between the victorious great powers.[2] However, this often self-inflicted political blindness was, in the same breath, an expression of a manifest, and almost universal, will on the Left to block the path leading anew to the irrationalities and injustices of the Versailles system, out of which alone Nazism could have emerged.

However, two fundamental features of this system of benevolent self-delusion on the part of both Eastern and Western Left cannot be defended even in terms of a 'retrospective understanding'. The first was the untenable hope (without which of course the whole perspective of a 'new democracy' could not have been established) that the alliance between the victorious anti-Nazi powers could, and should, be upheld even after victory. Moreover, Eastern and Western Left alike (with the exception of the communist apparatuses which had an uneven, but nonetheless incomparably more lucid awareness of the power game behind the scenes than the rest of the Left) regarded itself as the natural mediator amidst the tensions emerging publicly between the victors immediately after victory. In this respect, European leftists missed the crucial point. The alternative to the upholding of the wartime alliance was not a new war between the victorious powers (because of a general exhaustion, the latter was a virtual impossibility), but rather a re-distribution of world power undertaken in mutual mistrust and based in a mutual, if ill-defined agreement regarding respective spheres of influence. The partitioning of the world first involved three partners. When, however, the British Empire started to disintegrate, far more rapidly than anyone had expected, the system quickly turned into a bipolar arrangement. While a war between the new superpowers was more than unlikely, a renewed alliance was positively inconceivable. They had neither a common enemy, nor any mutually binding interest as the basis for an alliance.

The second, equally indefensible, illusion of the 'Eastern' and 'Western' Left was closely tied up with the first. It was displayed by a conciliatory and moreover, almost totally uncritical stance towards the USSR, a stance which harboured hopes of a 'radical change' in the regime once it was no longer surrounded by a threatening *cordon sanitaire*. A statement like this, of course, needs immediate qualifica-

---

[2] It is a fact though, amply demonstrated by F. Fejtö, among others, in his *A History of the Peoples' Democracies*, New York: Praeger, 1971, and in a more detailed manner using the example of the Czechoslovak coup in his *Le coup de Prague, 1948*, Paris: Seuil, 1976, that often even the communist apparatuses, hand-picked to be the local repositories of the central Soviet power, remained ignorant (for a while) as to the genuine role they were supposed to play in Stalin's plans.

tion. Not only did social democrats, Trotskyites and independent socialists of different kinds never forget the lessons of the twenties and thirties regarding communist politics, but there were, in addition, particular areas[3] where the conflicts between communists and other leftists resumed with unbroken vigour. And yet, an attitude of un-critical reconciliation was overwhelmingly predominant and for different reasons. Very often it was triggered by fear pure and simple. In the regions under Soviet occupation even leftists, with a clear memory of the Bolshevik terror, and perhaps precisely because of this memory, tried desperately to find some *modus vivendi* with Stalin's Russia as it emerged as an invincible world power after 1945. Other groups of the Left in other areas credited Stalin's system with the triumph over Nazism, although they did not have the slightest penchant for a totalitarian order. A third, and perhaps the most important factor in the (Eastern and Western) Left's uncritical attitude to the USSR can be located in its assumed and entirely illusory mediating role in resurrecting the impossible alliance of the victors. Much as this was a complete pipe-dream, if the left was to take its own strategic recom-mendation for a continuing alliance seriously, it had to display at least as much tact and caution as Churchill had done in handling his dangerous ally.

Up until this point, we have, for different reasons, deliberately omitted both the USSR and the United States from the analysis of the regions of 'Western' and 'Eastern' Left. As far as the Soviet Union is concerned, we have tried to show elsewhere[4] that Soviet society is neither capitalist nor socialist in any interpretable sense of these terms, and that therefore the distinction between 'Left' and 'Right' makes no sense at all in the officially tolerated political and cultural space. Two qualifications are necessary here. The party apparatus in power has constantly distinguished both 'rightist' and 'leftist' 'deviations' from the correct (that is, victorious) Party line. While the use of these terms has always remained sufficiently confused, initially, at least, they carried the sincere conviction of the first Bolshevik generations, who identified their own regime with socialism and saw everything to the right of them as threatening a new 'Thermidor' or relapse into capitalism. Later on, the distinction became one of the easily manipulable tools of power

---

[3] The most important example of such immediate postwar clashes is that of the resolute rejection of the German social democrats, under Schumacher's leadership, of what they regarded as Soviet imperialism. We have analysed this position in our *Eastern Europe under the Shadow of a New Rapallo*, Cologne: Index, 1985.

[4] F. Fehér, A. Heller and G. Markus: *Dictatorship Over Needs*, Oxford: Basil Blackwell, 1983.

technology. Secondly, the immediate postwar opposition to the Soviet regime, which emerged quite powerfully at the base but only sporadically at the top, could not help but be rightist in a very genuine sense of the word. At the base there was a protracted armed resistance against the reimposition of the Soviet regime in 'liberated' areas, above all in the Baltic states and in the Ukraine where Stalin's satraps, like Suslov, the 'hangman of Lithuania', for example, ruled with methods no better than those of Hitler's satraps, Hans Franck in the Polish 'Protectorate' or those of Rosenberg, the plenipotentiary of the so-called 'occupied Eastern territories'. The local guerrilla armies had often started their anti-Soviet crusade in open alliance with the Nazis (an alliance which was sometimes dissolved, as in the case of so many Ukranian nationalists who took Ukranian independence too seriously for German liking, but which sometimes remained in force, as with the Vlasovites). However, even without such an alliance, due to the fact that not even liberal conservatives in the West found it possible to offer them even nominal moral support, they became fanatically rightist to the extent that they had ideologies at all.[5]

As far as the sporadic emergence of an opposition at the top is concerned, we are indebted to Khrushchev for a symbolic story which has been preserved by his good, albeit arbitrarily selective, memory, even if he himself, due to his lack of culture, did not grasp its meaning. On the basis of circulating party gossip, he describes the trial of the 'Leningrad opposition' in 1949, the fate of the top *apparatchiks* who had allegedly wanted a measure of liberalization in the wake of the resounding victory guaranteeing the security of the Soviet state, and who were duly sent to the execution chambers. One of the main accused, Voznesensky, half a year earlier a rising star and the economic wizard in Stalin's entourage, burst out in fury against 'Leningrad, this city of Biron's and Zinoviev's' when he was 'sentenced' to death.[6] The message, although incomprehensible for Khrushchev, is clear enough. The curse against the omnipotent German minister of a Tzarina, and against the omnipotent Jewish apparatchik of Lenin was a curse against

---

[5] The chronicle of this armed anti-Soviet resistance is an extremely complex, bloody, filthy and in many aspects tragic story which has not yet found its proper historian. The only vaguely comparable events in modern history are the Spanish *guerilla* against the *Grande Armée*, with its mixture of legitimate national grievances, ruthless religious fanaticism and total disregard for the life of a captured enemy, or the *chouannerie* as described by Balzac. The social and national causes fuelling the wrath of the partisans of Bandera and several similar chieftains are clear enough. Equally clear and undeniable are, however, the bestial deeds they committed, above all against the persecuted Jews, that main target of Hitlerism.

[6] *Khrushchev Remembers*. Introduction, commentary and notes by Edward Crankshaw. Translated and edited by Strobe Talbott, Boston: Little, Brown and Co., 1970, p. 257.

Petrograd, and its 'foreign rulers' in the same breath. When Russian political opposition re-emerged, after a 30-year hiatus, and, ironically, on the threshold of the execution chamber, it immediately revoked not only Lenin's revolution or Plekhanov's social democratic reformism but also the idea of Russian Westernism, to return to the most reactionary version of Slavophile ideology.

It would be out of place here to try to account for the absence of leftist mass movements in the United States (and in addition, we do not have the competence for any such detailed history). In the present study, we can only draw certain conclusions from the much analysed fact that the United States of America started its existence without a feudal prehistory and an absolutist state. The fact that *ab urbe condita* there has constantly been a liberal state in America, had at least the following consequences for leftist mass movements. The country has almost never known a mentionable romantic anticapitalism of any kind as a large-scale movement, nor did any feudal or paternalist forms of socialism emerge. With the exception of the communists, no group of the American Left that deserves mention has had a political alternative to the existing liberal state, however much they have attacked its inconsistencies or 'sham-liberal' character. Anticapitalist feeling, although at times quite widespread, has therefore never found an adequate political channel of articulation, particularly in the period under investigation. Leftists of different kinds linked their political destinies with the New Deal (despite the fact that Roosevelt's reformed state was much less benevolent towards radicals than popular legends have it). In 1945–6, the American intellectual Left, anyway numerically weak, was living its most bitter hour. This was the time of the dismantling of the New Deal apparatus, and the first sign of a gathering storm which was to make the Left scapegoats for Roosevelt's strategic miscalculations concerning Russia. They therefore could not play any significant role in this period of 'great expectations'.

In short, there were two distinct contingents of the European Left in the period immediately following World War Two, a 'Western' and an 'Eastern', with different traditions and options but with the hope of a coming merger. Although the perspectives inherent in and expressed through this hope were more than mere pipe-dreams, their interaction never went beyond the level of the symbolic. However, this symbolic European leftist interaction, although doomed by superpower politics, established perspectives which are still not on the actual agenda but which have until now continued to shape the leftist imagination.

II FROM THE BEGINNINGS OF THE COLD WAR TO STALIN'S DEATH

We do not intend to sit in judgement on the feuding superpowers to establish their 'primary responsibility' for creating the dark era of the Cold War. The best account of the period can be read in A. Fontaine's excellent book[7] from which we can learn, if we had any doubts to that effect, that its deepest cause was the aspiration of two equally expansive 'imperial' systems to rearrange the map of the world. The effect was, particularly as far as the 'Eastern' and 'Western' Left was concerned, a total and rapid collapse of all their immediate postwar hopes and the mandatory need for a redefinition of their seemingly transparent concepts of the 'Left' and the 'Right'.

To begin with, in the West the short-term, always conditional, never formalized and increasingly conflict-ridden unity of the Left created by the 'Hitler experience' drew to its swift and dramatic end. The communist parties saw a very simple semantic task ahead of them. In their redefinition, the 'Left' again became identical, as it had been before the war, with the USSR (expanded by the apparatuses of the newly created East European states) and with all West European parties, groups and individual actors who supported the USSR unconditionally.[8] The social democrats, the independent socialists, and certain smaller oppositional Marxist groups (above all the Trotskyites) had an incomparably more difficult task of definition. They had no doubts, and here we speak mainly of social democrats and labourites, as to the threatening character of Eastern totalitarianism. At the same time, they had hardly any theory in terms of which they could have labelled it 'rightist'.[9] The postwar social democratic theory dismissed the Eastern bloc as a no man's land from the viewpoint of the Left much as they had done earlier with Germany under Hitler's rule. In the mainstream of the Western Left, the 'great expectations' of the aftermath of

---

[7] André Fontaine, *L'histoire de la guerre froide*, Paris: Fayard, 1965–6.

[8] Semantic difficulties only arose when an otherwise unmistakably monolithic communist apparatus like that of Yugoslavia broke relations with the Eastern bloc. From the communist viewpoint it immediately became a 'rightist' force, but communist theorists remained, for very good reasons, quite reluctant to provide a sociological explanation of this overnight change.

[9] It shows that poverty of Trotskyite theory that Trotskyites have ever since insisted on the antiquated, and even initially very questionable, terminology of the Stalin–Trotsky rupture. The Trotskyites regarded themselves then as 'leftist' and the Bukharin–Stalin coalition as 'rightist' in the sense of an allegedly imminent Thermidor, the supposed restoration of capitalism.

the war gave way to a deep resignation. The terrain to be used for leftist strategies, which had seemed to be almost endless in 1945 and 1946, shrank to a very limited region of Western Europe.

In the nucleus of the East, the USSR (where at that particular time there was almost no visible opposition and where, in so far as it did sporadically appear, it was, as we have seen, far from being leftist), Stalin's apparatus smoothly manipulated the terms 'Left' and 'Right' for its own tactical purposes. Although in the simplifying mirror of 'Marxism–Leninism' things seemed to be pretty straightforward, a certain awkwardness came to the fore. In principle, Stalin's apparatus kept operating with the binary categories of 'Left' and 'Right', a distinction which had already had a most questionable status at the very beginning in Lenin's polemics. Again in principle, the *apparatchiks* never gave up the option of terming certain 'deviations', or types of opposition, 'leftist'.[10] But there were very deep roots in their mythology (in this 'most scientific approach to social problems') which caused them to prefer the 'rightist' to the 'leftist' label. Namely, the 'Left' was incarnated in them, its cause was identical with their 'socialism', whereas everyone who was, potentially or actually, critical of them had to be 'objectively' promoting the restoration of capitalism. In that sense, the critic had to be a 'rightist'.[11]

A somewhat more complex situation was presented by the case of Eastern Europe. The seizure of power by the communist parties was gradually completed in a manner and rhythm varying from country to country between 1945 and 1948. In this period, the communist apparatuses behaved as they were ordered to by the centre. They had just as few semantic problems in redefining the 'Left' as their Western confrères. The non-communist Left, in countries where the mercy of history granted it an at least short-term existence, hung onto the shabby vestiges of its postwar hopes. Its politicians persisted for a while in terming the communists 'Left' while being gradually absorbed by them, and waited for the miracle that the immediate postwar rapprochement of the Left would be maintained.[12] Many a representative of the

[10] In the first Cominform document on the 'Yugoslav affair' the Titoist leadership was called 'leftist' and 'rightist' deviationist, to be promoted soon after to the rank of a paid agency of the Gestapo and the CIA. Later Khrushchev made some efforts, abandoned by his successors, to term the Maoist leadership 'leftist' deviationist.

[11] A very important pragmatic requirement followed from this myth for the Stalinist leaders: they could not tolerate competition on their 'Left', only on their 'Right'. Mlynář describes Novotny's shrewd advice to his followers never to have an opposition on their 'Left' but always on their 'Right', in Z. Mlynář, *Night Frost in Prague*, London: Hurst and Co., 1980, p. 67.

[12] A historical document, I. Bibó's article from 1947, 'The Crisis of Democracy' in *A harmadik út* (*The Third Road*) London: Magyar Könyves Céh, 1960 (which was,

so-called 'realist school' of historiography regards these gestures as so many acts of pusillanimity. No doubt, this obedient march to the execution chambers was full of humiliating scenes in which actors who were two steps from the gallows tried to convince themselves that the executioner, 'seen from a proper perspective', was their best ally. And if it is at all permissible to make reprimands to victims, it has to be stated of several non-Marxist leftist victims of East European Stalinism that they had surrendered the only weapon which could have weakened the position of their antagonists: the alliance with similar non-communist leftist forces across national borders. However, there was a realistic socio-psychological assumption behind this attitude which bore long-term fruits. The wisest intellects of the East European non-Marxist Left had a historical perspective of the meteoric rise of East European communism. They understood perfectly that political parties which had been minuscule groups in prewar times in all countries of the region, (the only exception being liberal Czechoslovakia) owed their rise to two factors. Firstly, and overwhelmingly, it was due to the unchallenged predominance of the communist superpower in the region, but there was also another factor. In the power vacuum created by the capitulation of almost all the traditional parties in the area in the face of Hitlerism, a capitulation which had many different forms but which was almost total,[13] the communists gained a broad and swiftly increasing following, not just as a premium for their traditional resoluteness in armed resistance but also by virtue of their manipulative self-identification with the cause of democracy. If the latter assumption were true, certain tactically-minded leftists contended, if millions joined communism because they identified it with 'the cause of freedom' (which is most understandable given the miserable prewar and wartime reality of Eastern Europe), then these millions could be influenced by arguments not to relinquish the relative freedom they had gained with the collapse of Hitlerism. In the short term, this hope proved to be totally futile. Its apostles were buried under the debris of the 'demolition job' of the governments of terror. However, considering processes in the *longue durée*, it is difficult to imagine where the actors of the East European 'thaw' could have come from if it had not been for those who had in fact joined communism for

---

ironically, and not at all to his glory, attacked, but not refuted by G. Lukács) is the best manifestation of these frantic efforts.

[13] In an interesting study, George Schöpflin analyses this power vacuum in Eastern Europe as one of the major causes of a swift and effortless communist victory. See his paper 'A kommunista hatalomátvétel fázisai Kelet-Európában' ('Phases of the Communist Seizure of Power in Eastern Europe'), *Magyar Füzetek*, Paris, 1984, n. 13.

freedom and who must have been influenced to a degree, at least in their 'political subconscious', by the arguments of those pusillanimous democratic leftists.

But by 1949, the darkness was complete. The relationship of the 'Eastern' Left (if there was still any force which deserved that name) to the 'Western' Left reached its absolute nadir. Communists in the West acclaimed the physical elimination of huge traditionally leftist parties enthusiastically and often unconditionally as a 'triumph of socialism', in spite of the fact that the latter embodied the only possibility of a leftist perspective without armed Soviet supervision. Western social democrats were fully aware of the Eastern catastrophe but they had no means, either theoretical or practical, of influencing the fatal course of events. Therefore they turned away from this truly abominable sight as from a homogeneously reactionary world. The Eastern communist apparatuses played their tactical games by terming occasional allies 'leftist', possible critics 'rightist' and often creating, not just designating, rightist forces by virtue of the fairly general outrage and repulsion in which their regimes were enveloped in the West. Genuine East European leftists, the dispersed survivors of a once existing political alternative, now hiding in the niches of history, inevitably lost their sense of orientation. As a result of the horrific reality in which they had to live, people who had been clearly aware of the genuine physiognomy of capitalism lost or deliberately blunted their critical edge against it. They embraced the West as a homogeneously free world as a reaction against the total loss of freedom which was their everyday lot. For them, any distinction in the West between 'Left' and 'Right' was either communist demagogy or a sterile terminological exercise when compared to the naked brutality and inhumanity of the conditions of their own lives. Very few of them could retain even the 'republican dimension' of leftist thought. Theoretical capitulation in front of liberalism pure and simple was, and had to be, a general feature of their ranks. By the time Stalin died, 'Eastern' and 'Western' leftist interaction no longer existed, nor, for that matter, did an 'Eastern Left' worthy of that name.

III FROM STALIN'S DEATH TO THE SYMBOLIC YEAR OF 1968: A NEW REDEFINITION OF THE CONCEPTS, THE RESUMPTION OF CONTACTS

The rebirth of the 'Eastern Left'

The very fact that the redefinition of the concept 'Left' resumed at all in Eastern Europe, and for a while in the USSR as well,[14] was a result of a shift within the Soviet regime. So unshakably set on a course which tolerated no alternative options under Stalin, it ceased for a moment to be totally resistant to new openings. Suddenly and unexpectedly, not only for the heirs to Stalin who had regarded the alternatives to the 'construction of socialism' as closed off for all eternity, new social options appeared on the horizon, both at the social summit and at the social base. The redefinition (or what seemed to be a redefinition) of the 'Left' took place in two distinct ways. On the one hand, rebels from the communist intelligentsia and, to a far lesser extent, 'defectors' from the *nomenklatura*, whose greatest and most paradigmatic, but not only example, was Imre Nagy[15] felt an urgent moral and political need to

[14] Here we wish to mention only one pioneer of a leftist opposition in the USSR, the magnificent example of Boris Weil who spent altogether 13 years in camps and who went to prison for the first time as little more than an adolescent for the 'crime' of distributing leaflets which defended the Hungarian revolution of 1956 as a socialist uprising. With him the Menshevik option reappeared, and while the historical viability of the option can be debated, its leftist character cannot be questioned.

[15] There are now dissenting voices in the salutary process of a renaissance of this memorable martyr of the socialist calendar. He is often presented as an accidental fellow traveller of History who, as it were,'bumped into' a situation which demanded emancipatory action, instead of deliberately choosing such a situation. Bill Lomax is the main representative of this view. But even he, as a conscientious chronicler of historical events has to admit, on the basis of newly discovered documents, that without Nagy's initiative not even an option comparable to the opening of Gomulka could have materialized in Hungary in June 1953 (see his 'The Hungarian Revolution of 1956 and the Origins of the Kádár Regime', manuscript). Against Lomax we would like to quote the extraordinary interview with George Krassó, a political prisoner after 1956, now an economist and an editor of one of the *samizdat* publications in Hungary, who defends the paradigmatic role of Nagy in creating an emancipatory space for the action of the 1956 rebels (although Krassó himself had turned against communism, reformist or non-reformist, a very long time ago). See his interview, 'The Memory of the Dead' in *Survey* 3 (1984). More complex problems arise in classifying Nagy as a 'defector from the *nomenklatura*'. In fact, he started his career as a Khrushchevite *par excellence* but in a rapid and dramatic development, with a gesture of relinquishing a sovereignty usurped by the Party to an uprising nation, he dissociated himself for good from the ruling apparatus. This intention is even more apparent in his last words in front of the Kádárist tribunal which was going to murder him 'legally' (see, Kopácsy's report on his last words as quoted in F. Fehér and A. Heller, *Hungary, 1956 Revisited*, London: Allen and Unwin, 1982, p. 136.) In order to substantiate our other statement that he was not the only, albeit the paradigmatic, 'defector' from the *nomen-*

return to the roots and save the concept of the 'Left' from the filth heaped upon it. And they did so increasingly in defiance of the whole system of domination. On the other hand, in the option called 'Khrushchevism', an extremely limited self-criticism of the regime seemed to negotiate a 'return to Lenin'. This attempt carried the message for many recipients, but only for them, (while those who launched the campaign had very different considerations) of a redefinition of the 'Left' this time by the ruling apparatus.

In the opposition, Leszek Kolakowski can be credited with the most spectacular attempt at a redefinition in his celebrated essay, 'The Meaning of the Concept "Left"' in 1957.[16] The essay proceeds from a total ossification of the Left, both in the East and the West, but primarily in the countries of Eastern Europe as a direct result of 'Stalin's crimes'. As a panacea, it postulates the need for a resurrection of the utopian dimension on the Left (in the sense of a constantly renewed querying of the dominant social imaginary). Not only was this gesture a brisk rejection of 'Marxism–Leninism', that 'scientific theory', but it was also tantamount to the first, cautious and tentative formulation of political pluralism in the communist-dominated press. Kolakowski made no secret about his conviction that, while the Left should be a unity of *vita contemplativa* and *vita activa* (including a firm moral code), and therefore, in that sense always include political action of a kind, it can never be exhaustively described in terms of political parties. Leftist activity, both in the East and the West, transcends the framework of party organization.

Indicative of both Kolakowski's redefinition and the atmosphere of the period was that, for him, the category 'Left' transcended borders, furthermore, that both Eastern and Western Left, as presented in his analysis, suffered from the same malaise and, finally, that no partial, but only a total regeneration was conceivable through a retrieved utopian dimension. 'Regeneration via utopia' means regaining the movement character of the Left which was lost in the stifling atmosphere of Stalinist 'bureaucratization'. However, whether or not he was then

klatura, we mention the example of Ochab, First Secretary of the Polish Communist Party between Bierut's suicide after the 20th Congress of the Soviet Communist Party (April 1956) and October 1956. Ochab was one of the very few communist leaders for whom his personal mythology of the 'Party's interests' (which was at least a collectivist ideal) was more important than his personal career. He abdicated in the face of a populace in revolt which, he was convinced, only Gomulka could appease. From here, he proceeded to participate in collective actions of protest against secret police brutality in the Gierek period, together with 'quite ordinary' oppositional intellectuals.

[16] 'Der Sinn des Begriffes "Linke"' in Leszek Kolakowski, *Der Mensch ohne Alternative*, Munich: Piper, 1960.

familiar with the work, Kolakowski is keenly aware of Hannah
Arendt's reminder in her *The Origins of Totalitarianism*. A constant
renewal of the movement character of the Party and the whole regime
which keeps society in a state of permanent turbulence can be (but is
not necessarily, contrary to Arendt's view) an important characteristic
and constant objective of totalitarianism. This is why Kolakowski
issues the warning that a 'utopian dimension' was also typical of
National Socialism which, in addition, had a pronounced movement
character. Therefore, the definition needs further substantive provisos.
Kolakowski's 'substantive provisos' already take account, instinctively
as it were, without at the time clarifying the deeper methodological
background, of the difficulties of a unified concept of the 'Left' if it is
extended to Eastern Europe. His postulates operate with an extended
sense of the anticapitalist dimension, similar to that suggested at the
beginning of our essay. He also makes use of a version of the 'republican dimension'. Such substantive provisos are, in the West and
the East alike, directed against traditional or newly created social
privileges, national dependence of any kind (at the time of committing
the essay to paper, the decolonization process was far from completed), a constant opposition to racism of any kind.[17] The provisos
pinpoint freedom as a central value. Additionally, Kolakowski empha-
sizes that the Left is a direct heir to the Enlightenment legacy. The Left
must not be 'sacral', he stresses, in the sense that leftist thinking and
action must not acknowledge any taboos to critical thought.[18]
Kolakowski's essay concludes with an appeal to political action. As
long as the Left, in particular in Eastern Europe, remains captive to
moral protest, however legitimate, it remains weak and largely in-
effective.

At the social summit, the attempts which were read by the oppositional recipient as efforts to redefine the Left, and which in fact had a
totally different meaning and function, are best represented by
Khrushchev's famous 'secret speech' at the 20th Congress of the Soviet
Communist Party.[19] Of course, Khrushchev remained convinced
until the day of his death that Stalin's regime, with all the butchery

---

[17] In particular, Kolakowski was fighting here, as elsewhere, the first symptoms of an
officially tolerated Polish anti-Semitism which later became the dominant demonology
deliberately manipulated by the ruling apparatus, above all in the USSR.

[18] To what extent here Kolakowski shares certain illusions of the absolute anti-authoritarian,
Karl Marx, illusions which he later criticized in Marx and in himself in the process of his
conversion to religion, is another problem.

[19] For an overall analysis of the 'secret speech' as the 'hermeneutical clue' of Khrushchevism,
see F. Fehér: 'The Social Character of Khrushchevism' in R. Miller and F. Fehér,
Khrushchev and the Communist World, London: Croom Helm, 1983, pp. 12–38.

committed in it (which he euphemistically termed 'violations of the socialist legality' and narrowed down to Stalin's purges of the loyal members of the ruling apparatus), had remained socialist, and in this sense leftist. Therefore, in his eyes the concept of the 'Left' needed no redefinition. Secondly, in marked contrast to Kolakowski's 'substantive provisos', the very concept of 'freedom' is missing from his text. That this secret speech was understood as a manifesto of restored liberties (or liberties to be restored) indicates more than a gross misreading; it is rather a classic example of the hermeneutical efforts of an age criticized and overruled by the hermeneutics of a later age. And yet the fact remains: the work of redefinition in Khrushchev's crucial document is tantamount to the postulate of 'restoring the Leninist norms'.

Nevertheless, Khrushchev's speech was an exercise in redefinition and it had a Janus face. On the one hand, his slogan of a 'return to Leninist norms' meant a step forward towards the consolidated rule of an oligarchy, as a collective body without a single despot. In this sense, it was received with relief by the ruling apparatus; at the same time, it was for two reasons regarded by its members as a mixed blessing. Firstly, the Great Experimenter was too unpredictable for this new type of rule. But going more deeply, it has been an inviolable rule in the USSR since the emergence of 'Marxism–Leninism', a rule which guaranteed the constancy of domination, that every period must be presented as superior to the previous one in the unbroken progress of 'the construction of socialism'. In this sense, any 'return' was a dangerous idea which, paradoxically, generated more suspicion towards Khrushchev than had been felt towards Stalin. The *apparatchiks* had the feeling that while the latter had threatened each and every one of them in their individual existence, he had never endangered their collective rule. But a reconsideration of Soviet history could have incalculable consequences. The other facet of this Janus-faced slogan was a practical end to Stalin's devastating 'revolutions from above' which was a relief for the populace. It was precisely because of the double and ambiguous character of this redefinition by Khrushchev that a text which was meant to be a new canon for the ruling apparatus was read by many living outside this stratum, and even by those in opposition to it, as a redefinition of the 'Left'.

For several years after Stalin's death, opponents and reformers at the top seemed to speak a similar, if never totally identical, 'language of regeneration'. However, at this point our earlier emphasis on 'Central', as distinct from Eastern Europe becomes extremely important. For it was only in 'Central', never in 'Eastern', Europe that the motif of regeneration *sensu stricto* emerged for a while as part and parcel of the official vocabulary. It first happened in the 'reformist communism' of Hungary and Poland in 1956, more than a decade later in Czechoslovakia but never in the USSR. The political explanation is at hand: it was only in these countries that a persecuted generation of communist leaders took over leadership from their own persecutors (to become, in turn, persecutors themselves). But there were previously persecuted communist leaders aplenty in Rumania or Bulgaria who never had a comeback – can this difference be explained by political factors alone? We believe not. The unfolding (and underground influence) of a once extant, now seemingly extinct, 'civil society' in Central Europe which was lacking in the Eastern European context seems to account for the return of a persecuted generation of political leaders (who promised a new beginning), as well as for the emergence of a 'vocabulary of regeneration'.

This (fairly superficial) semantic harmony between the ruling apparatus and the opposition was due to several reasons, one of them quite obvious. Even in the historical moments of a 'honeymoon with its subjects', the Soviet system remained harsh enough not to tolerate an idiom radically different from the official ideology. Therefore, the elements which separated the oppositional view from the official ones were far greater in number than those unifying (which were not just semantic in nature) them, and clashes immediately emerged.[20] The fundamental principles of 'freedom versus rationalized domination' (the first being the principal value of the opposition, the second the Khrushchevite recommendation) were so strongly conflicting that on this point there was no chance of reconciliation or even of a dialogue. Furthermore, the opposition worked with a strange dialectic in those years of self-delusion which could not be assimilated into the 'two legs bad – four legs good' Marxism of the apparatus. For the opposition, almost all the phenomena of the regime showed a distorted, threatening, negative face and yet, the 'essence', the 'deep text' remained mysteriously intact and sane. While this poorly founded historical

---

[20] The most important terminological clash was the one between the terms 'cult of personality' and 'Stalinism'. That the first had absolutely no explanatory value at all must have been, and indeed was, clear to every reasonable actor. The oppositional communist intelligentsia (which in those years borrowed its vocabulary to a very great extent from the Titoist ideology) worked out the counter-concept of Stalinism in the whole of Central Europe which suggested a systemic coherence between individual 'mistakes' and acts of 'violation of the socialist legality'. Its paradoxical fate was that the term proved unacceptable for the ruling apparatus (precisely because it suggested systemic coherence) and yet it remained captive, more than those who coined it wanted to admit, to the method of explaining history via moral monsters.

optimism betrayed a considerable degree of blindness, it also contained enough explosive material, as in the Soviet system all kinds of 'indirect apologies' do, not to be tolerated.[21] Finally, and perhaps most importantly, there was an inherent trend in the East and Central European (but not in the Soviet Russian) opposition which aimed at querying the whole system of the Yalta–Potsdam agreements. This trend became explicit in Hungary in 1956 when the declaration of Hungarian neutrality put a drastic end, even if only for three days, to the absolute prevalence of bloc politics in the region. No further explanation is necessary as to why the apparatus could not, and would not, go along with this sometimes implicit, sometimes explicit trend.

Even a superficial semantic harmony was doomed to a quick death under Khrushchev. The crushing of the Hungarian Revolution and the following 'conveyor belt executions' (as G. Krassó put it so aptly in his interview mentioned in note 15 above), the rapid disintegration of the elements of reform in Gomulka's regime as well as the first signs of opposition against it (the paradigmatic acts of which were Kuron's and Modzelewski's famous 'letter to the Party', and Kolakowski's celebrated speech on the tenth anniversary of the 'betrayed Polish October'), the crack-down on the Soviet intelligentsia who took the thaw much too seriously – all these events together sounded the death-knell to any semantic rapprochement between apparent partners with irreconcilable positions. After the *coup de théâtre* removing Khrushchev, in the wake of which a total continuity with the past was restored and the rule of the oligarchy introduced, even the appearance of any semantic harmony, or rapprochement, evaporated. At exactly the same time that in Western Europe and North America several new actors of the Left were emerging and were busy with the redefinition of the concept of the 'Left', any such attempt was branded as counter-revolutionary and was buried in the grave of the last Khrushchevite experiment during the occupation of Dubčekist Czechoslovakia.

However, it would be unfair to describe this process of disintegration of the oppositional Left in East Central Europe as a 'martyrdom of the innocent'. Disintegration had deep structural causes inherent in the very theory and practice of the leftist opposition. The fact that its

---

[21] We use the term 'indirect apology' exactly in the sense of G. Lukács coined for it in his *The Destruction of Reason* to describe a particular type of 'irrationalist' ideology. Its apostles vehemently criticized for almost all the surface phenomena of a pedestrian bourgeois civilization, they took risks and lived dangerously, but the medicine they recommended was either the defence of a 'sane nucleus in a decaying crust', or worse still, a transcendence in a negative direction, by intensifying the most fatal features of a harshly criticized reality. If the East European opposition was an indirect apologist in this period, it was only so in the first sense of the term.

perspectives were built on sand, that is to say, on the hope of an internal and radical reform of the system, was only one of them. For it is always only in retrospect that one can state with certainty of hopes that 'they were built on sand'. (Jaurès believed, a hundred years later, that Mirabeau's perspective of transforming the French monarchy into an 'English' (i.e. constitutional) one, which would have guaranteed evolution without terror and military dictatorship, had been a strong and viable option in 1789–90 and who can refute his view with 'scientific rigour'?) Two deep-lying causes established the inefficacy of leftist opposition. One of them was the insistence of its majority on a simple 'return' (to Marx, to Lenin or to both of them), a position which assumed a body of doctrine unaffected by the filth of historical events and waiting to be excavated from under the rubble. Our intellectual master, Lukács, with all his inflexible integrity, was the classic figure of this position (and we shared a considerable part of his view for a very long time). This stance did not allow for facing the inner problematic of the 'original' body of tenets, nor did it promote a tolerant view towards the legitimate, even salutary process of the diversification of the oppositional Left.[22] Finally, the idea of a 'return' brought the oppositional intellectuals, however dangerously they actually lived, dangerously close to the 'reformist' part of the upper stratum. This proximity caused them to appear suspicious to the silently but totally disillusioned'.[23]

A particular brand of the 'Leninist opposition' best exemplifies the reasons for this well-deserved fiasco. Initially it emerged in the USSR with the Medvedev brothers. It would be totally unfair as Solzhenytsin does, to deny their positive role, even more so to deny the personal courage continuously displayed by Roy Medvedev in a persecuted career. To call the key witness, it was Sakharov who confessed that Roy Medvedev's *samizdat* volume, *Let History Judge*, an eloquent

---

[22] There was, however, a disagreement between us and Lukács on this latter point as is clearly proved by an article of G. Márkus, 'Viták és irányzatok a marxizmusban' ('Debates and Trends within Marxism') *Kortárs* August 1968 (Budapest).

[23] Solzhenytsin's attitude, the grandeur of which is unaffected by the liberal virtues of justice and objectivity, is a good example of such suspiciousness. Here is what he wrote of Lukács who defended him in a series of articles which involved the author in serious conflicts: '"Stalinism" is a very convenient concept for those "purified" Marxist circles of ours, who strive to differentiate themselves from the official line, though in reality the difference is negligible (Roy Medvedev may be mentioned as a typical example of this trend). For the same purpose the concept of "Stalinism" is still more important and necessary to Western Communist parties – they shift onto it the whole bloody burden of the past to make their present position easier. (In this category belong such Communist theorists as G. Lukács and I. Deutscher.)' In Solzhenitsyn et al., *From Under the Rubble*, transl. by A. M. Brock (et al.) under the direction of M. Scammell, with an introduction by Max Hayward, Boston and Toronto: Little and Brown, 1975, p. 12.

summary of the *communist* martyrdom under Stalin, had been the first document that opened his eyes. But from this the Medvedev brothers proceeded to an unscrupulous 'indirect apology' (sometimes even a direct apology) of the regime, from branding all non-Bolshevik social-ists 'counter-revolutionary' to holding a now fashionable position in terms of which the USSR appears as a 'peaceful' power without any 'military–industrial complex'.[24]

However, the worst was to come from the GDR. (And even if a part of this story transcends the period under investigation, it should be scrutinized here for it belongs essentially to this context.) Even the first chapter of the story was fairly lamentable. In the East German counter-part of the Hungarian intellectual's revolt, Wolfgang Harich tried in 1956, in a clumsy attempt which he apparently regarded as a diaboli-cally skilful intrigue, to conspire with the Soviet ambassador against Ulbricht, and after ten years, he emerged from prison as an ultra-Stalinist.[25] Later the incomparable nobler figures of Havemann and Biermann dominated the very limited scene of East German opposi-tion. However, Havemann's theoretical framework was hopelessly and incurably obsolete. Theoretical and political degradation described a full circle with Bahro's book, *The Alternative in Eastern Europe*.[26] His personal fate, the circumstance that he was for years an 'object of progress' in Bautzen (we are using here Bahro's own term for the victims of dekulakization), makes even more conspicuous the danger-ous and characteristic features of his achievement, which are so deeply rooted in problematic national traditions. It is a recurring feature of the German Romantic tradition, to which Bahro organically belongs, that the vehemence of its attacks against a regime (and in Bahro's case, also the risk run by him) blinds the audience of such criticism to the indirect apology for the monstrosities of that very system which is being so vehemently criticized. Bahro, a romantic intellectual true to type, starts from the premise that Europe is dead (including its 'materialistic' working class with its petty struggles). His ultimate value is industriali-zation.[27] For Bahro, the epicentre of 'progressive' (or revolutionary) action has legitimately shifted to the third world (Russia, China and further). He feels a superior contempt towards the sentimentality of all

---

[24] Roy Medvedev and Zhores Medvedev, 'The USSR and the Arms Race' *The New Left Review*, 113 (Nov.–Dec. 1981).

[25] See his book, *Kommunismus ohne Wachstum*, Hamburg: Rowohlt, 1975.

[26] Rudolf Bahro, *The Alternative in Eastern Europe*, transl. by David Fernbach, London: New Left Books, 1978.

[27] Industrialization as a supreme value is, of course, a discrepant element in a romantic intellect. Therefore it is far from surprising that Bahro later progressed to an unqualified German nationalism and anti-industrialism.

theories of 'backwardness' whose authors weep crocodile tears on contemplating the inevitable results of the drastic attempts at modernizing backward countries, tears which very often flow from the eyes of those who have helped launch this avalanche of modernization. In contrast, Bahro provides an indirect but powerful plaidoyer for all that was worst under Lenin and Stalin. He watches with irony those hopeless interpreters who keep conjuring up the 'democrat' in Lenin or who believe that they can detect an abyss between Lenin and Stalin. Bahro rather sees their work as the continuous process of building a magnificent edifice. In this process of construction the victims do not count, for they are just 'objects of progress', the relations between *Volk* and *Regierung* being 'progressive' (Bahro, who never minces words, mentions specifically the years of the Great Terror). All that counts is the accelerated rythm of industrial development. The only problem with an emerging bureaucracy is that the latter counterposes its own *esprit de corps* against this miraculous pace of industrialization. A cultural revolution should therefore be launched against the bureaucrats in which the *party as movement* will be regenerated and, this goes without saying, will retain its power monopoly. Bahro's program is conceived of in deeply German Romantic terms. It implies a total rejection of political freedom as obsolete, but demands a resurrection of *Gemeinschaft* as coextensive with *Gesellschaft*. And although this position was already at the time of being committed to paper totally unacceptable to many *marxisant* oppositional groups (parts of the Czechoslovak opposition, the Budapest School, several Yugoslav theorists and the remnants of the Polish oppositional Left), this atypical personal career carried a far from atypical option. As such, it is an excellent exemplification of the leftist theoretical fiasco and its underlying causes in Eastern Europe.

However, the Bahro affair had one unique aspect. During his persecution, Bahro enjoyed an almost unanimous support from the West German Left, with the exception of the DKP. This unusually critical attitude to the GDR on the German Far Left was partly due to the circumstances that the years of Bahro's imprisonment were also the years of the important West German campaign against *Berufsverbot*. For the duration of this particular issue, the West German Left felt they had established an alliance 'across the Wall'. But this feeling of solidarity does not account for the universal acceptance of Bahro's book as a critical theory of Soviet societies (for many *the* correct criticism). This uncritical acceptance of a position as critique which was in fact, behind a barrage of attacks, an unrepentant defence of the utter inhumanity of Soviet societies, was a self-pronounced verdict on the theoretical half-heartedness of the German Far Left which is now, paradoxically, spreading over a considerable part of German social democracy as well.

The redefinition of the concept 'Left' in the West

The process of redefinition resumed in the West as well, under the impact of several interrelated factors. The first of these was the gradual end to the Cold War, the second was the same factor as was triggering a simultaneous process in East Central Europe. For Stalin's death, the ensuing revolutions and turbulences, the power struggle among his successors and the hopes of a reform in the East deeply influenced Western political actors. There was, finally, a third, equally important cause: the unexpected and unprecedented *pax Dei*, the postwar economic miracle of Western capitalism, the advent of the 'affluent society' which, on the one hand, seemed to have discarded several traditional leftist objectives for good, and which, on the other hand, required self-distancing from an obsolete orthodoxy and promoted the quest for new targets and methods of social struggle.[28]

As far as the redefinition of the Left in Western communist parties is concerned, to the extent that it occurred at all, it remained partial and extremely limited. They followed Khrushchev's recipe of a 'parliamentary road to socialism' (some of them reluctantly, others with enthusiasm). Whatever the meaning of this confused new edition of the 'Trojan horse strategy', it prescribed a mandatory new interpretation of social democracy. Most communist parties changed their Cold War vocabularies in a simple operation, and recognized the social democrats as 'progressive', 'potentially progressive' or sometimes even 'leftist' forces to a greater or lesser extent. For all practical purposes, this change of vocabulary remained a verbal exercise. Social democrats and non-communists nowhere and at no time entered into alliance with communists (the only, and then symbolic, exception being the loose

---

[28] Without doubt, the 'affluent society' was not a burning problem for the Eastern Left. And yet, here we witness again the relevance of the problem raised by Castoriadis and Touraine of a shared historicity of contesting actors with transcends distinct political systems and economic organizations. For the message of cultural criticism of the Western New Left found a surprisingly wide audience in the East (above all, Central) European countries, particularly in the younger generation. Issues like the communal way of life, the 'sexual revolution', a widespread acceptance of a new, urban popular culture and the like, made the younger Eastern leftist a cultural contemporary of struggles whose main political and economic objectives could not be his or her immediate concern, particularly in Hungary, Poland and Czechoslovakia.

contact between Spanish and Portuguese emigré socialists and communists.) Moreover, the only functioning cooperation between socialists and communists, the Nenni–Togliatti alliance, was disbanded precisely in this particular period as a result of the communist condonation of the crushing of the Hungarian Revolution of 1956. As far as Eastern Europe was concerned, the communist parties did not alter their ideologies and practical attitudes in the slightest. In many ways, they turned out to be more intransigent than some of their Eastern counterparts who lived under constant social pressure. Gomulka was forced at least to admit, if only temporarily and conditionally, that certain oppositional groups which had aided his rise to power with their propaganda were 'progressive' factors. Western communists may have and in fact did appraise the stormy events in Eastern Europe with varying degrees of realism but a crucial element in their body of doctrine never changed. For them, the 'Left' in the East was, and remained, identical with the ruling apparatus.

The social democratic parties started to see some light at the end of the Eastern tunnel, and in this new illumination, the seemingly homogeneous sight presented by the Eastern totalitarian societies started to separate out into its actual components. Naturally, they were above all concerned with the (almost always tragic) fate of their fellow social democrats in the East Central European countries and they made some attempts, mostly futile, to intervene on their behalf.[29] And yet, although Western social democrats had a very limited influence over the events in the East, their record of solidarity was, even within these limits, not particularly impressive. The later dissolution of the so-called 'Eastern bureau' of the Second International and the expulsion of veritable resistance heroes to the secret police of totalitarian regimes (the Hungarian Anna Kéthly in particular) when they no longer served 'useful' purposes, are acts which do not belong to the highlights of the history of social democracy.

The genuine problem with the attitude of Western social democracy towards a potential or actual Eastern Left lay, however, deeper: it followed from their strategy at home. A complex constellation of such factors as the economic miracle, Western integration and the Cold War atmosphere resulted in the social democratic parties gradually shedding their traditional Marxist ideology. Bad-Godesberg was only the

---

[29] It was a good test of the seriousness of Khrushchev's intentions concerning a 'parliamentary way' to socialism that Gaitskell's perfectly legitimate inquiries into the fate of East European social democrats who had disappeared without trace were greeted by him with outrage as an example of Cold War provocation during his 1955 visit to Britain. See *Khrushchev Remembers*, pp. 412–13.

most spectacular, but by far not the only example of this shift. Such a shift would in itself have been totally understandable, in particular if one takes into consideration the extremely old-fashioned versions of Marxist theory which miraculously survived in so many social democratic parties, precisely because they were so pragmatically oriented that party doctrine had ceased to be a concern for them altogether. However, given that their position as parliamentary parties made them extremely suspicious of movements of all kinds, their adoption of an increasingly uncritical stance to the whole Western establishment prescribed, or at least strongly favoured, the acceptance of theories of 'industrial society' which were just as deterministic as some older versions of Marxism and which at the same time proved to be incurably and naively evolutionist.[30] In their suspicion of turbulent movements and their exclusive sympathies for the projects (and actors) of 'industrial society' (various versions of which showed, in their view, an increasing degree of convergency), several leading social democrats were favourably inclined towards authoritarian but 'instrumentally rationalist' communist leaders. At the same time, they remained totally impervious to the message of 'riotous' Eastern mass actions, although of course, not without recognizing their antitotalitarian merits. Therefore social democratic parties 'naturally' sought contacts almost exclusively with the so-called 'moderate elements' of the communist apparatus and never with the opposition.

Space, as well as the character of the present study, does not allow for any detailed criticism of the theories of 'industrial society' with their implicit or explicit conclusion of a 'convergency'. It will suffice to mention here that the genuine testing ground of these theories was not what is usually described as the 'free world' where the industrial dynamic did integrate to some extent – although only to some extent – countries with liberal regimes, others with traditional or streamlined tyrannies, into one system. The genuine test was the value of the theory in explaining whether or not Western and Soviet-type societies, both

[30] This is of course a much too summary judgement which disregards important local and historical divergencies. Labour parties never had to shed an old-fashioned Marxism of their own, for they never had any commitment to Marxism. It was only from the late seventies onwards that the worst kind of Trotskyite simplifications started to play a crucial role in shaping the policies of the British Labour Party. In certain Scandinavian social democratic parties, above all in Sweden, an egalitarian critique of capitalism has always remained vigorous, whereas the Italian and German socialists and social democrats, shareholders in, or chief managers of, the 'affluent society', increasingly regarded the so-called 'social question' as closed, even if they admitted the existence of 'dysfunctions'. An additional factor was the rise of parties which persisted in labelling themselves 'socialist', instead of social democratic or labour. However vague the doctrinal differences, they still indicated a deviation from the social democratic pattern.

highly industrialized, would undergo the assumed process of convergency. The universally known fact is that countries with a Soviet
system did not take a single step towards a liberal social organization,
despite the formal abandonment of Stalin's theory of the 'two world
markets', and despite further industrialization and an increased
commercial relationship with the capitalist world market. Whenever
and wherever attempts at liberalization were made on a limited scale
(in Yugoslavia and in the last years in Hungary), they always took place
as a result of political considerations and were never triggered by an
industrial dynamic and its inherent, almost mystical 'laws'. Characteris-
tically, there has been only one paradigmatic advocate of the theories
of 'industrial society' among the Eastern dissidents: Sakharov, that
symbol of the social conscience of science who is, at the same time, an
almost naive believer in a liberal Enlightenment.

Western Maoism was almost the only intermezzo with participants
who for a time deluded themselves with the dream of unifying Western
and Eastern social aspirations in one movement. Once again, it is
impossible here to even try to interpret the framework of reference,
Mao's 'cultural revolution', a venture at which so many Western
analysts have boldly tried their hands. Even a much more modest
undertaking would be beyond our competence and the limits of the
present essay: namely a hermeneutical analysis of the term 'cultural
revolution' as it was used by the paradigmatic actors of the sixties. We
wish to briefly state only the following: a certain type of radical
theorist[31] understood Mao's totalitarian movement within a totalitarian society as a revolution with the double objective of transcending
both Stalinist 'bureaucratization' and modern and capitalist alienation
(by abolishing the division of labour, performance-centred work
activity in the factories and the like). One now needs no special
knowledge of the field to state that there was absolutely nothing in
Chinese reality, apart from the fanfare of Maoist propaganda (in itself
necessary for the emergence and functioning of the 'cultural revolution') which would have lent credibility to those pipe-dreams. More
importantly, those West European radicals who believed in the
creation of 'East–West cohesion' of the Left via Maoism overlooked
the fundamental fact that in Eastern Europe and the USSR there was
almost no echo favourable to Maoism in the opposition. As an almost
single exception, a minuscule Hungarian group can be mentioned in

---

[31] There is a vast and well-known literature on the subject written from this position. We
would only mention the most characteristic, and perhaps the best, specimen of the genre
(with which, of course, we radically disagree), K. S. Karol's *The Second Chinese
Revolution*, New York: Hill and Wang, 1974.

the late sixties, the majority of whose members have since disappeared from the political scene.[32] Perhaps certain aspects of Bahro's treatise, *The Alternative in Eastern Europe*, can be added to the list. In it, the whole idea of a 'cultural revolution', as well as some of its substantive postulates, clearly bear the marks of a Maoist origin. East European hostility to Maoism was, of course, not necessarily the guarantee of a more penetrating insight than could be perceived in the case of Western analysts and their endorsement of the phenomenon. The well-known analysis by G. Lukács of the 'debate between the USSR and China' (where the euphemistic title alone speaks volumes) can be regarded as a classic instance of misreading. For Lukács, Mao's China was a simple continuation of 'Stalinism', a reaction to the 20th Congress of the Communist Party of the USSR. What in fact transpired from this unmitigated hostility and almost unanimous rejection was, apart from Russian chauvinism towards the 'yellow peril', a negative attitude towards organizing opposition to the prevailing system around the category of equality, instead of freedom. This does not mean that people from all walks of life in Eastern Europe were satisfied in any degree with the level of equality in their society. They were not and they had very good reason not to be; moreover, their dissatisfaction with the prevailing inequality played, as we shall see, a special role in the East European world-view.[33] However, both the political activists and the proverbial 'man in the street' in Eastern Europe grasped the implications of the Chinese drama correctly. Without any kind of theory, but with a good political 'instinct', they had a legitimate fear of presenting social grievances in the vocabulary of equality instead of freedom. In a word, they feared that such an approach would result in the general equality of unfreedom. Precisely for this reason, the Western Maoist hope of a unified Eastern and Western left around the Little Red Book was an empty, if pernicious, illusion. But despite the Maoist fiasco in Eastern Europe, there were sporadic moments of encounter, if not an alliance, between Eastern and Western leftists which remained without a sequel but which deserve mention. We have in mind the famous meeting of Rudi Dutschke with Czech students during the Prague Spring, in 1968, the historical zero hour of our present discussion. As is well known, the dialogue was unsuccessful. Dutschke criticized the

---

[32] The only theoretically and politically 'surviving' member of the group is M. Haraszti, whose position has changed drastically and who has gained a deserved reputation both with his book, *A Worker in a Worker's State*, Harmondsworth: Penguin, 1977, and his courageous political activity.

[33] For a good analysis of the problem of equality in inequality in Soviet societies, see Pierre Kende and Zdenek Strmiska, *Égalité et inégalités en Europe de l'est*, Paris: Presses de la fondation nationale des sciences politiques, 1984.

Czech interlocutors for some of their liberal illusions, the latter detected vestiges of Leninism in his theory, and they were mutually correct almost to the same extent. And yet, this meeting marked a missed but genuine potential: the collaboration of Eastern and Western leftists for whom the realization of liberties was the royal, and certainly the only, road leading to socialism.

There was one monumental exception to the merely symbolic interaction between Eastern and Western leftists in the form of an unexpected upsurge of an American leftist movement during the sixties. In speaking briefly of this phenomenon, we must once again state our lack of competence as historians. However, even without a documentary history of the American movement, the following statement seems to be valid. This umbrella movement was a combination of several different factions, of which the campaign for civil rights and the opposition to the American war in Vietnam were the most powerful contingents. It was never centrally organized, not even synchronized, and even less ideologically homogenized. And yet it seems justified to call it the first leftist political mass movement in twentieth century American history. The movement was clearly political in character. It comprised an increasing number of participants from a younger generation who, as a result of the postwar importation of modern Marxist and other socialist literature had appropriated theories which suited modern American reality incomparably better than old-fashioned theories did. This was so in particular because of the anti-authoritarian character of both these imported theories and of the movement itself. The latter had a very vague anticapitalist character in so far as its participants, their ideological differences notwithstanding, were strongly opposed to the idea (and the dirty practice) of transforming the *pax Americana* into a new empire and a new imperialism. It also had, independently of its vague anticapitalist leanings, a strong anti-industrialization bias. However, this movement with its widespread anti-alienation cultural critique and its anti-imperialist tendencies never offered any generally accepted political alternative to the existing system of American liberalism.

The genuine novelty of the first American leftist mass movement was twofold. On the one hand, the movement was the single decisive factor in stopping the American war machine in Vietnam. In this sense, through the opponents of the establishment, the American democracy confirmed its *raison d'être* to a far greater extent than many vehement anti-American propagandists are ready to admit, whose own countries waged several unjust and cruel wars without their populace ever being willing or able to prevent them. The 'American shame' was transformed into a worthy democratic and radical tradition through the deeds of American leftists. This and above all, the far-reaching success of the civil rights movement, was almost the only victory of the democratic Left in a postwar world. On the other hand, the 'war against the war' meant an active interaction between the American Left and what it believed to be the 'Vietnamese Left', in a monumental act of self-delusion. Victory was achieved at the price of an inadmissible exoneration of the target and victim of American expansionism, itself an intolerably cruel totalitarian regime, a mistake which is apparently about to be repeated by the same actor, this time in connection with Central America.

The balance sheet of this period can be drawn up in a few words. The efforts to redefine leftism both in the West and in the East were parallel, but asynchronic, aspirations. While the leftists on both sides seemed to need one another, the interaction between them in fact remained symbolic. The only exception was the indirect but actual contact between the American leftist movement and the Vietnamese organizations of resistance to American expansionism, but only at the cost of inventing the fiction of a 'people's Vietnam', a 'Vietnamese Left'. Both trends had the same zero hour. This was the year 1968 in which communist reformism, both at the top and at the base, suffered a resounding and, it seems, final defeat, the West European New Left reached its peak without achieving its objectives, and the American Left embarked, after having achieved its own strategic objectives, on a gradual process of disintegration.

IV EASTERN LEFT, WESTERN LEFT – AFTER 1968

The Western Situation

A number of factors which emerged and remained in force in the seventies on the Western scene promoted the redefinition not so much of the concept of the 'Left' but rather of the framework in which a Left of any kind could operate. This does not mean that there were no genuine efforts to redefine the concept itself in this area. On the contrary, the media (and the public opinion) of the mid-seventies were full of news and speculations about the most spectacular manifestation of such experiments, the celebrated 'Eurocommunism'. If anything, the Eurocommunist escapade (we have to use this term after its inglorious demise) was an attempt *par excellence* at redefinition. The communist parties involved in it (above all the Italian Communist Party, the leading apparatus of which took the challenge seriously, and not just as a new chapter in the detailed manual on the 'Trojan horse strategy') wished to understand their own identity anew. They also sought for a reply to the tormenting dilemma: what should the Left in general stand for? The fiasco of this experiment is now a well-known fact.[34] The reasons for such a fiasco, some of them clearly predictable, have also been analysed to a sufficient degree. The problem with these analyses,[35] consists in the fact that they operate within the framework of political organizations, their composition, power structure, history and tradition, and in this sense are almost all internal explanations. However, if we take into consideration the fact that a process of self-redefinition was also taking place in this period among the socialists and social democrats (see the rise of Mitterand's party and the first signs of its disintegration, as well as the changes in the British Labour Party and German social democracy), and that they also remained equally unsuccessful for different reasons, we have to come to the following conclusion: new attempts at the redefinition of the Western Left can only be understood if they are inserted in the broader context of the new Western constellation.

The main factors of the general Western constellation can be expressed in abbreviated form as follows. Perhaps the longest, although certainly not the stormiest, of all depressions in the history of

---

[34] Eurocommunist aspirations never went beyond the Italian–Spanish–French triangle, although many of the minuscule Western communist parties, with the exceptions of the two arch-Stalinist ones, the Portuguese and the West German, had Eurocommunist factions. The first defectors were the French whose credibility as 'democratic socialists' was anyhow next to zero. They did not need the test of their enthusiastic endorsement of the Soviet invasion of Afghanistan and their unequivocal condemnation of Solidarity, the only autonomous working class movement in Eastern Europe, to press home this message. Once they broke with the *alliance de gauche*, this gesture also put an end to their Eurocommunist fling, to which they did not return even during their years in government under Mitterand. The Spanish communists had some surprises in store: their ex-leader, Carillo, proved to the world in a negative way that he had genuine political talent. For a while, he was able to convince even the most sceptical observers of the sincerity of his convictions, only to shed his new creed again when his party was reduced to insignificance and his position was threatened, and finally undermined, by the unrepentant Stalinists. This development left the Italian communist leadership (and their internally split, outwardly unified party) as the only Eurocommunist force, which meant, for all practical purposes, the end of the experiment.

[35] The most important literature on Eurocommunism consists of the following works: F. Claudin, *Eurocommunism and Socialism*, London: New Left Books, 1978; Carl Boggs and D. Plotke, eds, *The Politics of Eurocommunism*, Basingstoke/Boston: Macmillan Free Press, 1980; C. Boggs, *The Impasse of European Communism*, Colorado: Westview Press, 1982; G. R. Urban, ed., *Eurocommunism*, London: Temple Smith, 1978.

capitalism set in during the seventies, the end, or even the outcome of which is still not visible. The long depression buried a number of the leftist strategies and theories of the sixties and at the same time it shook the self-confidence of capitalist technocracy and its 'infallible' economic doctrines. But it also demanded new approaches by the Left which the latter has not been able to provide up until now. The American global hegemony started to disintegrate under the impact of several different factors which we shall not analyse or even list here. The heavy-handed American presence in world politics was still felt by everyone, however, this time without the clout it had carried in the postwar period before Vietnam and, more importantly, without the economic benefits which had poured into Europe after 1945 in an apparently unceasing stream. Moreover, American capitalism and the United States administration passed on a good deal of their own economic difficulties to their partners. The Western alliance entered a critical phase, with a possible outcome of total disintegration and the return of the United States to its isolationist policies. An upsurge of anti-American feeling accompanied this process which consisted of a combination of undeniably legitimate criticism and the worst kind of nationalist demagogy, fuelled by contempt for a superpower losing its grip over world affairs. The hopes of the sixties for an internal Soviet reform evaporated in a similar fashion. In this regard, 'great expectations' gave way to a so-called 'pragmatic attitude' to the Soviet Union on the Left. 'Pragmatic attitude' carries the following connotations. Leftists no longer nurture, in so far as they ever did, 'chiliastic' hopes about the Soviet Union and its social system. The myths of the Left have been shifted from an 'East–West' to a 'North–South' axis. On the other hand,leftist actors *en masse* seem to have forgotten the elementary lessons of the de-Stalinization process, those facts and historical events which together with their structural consequences were common knowledge in the sixties. Lack of expectations on the one hand and lapses of historical recollection on the other have resulted in a readiness to enter into compromises of the most questionable kind with the Soviet regime on the part of the most unexpected contingents of the Western Left. When the British TUC remained reluctant to recognize the existence of Solidarity even at a time when the Polish authorities had already made a tactical and short-term compromise with its rebellious existence, when German social democracy went out of its way to 'display self-restraint from anti-Russian demagoguery' during and in the wake of the Polish military coup in December 1981, when the socialist Papandreou approves without reservation the suppression of Solidarity as a 'historical necessity', we are only facing the most conspicuous, and the most despicable, examples of this newly born pragmatism.

This pragmatism has one particular cause among many others: the *horror vacui* of the Western Left, a new phenomenon which is seizing many a genuinely democratic leftist these days. Whatever illusions democratic leftists might be displaying towards the Soviet regime for tactical reasons, there can be very little doubt that they are perfectly aware, at least in their 'political subconscious', of what a threatening phenomenon they are facing. At the same time, all efforts to create a lasting version of democratic socialism have failed up until now. At present the French Left is facing a new phase of self-imposed disintegration and an impending electoral defeat. In addition, leftist actors have disappeared from the American scene as a mass movement. There is no force in sight which could curb the economic strategy of a conservative administration so harmful for its own allies, or which could control its expansionist escapades (consider Grenada). These factors together impress upon the democratic and realistic part of the Western Left the suffocating, albeit correct, feeling that they are between and against two worlds, without being able to identify with either of them and equally without any imminent chance for creating a third, alternative world of 'their own'. And since reality is normally preferred to potentiality in political activity, in this atmosphere the utopian dimension, so rightly demanded by Kolakowski a quarter of a century ago, is being successively discarded by the Western Left in favour of an upsurge of pragmatism. Finally, it is very difficult to translate a particular feeling reigning supreme in the overwhelming majority of the democratic Western Left, into a political vocabulary. The feeling in question is that the world in which they live, against which they fight and which they intend to transform (under the penalty of ceasing otherwise to be Left at all), is still the more habitable part of our political universe. The constant, and in itself not at all illegitimate, fear of becoming apologetic for Western liberal capitalism contributes to the paralysing atmosphere of the *horror vacui*.

The structural problems of the 'crisis of the West', together with the accompanying feeling of *horror vacui*, are the genuine causes behind all the failed attempts at leftist self-redefinition in the West. They are also the real causes of another, even more important phenomenon which is generally denied but which undeniably exists: the almost total indifference of the Western Left towards the Eastern Left, its existence or non-existence, its self-definition and potential. This extremely negative development, even when compared to the merely symbolic interaction of the sixties, is basically the result, as well as the expression, of the impotence of the Western Left. Of course, time and time again there are outbursts of indignation and despair among Western leftists when an unusually 'depressing' event, for example the crushing of Solidarity, happens. It is also a matter of course that people sign protest letters on schedule against yet another act of imprisonment of yet another dissident. However, Western petitioners feel increasingly that they can hardly change anything in the system of oppression in the Soviet regimes and, in the spirit of the above-mentioned pragmatism, they also feel that Eastern dissidents, leftist or not, cannot contribute to ways out of *their* predicament, which is undeniably true. A certain 'humanitarian self-restraint' prevents people on the Western Left from admitting the prosaic fact that they are bored to death by the endless stories of vicissitudes and persecutions of dissidents. The only exception seems to be in relation to the peace and anti-nuclear movements where, for a while, and in particular in Germany, an 'East–West' unity suddenly emerged as a strategic recommendation. We do not wish to enter the debate on the anti-nuclear movements here, but simply add the following. The German experience is particular, not general. In all probability, further efforts will be made in that region in the direction of an 'East–West' unity. However, what is at stake there is not the anti-nuclear problem but that of the unification of West and East Germany in some form.[36] In all the countries with a Soviet regime, the attempts at an 'East–West unity' of the Left have degraded into the not totally innocent farce of Western delegations banqueting with official Eastern peaceniks who take their instructions directly from Party and security organizations. Finally, it is extremely questionable to what extent the anti-nuclear movements, in themselves cross-party and cross-class phenomena *par excellence*, are 'leftist' in any sense of the term.

The indifference of the Western Left towards the existence or non-existence of an Eastern Left, its chances and perspectives, has broader than moral connotations. Put simply, by its newly arisen indifference, the Western Left relinquishes its universalistic claims in a highly contradictory process. On the one hand, Western leftists live and act in an ideological context which strongly influences the Left as a whole, and not just its intellectual component, in favour of a special brand of hermeneutical thinking: the anti-ethnocentric. Its totally relativist versions, widely rampant on the Left, regard 'endogenous' problems regarding the existence of specific forms of the Left as an issue concerning that particular culture, without any more general relevance.

[36] We set forth our views on this matter in our *Eastern Europe Under the Shadow of a New Rapallo*, Cologne, Index, 1985.

As a reaction against earlier European superiority and the imposition of European categories on the Left all over the world, the anti-ethnocentric drive is understandable, even legitimate. It can, and indeed does, trigger efforts on the part of the Eastern Left to excavate their own specific contribution to the common cause of the West. However, a total abandonment of leftist universalism reduces what was originally conceived as a universal answer (or an ensemble of several universalistic answers) to the capitalist cosmos to the meagre level of a 'regional dilemma'.

The Eastern situation

There can be very little doubt that this increasing, albeit publicly never admitted, indifference of the Western Left towards a potential or actual Eastern partner has significant roots in East European reality as well. For one has to ask the seemingly astonishing question: is there still an East Central European Left? We sadly believe that this distinction between the factions of opposition is progressively losing its meaning and relevance, at least for the militants. Any such seemingly radical statement calls, of course, for immediate qualifications. Firstly, when we mention the progressive loss of the meaning of the term 'Left' among the militants, we do not mean that there are no longer activists among them who would describe themselves and their *Weltanschauung* as leftist. They are still there, to a degree which varies from nation to nation. (And the Central European aspect of the problem has a particular importance in this respect.) For reasons which we cannot analyse here, Czechoslovakia seems to be the country in which a definite contingent of the opposition terms its aspirations 'leftist' in a self-conscious manner. On the other hand, it would be very difficult to find its counterpart in Poland. At a certain point, the Polish Left almost unanimously joined the overwhelming nationalist and Catholic trend of the resistance.[37] Its affiliation became, gradually and imperceptibly, a merger. In the USSR, one can hardly find leftist dissidents, however vaguely the term is defined, whereas there are groups which can clearly be labelled rightist. Hungary stands somewhere in between. Once, but not any longer, the last bastion of an oppositional Marxism, there are still sporadic, albeit important, theoretical efforts which are unequivocally socialist in nature.

---

[37] A. Michnik's book, *La gauche et l'église*, Paris, 1976, is the most important theoretical document of this conversion.

A further problem of qualification arises if we include emigrés within the ideological map of internal dissidence, a procedure which is unquestionably problematic for many reasons. In this respect, cultures again differ widely. The Polish tradition has been to regard those forced to emigrate as emissaries abroad of the national culture; the Hungarian tradition is to forget them. Furthermore, it is entirely true that emigrants also inevitably obtain a 'double cultural citizenship'. Even those most impervious to foreign experience, the Russians, are influenced by certain crucial events in the West. This assimilation process makes their simple integration into the home resistance a problematic operation. At the same time, it becomes incomparably clearer abroad what was 'leftist' or 'rightist' in their original objectives, for these objectives are inserted, as it were, into a Western framework where such categories make perfect sense. No doubt the Western observer can and often does draw up an entire map of the divergent forces of national dissidence, attempting to predict from such purely ideological manifestations the future emergence of distinct political parties and their behaviour in case of sudden collapse of the regime. Occasionally, one hears forecasts about a Russian liberal party organized on the principles of Sakharov, a Russian fundamentalist movement based on tbe premises of Solzhenytsin's ideology, a minuscule oppositional Marxist–Leninist group shaped by the extremely contradictory ideology of the Medvedev brothers and perhaps some kind of a renewal of the Menshevik (or social democratic) type of socialism, together with a number of regional and nationalist parties and movements. These predictions are not necessarily false, at least, they cannot be falsified with any kind of 'scientific rigour'. The problem with predictions of this kind is that Eastern actors are viewed with Western eyes, that is, it is the regard of the observer, not the actor that creates the division.

There exists an extremely superficial account of the progressive loss of relevance of the term 'Left' in East Central Europe. Western analysts often state that Eastern actors simply cannot call themselves 'leftist', since the term is occupied; it is their own oppressive government that claims to be the official incarnation of the Left. This view cannot account for the shift in collective behaviour. East European regimes 30 years ago were incomparably more oppressive in a physical sense than today, and yet, as we have tried to show, there were then clearly definable collective oppositional actors who called themselves leftist and went to great lengths to separate and guard themselves even from the appearance of rightism. What happened to change these attitudes?

The genuine explanation for this shift is extremely complex. The collective political actors of the opposition have in the last 20 years, in different countries in different ways, and each and every one of them in their own distinct idiom, come to the following common conclusion: the Soviet system cannot be reformed on its own premises. This does not mean the impossibility of changes, even sometimes quite important ones which alleviate the suffocating atmosphere. Nor does this mean that a militant who is full of resignation concerning structural reforms should be indifferent to such changes. Furthermore, the regime is not regarded by its subjects as either 'transitory' or 'mortally wounded'. (If anywhere, in Soviet societies there are certainly no recipients for the voguish Western theory of a 'society in transition'.) After the immediate post-Stalin convulsions and the consolidation of the collective rule of the oligarchy, Soviet society emerged as a frighteningly lasting historical formation even for its most rebellious subjects. Therefore it has to be understood in terms of its own functional principles, and not by any kind of analogical thinking. Finally, the political militants of the East European opposition (but also, for that matter, the politically lucid, albeit politically passive, wider strata as well) understand that their society is neither capitalist nor socialist but 'something else'. We can give the following rejoinder to the obvious objection that people in the Soviet regime could not care less about the labels of socialist doctrines (which is, by the way, perfectly true.) The message that Soviet societies are not capitalist in nature, is brought home by the most elementary daily experiences of the inhabitants of that world. None of the typical modes of behaviour necessary in capitalism would be of any use to them as guidelines for a successful career. In this respect, they are perfectly immune to the theoretical hair-splitting of Western observers. As to the allegedly socialist character of the regime, its inhabitants are, without the slightest commitment to leftist tenets of any kind, familiar with a fundamental fact of the 'Soviet way of life': its blatant and scandalous social inequality, from decision-making to material remuneration and a well-defined system of prerogatives. And a formalized, although officially denied and concealed system of rigidly upheld inequality which is political, budgetary and national, cannot be reconciled with 'socialism', even in a popular imagination which is hostile or indifferent to socialist doctrines. This is only an apparent contradiction of our earlier statement about the negative attitude of oppositional movements in Eastern Europe towards egalitarianism. It is one thing to organize resistance to a regime around the overarching category of absolute equality (an attitude that citizens of the USSR and the East European countries refuse to adopt), and another to condemn the formalized system of a rigidly hierarchic and unequal society. If, however, people are convinced, as they are, that this society is unreformable, that it is not transitory but a lasting condition of their lives, and, finally, that it is neither capitalist nor socialist, they cannot put to any use the fundamental dichotomy of the Western (and the historically traditional) Left which divides the world into capitalist and socialist. This negative aspect of a long intellectual process has been dawning upon people gradually in the last 15 to 20 years in Soviet societies.

Let us make an intellectual experiment and try to find out what course of action an East European oppositional actor would follow, were s/he ready to accept *either* side of the Western leftist dichotomy. If the actor regards Soviet society as a special type of ('bureaucratic' or 'state') capitalism as so many theorists of the Western Left suggest, should s/he strengthen the trend of capitalization? Frankly, there is a certain, although we believe limited, sympathy for such a course, and there have also been attempts (in Yugoslavia in the sixties, in Hungary more recently), at a partial recapitalization.[38] Apart from the obvious fact that many militants of the opposition still have a traditional resistance to recapitalization, there are two serious objections of different kinds to promoting such a course. First, there is plenty of historical evidence that such a course would necessarily remain limited in its scope and duration and that it would sooner or later share the fate of similar tendencies during the NEP. Secondly, Soviet societies are the living refutation of historical materialism. There is no likelihood whatsoever that any extensive tolerance of partial recapitalization would lead to any genuine, i.e., institutionally guaranteed political pluralism. What people could expect in all probability would be an anarchically functioning capitalist enclave (reaping extensive profits in the absence of an adequate taxation system), a further increase in certain aspects of social inequality and the unharmed survival of an oppressive paternalistic state.

Should the militant then, if s/he accepts the Western analysis and regards his or her society as capitalist, make efforts to 'transform it into

---

[38] By this process we mean economic recapitalization *sensu stricto* and not a return to market economy, a notion which scandalizes the Marx-orthodoxy of so many Western leftists. In contrast to them, and following the very interesting remark made recently by I. Szelényi that in the particular context of Soviet societies, market relations have an equalizing, rather than de-equalizing effect, at least in one fundamental aspect of the socio-economic relations, we believe that certain undeniable truths of Marx's position vis à vis a liberal–capitalist market system simply cannot be transposed onto the Soviet societies. (The remark is to be found in R. Manchin and I. Szelényi, 'Social Policy Under State Socialism: Market, Redistribution, and Social Inequalities', 1985, manuscript). Recapitalization, therefore, means to us the legal or semi-legal tolerance of private enterprises, overtly or under 'socialist' guise, which employ wage labour on a smaller or larger scale.

genuine socialism'? This is precisely the advice that the Eastern
opposition has so often been given by the Western leftists. What we are
criticizing here is the circularity and the ineffectual character of
Western leftist recommendations. For these advisers either depart
from the conviction that Soviet society is a socialism 'of sorts', in which
case they find a totally unreceptive audience, or else they believe that it
is not socialism, and must therefore, according to their vocabulary, be
capitalism 'of sorts', in which case they are in no position to give advice.
The recipient will simply reply by saying: realize your own, better
socialism first, and give advice afterwards. And this would be a correct
argument, given that up until now, following Western precepts has
always resulted in Eastern conditions.

If the Eastern political actor regards his or her society as a form of
socialism which is 'perverted', 'degenerated', 'bureaucratic' or 'transitory', what is s/he then supposed to do? Should s/he attempt to transform it into some form of capitalism? We have already dealt with this
option above. Should s/he 'protect the socialist achievements'? This
would simply be tantamount to an appeal to collaboration with the
ruling apparatus which is undesirable both for the former and the
latter. The structural character of Soviet societies tolerates no partner-
ship based on the recognition of even a measure of pluralism.[39] Should
s/he, finally, make an effort to render this socialism 'more socialist'?
Apart from the fact that the problem of 'how' remains unresolved in
this recommendation, it offers a further inherent difficulty: who would
be prepared to partner the opposition in this process of perfection?
Reforms of limited range and scope can easily find partners for their
purpose. The so-called ideological and 'creative' intelligentsia is a
ready, although fairly sceptical, partner in all experiments involving a
new 'thaw'. Intellectuals no longer expect miracles from any such thaw,
but they have the cynical wisdom that the more short-term tolerance,
the better. The peasantry of the cooperatives is an agreeable and enter-
prising partner, as the Hungarian example shows clearly, in all efforts
to make agricultural production more lucrative and more rational. The
technocracy is a somewhat reluctant, and certainly extremely demanding, yet available partner for certain projects of industrial re-
organization. But who would wish to be the partner of the dissidents in
a process aimed at 'perfecting the socialist character of the regime'?

All interpretations of modernity operating with the manichean

---

[39] The more recent theories of A. Hegedüs who recommends a collaboration of this kind is,
  in our view, in part a pipe-dream, in part an apology for the system. See his interview
  'Gorbatschow kann von unserem Reformkurs lernen (Gorbachev can learn from our
  reformist course') *Die Weltwoche*, 49 Hamburg, 5 December 1985, p. 13.

dichotomy of 'either socialism or capitalism' clearly break down in dealing with the Soviet societies. Neither their vocabulary nor, therefore, their strategic recommendations are applicable to this area. If Western leftists feel disillusioned with the Eastern dissidents who fail to show an understanding for the terms of their analysis, their recommendations and their labels, they should above all blame themselves and their obsolete theory. We do not intend to rationalize, even less to idealize, the turbulent theoretical and practical constellation of Soviet societies. We witness a process of total political apathy among a great number of socially conscious men and women in Eastern Europe and rightist political actors and theories can easily penetrate into the dangerous vaccum thus created. However, a very important process of reformulating and replacing antiquated social theories is also taking place in this region. Eastern theorists now produce a number of new approaches[40] which can be put to practical use in the East and serve as a memento for the Western Left in that these new approaches prepare the ground for a new theory of modernity. We shall briefly list the problems on the agenda of Eastern theoretical and political actors.

Three options seem to occupy the foreground of the political agenda. What can, after a fashion, be called the liberal option is, without doubt, the prevailing one among them. Its advocates have one overarching, sometimes exclusive, concern: the emancipation of civil society from the yoke of an oppressive state, the restoration of a measure (optimistically a full system) of pluralism. A conservative and fundamentalist opinion appears to be surprisingly strong (and it should be noted here that the terms 'conservative' and 'fundamentalist' are neither identical nor necessarily interrelated or combined). Solzhenytsin's political development is the paradigmatic exemplification of this option but we have seen analyses of the Solidarity years which are totally hostile to the communist regime but which are equally hostile to any workers' attempt at self-management and which favour a 'strong' government based on a nationalist consensus.[41] There

---

[40] Without excessive patriotism, we would suggest that 'Budapest' (in a symbolic sense which includes many efforts originating from there but sometimes realized in emigration), became the centre of such a rethinking of a new theory of modernity. The writings of G. Konrád, I. Szelényi, G. Bence, J. Kiss, M. Vajda, G. Tamás, A. Arato (who belongs here not just by birth but by virtue of his close contacts with, and active participation in, the metamorphoses of 'Budapest thinking') are exemplifications of this thesis. We add to this list our *Dictatorship Over Needs*, op. cit., written together with another protagonist of this 'rethinking process', G. Markus. And it would be unfair not to mention F. Fejtö, whose intellectual origins can be traced back to this symbolic 'Budapest' as well as to Paris and who, almost single-handedly, created a history of the peoples' democracies.

[41] This argument can be found in A. Walicki's paper, 'Myśli o sytuacji politycznej i moralno-psychologicznej w Polsce (Remarks on the Political and Moral–Psychological

is, finally, the option of a future regime based on self-management and self-administration, which is theoretically always marginal but in practice almost invariably the dominant option when it comes to a collective action in the moments of 'thaw'. It is only the second of these options that is incompatible with Western leftist positions for reasons of principle.

Economically, even more options seem to emerge. One of them recommends, in a paradoxical and complete reversal of Marx's original conception, the generalization of unobstructed market relations as the task *sui generis* of socialism. This astonishing suggestion coming from the Hungarian economist, T. Liska, does have some arguments, the basic one being that capitalism, through the system of monopolies, has obstructed, rather than expanded pure market relations which, if they were to come to full bloom, would guarantee an at least economic rationality. This is certainly an extremist and marginal view, much more so than the recently emerging recommendations for partial recapitalization. The partisans of the latter option never call a spade a spade, they speak rather of 'healthy competition', 'freedom of initiative' and the like. Without doubt, they have a strong economic argument: the poor performance of the command economy with the exception of the military–industrial complex. However, the partisans of 'healthy competition' are almost totally uninterested in any values other than economic ones, a state of affairs which is unacceptable to the populace, paradoxically, because it is used to state paternalism. The dominant option favours a mixed economy (with liberal state supervision and wide-ranging competition between the units of production), in other words, a particular version of the model of 'rational redistribution' suggested by Konrád and Szelényi. The once so popular option of general self-management is again fairly marginal for two reasons. The first and main reason is the continual failure of the (admittedly very fragmented) experiments with this system in the only country where they were actually put into practice, in Yugoslavia. Another is the vast number of theoretically unresolved problems in the blueprint of this system. Paradoxically, the various economic options can be, and indeed are, combined with the most unexpected political ones, and vice versa. Solzhenytsin favours a new, sturdy, individual Russian 'farmer'

Situation in Poland') in *Aneks*, London, 35/1984. The paper, with which we disagree totally, but which is beyond doubt one of the most original presentations of the Polish dilemma, was discussed, in the same issue of *Aneks*, by W. Kuczynski, J. J. Lipski and K. Pomian; the journal also published Walicki's 'Reply to my critics (Odpowiedz moim krytykom').

and a strong political and religious authority in the same breath. The
model of 'free and generalized market relations' implies a government
with stronger prerogatives in at least all matters economic than most of
the reformers or, for that matter, the designers of the project, would be
prepared to accept.

In an ideological field marked by strongly clashing views there are
four complexes which dominate the debates: nationalism, religion, the
way of life and social pluralism. Since the last one is closely tied up with
the political, if not necessarily with the economic, alternatives, there is
no need to analyse it further. Nationalism can appear in several distinct
and moreover radically different forms, from a perfectly legitimate,
even emancipatory defence of a national existence (see the example of
the Crimean Tartars and their struggle to regain their homeland) to the
equally legitimate quest for an at least extended version of nominal
sovereignty in the East European countries, up to the archreactionary
manifestations of an almost racist national (above all, Great Russian)
supremacy over the other nationalities of the USSR. Several representatives of the latter position had to share the fate of the opposition
under Brezhnev solely because they had spelled out semipublicly the
covert objectives of their own government.

Religion is at present experiencing a partial resurrection in Soviet
societies, much as in other regions of the world, again with many
different faces and functions. Here we cannot even attempt to analyze
but merely indicate, the contradictory character of the Polish Catholic
upsurge, the rise of a religion and a Church which has always had
considerable power and which has now ascended to a position of
almost exclusive spiritual monopoly. This is certainly a contradictory
process, to say the least, from a traditional leftist position. On the one
hand, the Polish Catholic Church does not only fight for religious
freedom *sensu stricto* but has also become a vehicle and an agent, albeit
a very cautious one always ready for questionable compromises, of the
self-liberation of civil society. On the other hand, all this had happened
at the price of an almost complete conversion of the opposition to a
traditionalist and self-righteously hierarchic doctrine and institution
accompanied by an increasing social intolerance towards dissenting,
i.e., lay, opinions and attitudes.[42] In several cases, above all in that of

---

[42] The 'Catholic conversion' of the Polish opposition and the hostile reception of this fact by
many Western leftists, blinding them to the overall importance of the Polish resistance, is a
classic example of a situation in which the cultural dimension of the complex leftist
tradition gains the upper hand over all others in assessment. Those who would otherwise
not be at all unsympathetic to the struggle of the KOR and the social objectives for which
Solidarity stood, find it often impossible to identify with a cause the proponents of which

Soviet Jewry, the return to religious rites is the expression of the growth of ethnic identity in the face of a dangerously increasing, and partly government-sponsored Soviet anti-Semitism. In several other cases, especially in those of disillusioned intellectuals, conversion to religion is a reaction *sensu stricto* to the Soviet system as a monstrous version of modernity. Just like economic options, religious ones can be combined with extremely diverse political and economic alternatives.

This catalogue of the issues on the agenda of the East European opposition has served three purposes. It has exemplified the difficulties of the Western leftist in finding his or her 'natural ally' in Soviet societies. There is a very good reason for such difficulties. In contrast to earlier periods, there are allies but they are far from 'natural' in the elementary sense that they speak an idiom at least partly alien to the Western leftist. Not only do the militants of the Eastern opposition advocate tenets, some of which are clearly incompatible with several dimensions *but one* of the Western leftist tradition, but more importantly, the majority of them also present such unexpected combinations of options for the Western observer that the latter can hardly fit them into a Western theoretical framework. This new constellation is, further, caused by the deliberately detotalizing attitudes of the Eastern opposition. Philosophy (of any kind) is not in vogue these days in Eastern Europe and the USSR, in countries which were in the past mostly recipients rather than protagonists in the great philosophical debates, but always enthusiastic and committed recipients who occasionally rose to the level of innovation. Holistic philosophy is now a prime suspect for the opposition: totality has become a hallmark of totalitarianism. This situation has blatantly negative features for all Western leftists, theorists in particular, and it would be puerile to deny the existence, and the negative character, of this theoretical vacuum.

However, there are, finally, two important theoretical results, at present implicit rather than explicit, at which we can only hint here. The first is the total collapse of the Marxian 'paradigm of production' among the militants of the East Central European opposition (which remains a fact irrespective of the almost total indifference of the majority of them to doctrinal issues within Marxism). Castoriadis was perfectly right: it is not Russia which has to be read in the light of *Capital*, but *Capital* which has to be critically re-read in the light of Russia (and Soviet societies in general). Much as people are, in their

---

speak a language belonging to an outright reactionary Western past or present. However, there is always context beyond the text, and it is highly to be recommended that the Western Left penetrate into this context.

daily discussions and concerns, focused on economic hardships caused by a permanently ailing economy, no East European actor seems to suggest practically that, as Marx believed, 'economy is the heart of civil society'. Nor do they believe any longer, as people did decades ago, that an economic reform would imply a political restructuring of society as a 'historical necessity'. If such a restructuring can be done at all, people now know, it cannot be achieved without the republican dimension, a fight in and for a new public space. The second theoretical result is even more complex. Since the opposition no longer thinks in terms of a 'socialism versus capitalism dichotomy', in so far as they think theoretically at all, they render a new meaning to the seemingly mythological category, 'the cunning of reason'. They understand in their practice that the *cunning* of reason is precisely a cunning of *reason*. No level-headed exponent of this opposition would question the initially socialist intention of the project undertaken by the generation which created the present monstrous society. At the same time, for reasons analysed above, no one agrees that the result is socialist in character, irrespective of his or her individual attitude to socialism as a project.[43] This 'cunning of reason' through which an initially socialist project has resulted in the present miserable social conditions is the historically deserved punishment for a haughty rationalism which promised a guaranteed and planned society. This project, so impervious to the limits of rationalism, and almost invariably resulting in social catastrophe, is precisely the 'cunning of reason' in that it is the living refutation of the project from which it departs. Thus, from an often totally pragmatic criticism of the planned economy, a much more 'totalizing' theoretical result has emerged as the message of the East European social struggles (even if not necessarily conscious to the actors themselves).

V THE PERSPECTIVES FOR A DIALOGUE OF THE WESTERN AND EASTERN LEFT

The chances for a resumption of a now almost totally defunct East–West dialogue on the Left can be viewed from two different

---

[43] The only exception to this was the group around Solzhenytsin which collectively published the volume *From Under the Rubble*, op. cit. Apart from the outspokenly conservative character of their collective manifesto, they could only identify socialism with the present regime, sometimes in positively low-quality contributions, at the cost of deliberately ignoring fundamental parts of the socialist tradition, not even the trace of which can be found in the Soviet system.

perspectives. The present situation can be first of all regarded as a temporary dysfunction which will sooner or later lead to new alliances without the need for a process of radical rethinking and a change of perspectives in traditional leftist projects. The advocates of this option persist in watching the Eastern terrain with Western eyes, and sometimes they arrive at surprising results but almost never at a comprehensive identification of their allies.[44] From a pragmatic point of view, it is a perfectly sensible undertaking for the Western leftist to separate the 'Left' from the 'Right' on the Soviet scene on the basis of traditional

---

[44] A typical example of a reading (or rather gross misreading) of Eastern actors through myopic Western eyes is to be found in E. P. Thompson's 'Comment' (*Praxis International* 5, No. 2, 1985). This is all the more regrettable as the republican dimension is a dominant feature in Thompson's intellectual make-up; he really intends to find allies in Eastern citizen movements. It is another issue altogether that there are incurable flaws in the Western part of his analysis. He presents what he calls the 'Western security state' as a new absolutism, an almost totalitarian regime which has devoured public space and citizens' rights almost totally. Parliament and the law are thugs, in his view, a statement which makes his recommendations of non-violent resistance more than questionable, since people normally and legitimately respond with violence to the incursions of thugs. This description of the state of affairs in the West makes the option of incitement to civil war, an option which Thompson explicitly rejects and describes as gossip, the almost inevitable logical conclusion to his position. This is even more so given that he tentatively rejects the acceptance of majority decision on defence issues by the simple means of terming defence as such a Cold War fiction. However, what is demagogic and dangerous but could become ominously realistic in the Western part of his analysis (in the sense that it could become an actual course of action if a minority were desperate and adventurist enough), turns into outright parody when Thompson comes to discuss Eastern Europe. As befits his prophetic stance, Thompson feels no hesitation in lecturing and preaching to Eastern movements whose actual room for manoeuvre he hardly seems to understand. His *bête noire* is Solidarity, against which he adopted an outright negative position when it was crushed in December 1981 by Jaruzelski (for whom Thompson then displayed a fine understanding). Now he has changed his mind and has more recently discovered certain 'citizen potential' in Solidarity in retrospect. However, according to his argument, Solidarity made one fatal mistake which seems to have contributed crucially to its doom: it did not find any allies in the Western anti-nuclear movements. In lieu of a refutation, a few questions will do. How was Solidarity to find allies among actors in the West, given that a great many of them were more reluctant to recognize its existence than its own oppressive government and were immediately ready to take sides with those who crushed the movement? What would it have added to the chances of Solidarity if its leaders had made even the feeblest attempt to threaten the most protected Soviet prerogative, that of strategic power, given that their much more limited political presence was in itself intolerable to the rulers of a genuinely totalitarian state? (It is by the way a historical fact, recommended to the attention of the historian sensitive to the ignorance of others in historical matters, that the Polish government made it unambiguously clear even during the months when it seemed to tolerate Solidarity, that any such politicized, indeed inappropriately over-politicized trade union was an undesirable presence in the military complex, which would be countered by force). All this is not to deny the many illusions which Solidarity did harbour, but to refute the superior gaze of the Western observer and the lofty prescriptions of the Western leftist imagination, which find deserved indifference, if not outright contempt, among political actors in the East.

insignia and vocabularies. And yet, comprehensible as this may be, it can only produce short-term results and options valid only for the West. An operation like this will never transcend the limits of an extremely reductive reading of both actors and their field of manoeuvre. Historical perspectives have changed so dramatically in the last decades that an exclusively Western gaze cannot help but constitute the phantom figures of its own projected social imagination. The second option must have become unambiguously clear from our preceding analysis. It should be based on the preliminary assumption that modernity is an open-ended totality which has several unexplored potentialities.

Frankly, we have no exaggerated pragmatic expectations for the resumption of the dialogue in question. The global equilibrium, as it now stands, cannot be upset either in a positive or in a negative way even by the whole of the West, let alone by one single actor in the shape of the Western Left. The vain hopes that the protests of Euro-communist parties would bind the hands of the expansionist Soviet *apparatchiks* proved futile, and not only as a result of so many *volte face* by so many Eurocommunists. It also happened because Soviet politics is guided by Brezhnev's celebrated paraphrase of Stalin's historical query: how many divisions does Comrade Berlinguer have? Pinpointing this painful reality is not meant to be an apology for any kind of cynical *Realpolitik*. Apart from the moral obligation of a political activity with a minimum of liberalism, an obligation which, despite well-entrenched views to the contrary, does exist, there are also strictly pragmatic political considerations which demand that the 'watch and protest' attitude of the Western left be upheld. There is simply no knowledge as to when, in a state of inner turbulence within the Soviet Empire, the 'broadcasting of a democratic imaginary' could ignite collective democratic actions which could properly be called leftist. The ruling apparatus is indeed not fooling itself when it incessantly speaks about 'ideological diversion'.

Despite this new complexity of the Eastern situation created by an increasingly lucid awareness of the real character of Soviet societies, there is still a firm basis for a dialogue between the Western leftist and his or her ally which can contribute to the emergence of what could be legitimately called the 'Eastern Left'. This firm basis can be neither the anticapitalist dimension of the leftist tradition, for reasons repeatedly analysed above nor the cultural dimension. (We repeat, the anti-capitalist dimension only plays a negative role in so far as those embracing the recapitalization project exclude themselves from an East–West leftist dialogue). The firm basis can therefore only be the republican dimension. The Eastern militant is, irrespective of his or her brand of *Weltanschauung*, a citizen without being a Jacobin, as long as s/he does not embrace fundamentalist options. The republican dimension shared in common between the Eastern and Western opposition does not mean a homogeneity, not even a strong similarity of viewpoints on several crucial matters. And yet it is incomparably more than a mere abstraction. It is precisely the type of public virtue demanded by Arendt, Castoriadis and others which alone can serve as ground for a free society beyond liberalism which, at the same time, reconciles important parts of the liberal tradition with its own concerns.

The pluralization of modernity is at the heart of this dialogue to be resumed and neither of the future partners is in this respect in a position of initial superiority. Eastern militants now experience a new and unexpected version of modernity via their incomplete project, which can in part be incorporated into Western leftist traditions but which in part explodes this tradition. The best of the Western leftist theory is in a process of appropriating the implications and consequences of this new situation. While we are at the very beginning of a process of fathoming the new features of modernity, there is no other vehicle of exploration but the open-ended dialogue itself.

What are the obstacles to such a dialogue? Above all, the traditionally manichean attitude of the Left that divides the world into 'progressive' and 'reactionary' halves, on the basis of an already obsolete dichotomy. The second obstacle follows from the former one: it is the difference of vocabularies or of respective cultural dimensions. Semantic and cultural factors of this kind are never without importance. A particular vocabulary can express a particular imaginary; it can integrate certain social experiences while it breaks down in front of others. We will only mention two examples, one of them integrating, the other divorcing Eastern and Western leftists. The vocabulary of 'needs' which is central to the discourse in both worlds is certainly an integrating factor. 'Dictatorship over needs', even regarded as a mere negative utopia of the Soviet system, is a central category of the Eastern world, the 'manipulation' or the 'paternalistic supervision' of 'acceptable' or 'unacceptable' needs is equally central in the West. On the other hand, the vocabulary of 'human rights' is a dividing factor. Leftists, otherwise extremely jealous of their human rights and publicly indignant at all cases of their violation in liberal countries, tend to regard the problem as historically resolved, therefore obsolete. (And this is true of leftists who have never been trained in the Marxist school of contempt for 'bourgeois rights'). And for obvious reasons, the demand for human rights unites almost all parts of the East European opposition.

Differences in vocabulary notwithstanding, we have already pointed out the single, but undeniably extant basis for an East–West dialogue. We also mentioned in our expectation that such a dialogue could, but not necessarily would, recreate an Eastern Left, as well as redefine the central categories of Eastern and Western self-understanding. The basis for this dialogue is, to return to the beginnings of this train of thought, the republican dimension of the leftist tradition.

2

Are There Prospects for Change in the Soviet Union and Eastern Europe?

Ferenc Fehér and Agnes Heller [1]

The USSR is the centre of a world empire (in the sense Immanuel Wallerstein uses the concept in a recent paper),[2] whereas East European societies are located on the inner periphery of the Soviet world empire. (The outer periphery is constituted by the directly dependent outposts and close allies of the USSR which have occasionally a social system different from the Soviet system in one or another respect.) Certain units of East European periphery are closer to the centre than others, and the difference is only partially determined by geographic location. Socio-historical factors play an incomparably more decisive role in determining proximity and distance respectively (a spatial–social relation which is never final) than do geographic ones. Re-arrangements have occurred more than once and can happen again in the future. Yet, if we abstract from accidental events and rather focus on the working determinants of the system itself, the varying degree of possibility and likelihood of changes in the centre and on the periphery are of extraordinary importance. In a rough approximation one can contend that certain reforms from above, eventually supported by movements from below, can be implemented more easily in the periphery than in the centre. However, the fundamental structure of domination must change in the centre for the periphery to change, at least in a thoroughgoing and final sense. Our second statement is in no need of extensive corroboration. Brezhnev stated openly, in his final

[1] Originally published in English in *Praxis International*, Vol. 5, N. 3, Oct. 1985.
[2] Immanuel Wallerstein, 'The Modern World-System as a Civilisation' paper given on the conference 'Civilisation and Theories of Civilising Processes: Comparative Perspective', University of Bielefeld, 15–17 June 1984.

meeting with Dubček and the Czechoslovak leadership, then captive in Moscow, that the Soviet Union regards the borders of the East European states as its own.[3] As a consequence, the Soviet Army will, directly or indirectly, intervene in each and every case when, in the view of the Soviet leadership, the common system of domination is under threat in any East European country. It is rather our first statement which has to be argued for.

The Soviet Union has been a totalitarian state (in a simple definition: a state in which pluralism is outlawed) from 1921 onwards. However, the totalization of society takes an extremely long time. In the main, it happened under Stalin's rule, and the result was a total atomization of society and an equally total transformation of human attitudes which, in the final analysis, led to the ultimate subjection of all aspects of civil society to an omnipotent political sphere, as well as the legitimation of domination thus created. However, in the periphery there was no time to accomplish this total transformation. Stalinism proper only lasted a few years, and civil society quickly recuperated, if in an extremely fragmented way, after the dictator's death. Human attitudes continued to be pluralistic, as did social imagination. The system of domination has not become legitimized. Reawakening civil society broke through via revolutions, the yield of which was total, albeit short-lived, collapses of the system or a strong and public challenge to them, in Hungary, Czechoslovakia and several times in Poland. The more resolute the rebellion, the less civil society could be totally subjected to state control.

Communist governments in Eastern Europe faced a double task. They had to keep the system of domination intact, but at the same time tolerable for the population in order to prevent new outbreaks of rebellion. Some of these governments, first and foremost the Hungarian, have increasingly developed a vested interest of their own in pursuing such manoeuvres within their own 'estate'. Additional factors contribute to the eventual, and always relative, success of such manoeuvres: the smallness of the countries in question (at least compared to the USSR) national homogeneity (in Hungary and Poland), and the like. Other factors operate as motivating forces: leaders of a particular 'unit' on the periphery of the Empire prefer to be genuine national chiefs to being the mere executors of a foreign will – if they can afford it, which is always dependent on (several) circumstances.

The Soviet leadership always had an ambiguous relation to the eventual detours and 'own ways' of the periphery of the Empire.

---

[3] Z. Mlynář, *Night Frost in Prague*, London: Hurst and Co., 1980, p. 240.

Formally, the option to integrate these countries into the Empire even nominally, or at least to impose the exact replica of the model existing in the USSR, is always there. In terms of a Machiavellian politics, a solution like this would sound plausible, and the Soviet Army would guarantee the success without fail. However, Soviet leaders always refrained from such solutions since Stalin's death (to whom, as exemplified by the fate of the Baltic states, such an option was not alien), and for very good reasons. Economy operates incomparably better at least in certain regions of the periphery than it does in the centre, and whatever their theoretical explanations for this 'irregular' phenomenon, what we call the restoration of the elements of civil society has to be, even if in a distorted form, part of the Soviet leadership's consideration. And as long as the Soviet economy badly needs to import consumer goods, providing the Soviet populace with consumer goods of East European origin would be much more endangered, were the latter region wholly and nominally Sovietized. Only if the USSR could, by political means, subject a few highly developed and industrialized Western countries to its influence (in the main, this option means the 'Finlandization' of West Germany), would the idea of the complete Sovietization of East European societies gain the upper hand in the considerations of the Soviet leadership. The reason is obvious: further 'Finlandization' would guarantee an incomparably wider and richer influx of the much desired consumer goods than the amount available from the East European periphery.

Thus the question of whether or not there are prospects for change in the USSR and in Eastern Europe has to be addressed in two consecutive steps: first, the prospects in the centre, then the prospects in the periphery have to be scrutinized.

Starting with the centre, it has to be emphasized that the notion of 'change' can be vague to the point of being misleading. Namely, all modern societies undergo changes, including short-term ones, and the USSR is no exception. Changes of what kind is the crucial question.

A striking change has taken place in the USSR since Khrushchev's fall, which has had several directions and implications.

First, a new kind of rule emerged: the collective rule of the Soviet oligarchy. Like all oligarchies, this too has a vested interest in conservatism, in minimizing internal conflicts and abandoning all socio-economic experiments. It has been a fact beyond dispute for two decades now that the Soviet oligarchy renounced all attempts at 'reforms from above', even if it pays totally empty lip-service to an extremely reduced version of merely economic reforms. On the other hand, in order to reduce actual and potential conflicts, the Soviet oligarchy embarked, after Khrushchev, on a political expansionism, which is an 'export of internal tensions' on an unprecedented scale. It is inadequate to term Soviet expansionism 'imperialism', for Soviet society is not profit-oriented, rather power- and control-oriented. Expansionism performs two tasks at once: it increases the global power of the Soviet oligarchy and it stabilizes its rule at home. The two aspects are organically interconnected. Having abandoned self-legitimation through constant changes and advertising so-called successes at home, they now draw legitimation from nationalism and chauvinism which are fueled by 'successes abroad'. This modification of policies goes hand in hand with the de-ideologization of the regime. Neither the *nomenklatura*, nor the populace believe in the hackneyed slogan of 'the construction of communism'. Victor Zaslavsky has pointed out in an interesting analysis that while the term 'communism' became a laughing-stock, both at the top and at the bottom, it has been replaced by the propagandists of the regime by references to 'the Soviet way of life', allegedly superior to all others.[4]

De-ideologization left its traces on the attitudes of the populace, including the oligarchy itself. What is normally labelled increasing corruption within the ranks of the oligarchy is a far more complex phenomenon than the terminology suggests. The need structure of all layers of the oligarchy is officially defined by the institution of the *nomenklatura*. The *nomenklatura*, a system of written and unwritten privileges, prescribes the exact amount of consumer goods and services a particular member of the ruling apparatus may enjoy and possess. (They are generally goods and services of much better quality than those available to the rest of the populace, often of Western origin, and they can be purchased for special prices in closed shops or are allotted to the members of the apparatus according to their rank in the *nomenklatura*, from special stores.) It goes without saying that if someone is not a member of the *nomenklatura*, he is excluded from the enjoyment of all such goods and services. Now, if we disregard the 'common people' and we speak exclusively of the members of the oligarchy, the system of *nomenklatura* makes the single participant in the corporate property of the oligarchy (euphemistically called 'socialist property relations') totally dependent on the corporation (the party and its apparatus). Odd as it may sound, corruption is the means of securing a degree of independence within the oligarchy. (This is why the conservative French Soviet scholar, Besançon, termed Soviet

[4] Victor Zaslavsky, *The Neo-Stalinist State*, New York/Brighton: M. E. Sharpe/Harvester, 1982, pp. 86–90.

corruption the embryonic rebellion of brutally oppressed civil society.)[5] If A, in position Y, accepts bribes in cash or *in natura* for services or for the simple tolerance of practices illegal in Soviet terms, he can amass a private fortune, whereby not only his, and his family's, actual standards of living will improve, but also the chances of his children for greater independence and room for manoeuvre within the Soviet society. The conflict between the common interests of the corporation and those of its individual members gained momentum immensely under the rule of Brezhnev. The individual members of the corporation started to understand themselves as members of a ruling class, whereas it is a vital interest of oligarchic self-legitimation that they should remain a corporation and not be transformed into a new class.

'Corruption' has an even wider connotation. It is deeply intertwined with the emergence of a (fragmented) market system in the midst of an anti-market command economy. Market relations (except those called, euphemistically again, 'socialist market relations') are illegal, yet they can in fact flourish, provided that the functionaries in charge are regularly bribed. A new stratum of black marketeers is in the making, the members of which are extremely wealthy but who, at the same time, take an extreme risk. They can be imprisoned, even executed, any time that the corporate interest gains the upper hand. It is, however, worth noting that precisely this illegal market provides, through devious channels of distribution, not only the lower ranks of the oligarchy, but the populace outside the *nomenklatura*, with a certain ever-increasing amount of goods otherwise unavailable.

It has become increasingly clear during the long rule of Brezhnev that a gigantic, modernizing country like the USSR, a country which puts such an exorbitant premium on industrial progress (particularly in military-related areas), is simply incapable of propelling industrial and technological development through its indigenous logic. The fact is that, apart from certain branches of military technology, the USSR either imports or simply steals its technological innovations from the West. In terms of population transfer from agriculture to industry and those of a curve of a forced industrial growth (which necessarily had to slow down for decades now), the country has accomplished the transcendence of the extensive phase of industrialization, without entering the intensive phase technologically, as well as in many other respects. Under such circumstances, and despite the gigantic industry,

---

[5] Alain Besançon, 'Preface' to Ilya Zemtsov, *Corruption en l'URSS*, Paris: Fayard, 1982, p. 4.

command economy reproduces scarcity. Moreover, continued scarcity should not be defined in comparison to earlier periods when millions were starved to the death (consider the artificially created famine in the Ukraine in 1932) but to the actual need structure which has slowly developed under Brezhnev's rule. This need structure has its origin in the upper strata of the oligarchy (which, in turn, simply imitates what is worst in the Western rich) but it permeates society as a whole. This is natural. It was the upper stratum of the oligarchy which, in an originally hermetically sealed society, first acquired knowledge about the existence of certain consumer goods which then existed in capitalist countries. This knowledge reached the lower ranks of the oligarchy only gradually, and even more slowly those strata which are not included in the *nomenklatura*. This is one reason why imports from the periphery cannot be dispensed with. In addition to producing scarcity in state-owned industry, the decennial agriculture crisis (which, according to Khrushchev's officially published data, brought the Soviet agricultural production in 1953 to a lower level than that of the last year of peace under the Tsar, 1913) drags on. Not unrelated to the agricultural crisis, but reinforced by other, hardly known, factors, the USSR is undergoing a peculiar kind of demographic crisis as well. The decrease in life-expectancy, quite a unique feature in any modernizing country, tells one half of the story. The other half is that the USSR does not suffer from a population explosion; just the contrary. The Russian contingent of the populace is decreasing in proportion to other, non-Russian ethnic groups, in particular to various Moslem groups. This spells trouble for the centre of the Empire.

As far as we can see, the Soviet leadership is more or less aware of this situation. The question is rather whether they can, or will, act against these continuing trends. Roughly, there are two attitudes among the members of the oligarchy towards the illegal market economy. The first contends that every economic activity outside the state-owned industry is, irrespective of its material yield, a production of waste. The other, with incomparably less chance of public self-articulation, asserts that it is precisely the state-owned economy that produces waste. The two attitudes imply two irreconcilable options to which we will return shortly. However, given that the option of imitating the Hungarian model has also emerged in Soviet considerations (just as in earlier times, members of the oligarchy experimented with the idea of introducing elements of the Yugoslav model and never realized it), we have to glance briefly at this model.

As mentioned, civil society was, partially and gradually, restored in Hungary after the Revolution of 1956. As a result, there exists now certain social conditions for certain reforms in Hungary but these social conditions are absent from the USSR. A prominent feature of such differences is the dissimilarity between Soviet and Hungarian collective farms, as far as (restricted) market conditions and internal structure are concerned. With respect to industry, there are now in Hungary not two, but three distinct types of economy: a state-owned economy: a private market economy operating under more or less severe restrictions and an illegal but tolerated market economy within state-owned industry. The latter has quite unique features. Formally, this too is based on bribery, but on a kind which does not include, nor does it presuppose the bribery-based collusion of the oligarchy. The third market operates in the following manner: if factory X needs spare part, machine or raw material A, the management of the factory in question will transfer (under semilegal pretexts or in cash) a certain sum to the management of the unit which possesses the goods in question. However, this sum will not, or only in small part, end up in the pocket of 'bribed' management. Rather, the latter will 'invest' it in the same strange fashion in order to obtain spare part, machine or raw material B, from productive unit Y, and so on. Thus 'bribe-taking' becomes a productive procedure.

What kind of changes are, then, conceivable, or even likely, on the basis of this state of affairs in the USSR? The discussion has to be conducted on two levels. First we envisage the logical possibilities of change, then we shall turn to the question of 'what is likely to happen'.

The first logical possibility is the implementation of what can be termed 'the Andropov line', in other words, a more or less extended, novel and streamlined version of Stalinism. It is not by chance that we termed this option 'the Andropov line'. Andropov's main slogan during his short rule, 'the elimination of corruption', stood for a policy with broader connotations, a policy aimed at the destruction of the class-in-the-making, as well as the second (resricted market) economy, by sheer force. It implied the reinforcement of the absolute power of the corporation as against its members and their dynamic of 'privatization', by making need satisfaction completely dependent on the *nomenklatura*, on the position of the individual within a centrally and rigidly stated social hierarchy, inside and outside the *nomenklatura*. It also implied a forced attachment of the workforce (in a country where there is a legal obligation to work, that means all members of society) to productive units by coercive central planning authorities. This would deprive the workforce of the only liberty it enjoyed under Brezhnev: if not the right, at least the actual chance of inner migration and of changing one's work place. This 'liberalization', as we learn from Victor

Zaslavsky, led to a degree of improvement of the standards of living and working conditions of the workforce, for the productive units had to compete to some extent to keep their workers within the factory.[6] However, 'liberalization' can be revoked and workers can be forcibly attached again, as they used to be under Stalin, to the centrally allotted productive units for a lifetime. This would inevitably lead to a policy of filling the concentration camps with those resisting the new policy, thus creating a new mass of slave labourers. Even money could be practically eliminated and replaced by direct exchange based on ration cards, an option, which emerged, as we know from none other a source than Stalin himself,[7] at the end of his life. The second logical option is to launch a campaign of rationalizing the economy by granting greater freedom to individual enterprises, by endorsing effectivity in the form of including technocrats in the decision-making process also at the level of the factory. Under this option, the Party would retain its political monopoly but it will increasingly abdicate from its economic monopoly position of disposing over national wealth. The third logical option is the combination of the second option with a measure of social liberalization. This option would include legalization of certain non-political organizations, such as independent trade unions, independent industrial, agricultural and cultural associations and the like. A half-hearted type of self-management program (somewhat similar to the Yugoslav model) might also be encouraged. However, even in terms of this option, the political monopoly of the Party would not be affected.

Although we associated the project of 'social liberalization' only with the third option, even the second is inconceivable without social reforms, above all, without the radical structural reforms of agriculture. For the time being, and in sharp contrast to Brezhnev's solemn promise to that effect, internal passports are still not issued to peasants working on collective farms. As a result, they cannot leave their villages freely, without the authorization of the leadership of the collective farms, they are bound to earth just like their forefathers used to be under the harsh conditions of a 'second serfdom'. But the perpetuation of such conditions is at cross purposes with even a minimum of rationalization. A further condition would be the lifting of the most severe restrictions on the circulation of information or at least, and this is not an excessive amount of liberalization, that a formalized political censorship be substituted for centrally organized systematic misinformation.

[6] V. Zaslavsky, *The Neo-Stalinist State*, New York/London: M. E. Sharpe/Harvester Press, 1982, pp. 46–48.

[7] Joseph Stalin, *Economic Problems of Socialism in the USSR*, Moscow: Foreign Languages Publishing House, 1952, p. 27.

These logical options for change can be associated with the concept of 'reform', for the latter implies that change is either promoted, or eventually even implemented, from above, under substantial pressure from below. Of course, a fourth type of change, that of sovereignty, which is revolutionary change *par excellence*, cannot be ruled out logically. However, as far as things stand now, there are no signs of the possibility, let alone the likelihood, of a revolution in the centre of the Soviet empire. Therefore, all speculations about its eventuality would bring us beyond the subject matter of this paper: 'change' in Soviet society.

Finally, the last logical option, which cannot be described either in terms of reform or in those of revolution, means the simple continuation of the present trend. Under this course, certain feeble attempts at economic reforms would be followed by certain, equally feeble and inconsistent, attempts at streamlined re-Stalinization, and in the process, a proper balance would be kept between corporate interest and the individual interests of the members of the oligarchy. One may ask: how long can the present technological, economic and demographic crisis be prolonged? Our straightforward answer to the question is that it can be prolonged for a very long time. It is a typical Western misconception of Soviet society to contend that it can collapse, or the power of the ruling oligarchy can be substantially reduced by an ongoing economic crisis. The Soviet leadership was capable of surviving vigorously in times when millions died of famine. Should dissatisfaction reach a dangerous level, a revived system of the Gulag is a constant option. In addition, Stalin's long and efficient training wiped out the spirit of rebellion from a populace which assesses its social conditions more realistically than do Western observers. Heroic individuals can challenge the system against overwhelming odds, people *en masse* rarely do, if at all. In addition, a rising and ever-stronger nationalist identification, combined with the lack of imagination aimed at possible alternatives, legitimizes the regime sufficiently as it stands now.

On the second level of argument, the relevant question is the following: which of the logically enumerated options is the most likely to determine the immediate future of the USSR?

Attempts at a streamlined version of re-Stalinization can be made, but without doubt, they will fail or will not be carried out at all. The oligarchy, after having established its collective power, does not have the slightest inclination to subject itself to the whims of a new dictator, and there is no new Stalinism without a new Stalin. They fear for their lives, their power, their wealth. It will suffice to threaten the third alone for any political actor to be brought to a halt by a jealous oligarchy. The 'big families' have become untouchable. Andropov came close to laying his hands on them, in particular on the proverbially corrupt Brezhnev family. But Chernenko stopped this 'deviation': he satisfied the 'purists' with a few token executions of corrupt managers (but no longer highly placed functionaries, whereas a former All-Union Deputy Minister of Fisheries was executed under Andropov for embezzlement). Chernenko's protection of the big families shows that the fear of all kinds of change threatening the prerogatives of the oligarchy, including even one which is seemingly close to them in ideological terms, is a substantial enough obstacle for the actualization of any such option.

But this very factor is the absolute obstacle to the implementation of the second option as well, although a considerable part of the oligarchy emphatically favours it, at least in principle. The reason is simple: there is no ruling elite which would not prefer a functioning economy to a dysfunctional one, at least in modernity. In addition, the Soviet oligarchy shed the ideological straightjacket a long time ago, its members think in straightforward pragmatic terms with a fair amount of cynicism. Therefore, the objection to the second option is not over-whelmingly ideological in nature. However, it is precisely pragmatic considerations that act against the acceptance of the second option. The Soviet leadership and party apparatus know full well that there is no economic rationalization without some kind of structural and social reform. And it is exactly the prospect of the latter that deters them from experimenting with economic rationalization. Put bluntly, the Soviet oligarchy subscribes to the domino theory, perhaps to a greater extent than would be necessary for maintaining their rule. (Which, of course, does not exclude the theoretical possibility that a new generation of leaders will make another attempt at squaring the circle, implementing economic, without social, reforms.) In a word, the accumulated social experiences of the oligarchy, from Hungary 1956, through Czechoslo-vakia 1968, to Poland, from the mid-seventies onwards, preclude the likelihood, if not the physical possibility, of Soviet experiments with economic rationalization.

Among all the courses briefly discussed in enumerating the logical possibilities, the continuation of the present one, with vacillations and slight modifications, seems to be the most likely alternative. Up to this point, our main argument has been the vested interest, rigidity, fears and conservatism of the ruling elite. However, the presentation would remain one-sided without taking into account the vested interest and behavioural patterns of certain wide strata of the populace outside the

ruling apparatus who support a 'no change' policy, and the continuation of the present trend, for different reasons. The opposition,
however much silenced, of the population to any attempt at reviving
Stalinism, is too obvious to be explained. However, a fear of changes, in
themselves apparently only beneficial, does need explanation. The
main explanatory factor is the circumstance that Soviet society, as a
result of Stalin's education, and even after the cessation of his cataclysmic 'revolutions from above', is an epitome of coercive paternalism.
The state's subjects have here one right only: the right to supplication.
They are asking for 'favours' from the state, and the term 'favour'
encompasses the whole (usually modest, if not outright poor) amount
of social services and amenities which are necessary for social and
physical reproduction but which are not rights. However, total
dependence on the state has the obverse of 'being taken care of' by the
state (excepting periods of mass reprisals), of being free from the
burdens of choices and of assessing alternatives. Much as it sounds
odd, the comfort of unfreedom can become a widely held social habit
and need. It has the special advantage that incompetence (with the
exception of highly placed and extremely sensitive jobs) is not a factor
one has to consider in one's life strategy. And a whole array of high-
and medium-placed incompetents are afraid of all reforms which
would introduce effectivity into social yardsticks to measure individual
performance. This is a distorted form of 'popular support', lent to a
conservative oligarchy, which has quite different kinds of reasons for
opposing reforms (although guaranteed incompetence is certainly one
of them).

The option to continue the present trend without experiments must
not be described in exclusively negative terms. The objective of export-
ing conflicts in order to counterbalance internal impotence and tension
does not necessarily exclude the temporary acceptance of a new
version of detente. The precondition is that it should bring economic
advantages, recognize the actually acquired Soviet sphere of influence
and that it should not impose any obligation on the Soviet Party to ease
state control over the populace. We have mentioned above a more
ambitious version of the same project: the 'Finlandization' of at least a
part of the West, with all its possible advantages for the Soviet
oligarchy.

East European Soviet societies have greater chances for internal
change. At the same time, they are dispossessed of all means of export-
ing their internal conflicts. The denizens of this part of the Empire are
not used to a complete version of paternalism, or at least much less than
people in the USSR. Practically no one is afraid of reforms: moreover,

almost everyone would support reforms: the more the better. National governments in these countries can use this motivating force on behalf of their own rule. They can mobilize this feeling now in particular, since, after the defeat of the Hungarian Revolution of 1956, the Czechoslovak 'reform from above' of 1968 and 'Poland's peaceful revolution', the hope for a radical change is gone in the region, at least for the foreseeable future.

As a consequence, in East European societies, the second option (that of economic rationalization and economic power-sharing with managers and technocrats) is, in principle, open to implementation. Moreover, in certain states, first and foremost in Hungary, rationalization processes are already under way. The first option, that of re-Stalinization, is emphatically excluded here, unless the Soviet leadership is prepared to eliminate the formal or nominal sovereignty of its satellites. The fourth option, change without reform, can be supported by the oligarchy, but it is completely rejected by the populace in this region, so it has a very limited chance, unless it is coupled with nationalism of a kind. However, this is only possible if the totalitarian state pursues an anti-Soviet, seemingly independent foreign policy, and a policy of excessive cultural nationalism. But it is highly unlikely that the Rumanian game could spread to other states as well. Even in the case of Rumania it was a precondition of the detour that, for a number of reasons, Soviet Army units were not stationed in Rumania.

What are the chances for the third option, that of structural and social reform, initiated from below and supported from above or, respectively, initiated from above and supported from below? Some structural and social changes are not altogether excluded as long as they do not affect the system of political domination. A complete detotalization of East European states is an excluded possibility: it is precisely the totalitarian character of the state that makes these countries part of the Soviet Empire, and if this is questioned, force prevails. The available maximum is a social structure similar to the Yugoslav model, but now without the national independence Yugoslavia enjoys.

Nonetheless, East European social fantasy has always transgressed the boundaries of the possible; movements in the region have reached out, time and time again, for the idea of the Great Republic. This idea was conceived in Central and Eastern Europe in social upheavals at the beginning of this century, and its memory has not completely faded away. It was this idea that fuelled the workers councils in Hungary in 1956. It has been revived in the Solidarity movement. Space does not allow us here to describe the utopia of the Great Republic in full (but see Chapter 8 below). We can only sum up its most important features. They are self-management in the social sphere, the combination of direct democracy and representative democracy in the political sphere. Despite an explicit aversion to all official ideas of socialism (which is often identified with socialism in general), the democratic socialist model of the Great Republic is in fact the leading version of social imagination in Central and Eastern Europe. Of course, with a long-lasting rule of the Soviet system this idea, too, can disappear, or at least be relegated in the background. But this is the utopia to which the writers of the present paper are committed.

When we mention, among the merely logical options, revolution, we do not have in mind bloodshed, barricades, stormtroops. Nor do we believe that revolutions can be prepared by conspirators and underground organizations. Revolutions 'happen' when the power lies on the street and can be picked up. Since in Eastern Europe the system of domination is not legitimized, even if certain governments are tacitly accepted, a revolution aimed at the model of the Great Republic would inevitably take place given the non-interference of the Soviet Army. Eastern Europe is ready for the change of sovereignty, but this is exactly the most unlikely change to happen.

As mentioned earlier, this statement does not apply to the USSR. Social agents of a revolutionary change are not visible on the Soviet horizon. And if they were, it is anybody's guess what direction their action would take. In principle, one cannot exclude that in cataclysmic times, the model of the Great Republic could gain momentum in certain regions of the USSR as well. So could, unfortunately, new brands of conservatism and fundamentalism, whose ascendancy would inevitably be accompanied by massacres. Not even the bleak perspective can be excluded that the Great Eastern Empire, even after a victorious revolution, would remain imperialist and hostile to democracy or liberalism, to the same extent it is now. Yet, Kant advised us to make a firm distinction between what we can know, what we should do and what we can hope for. We can hope that the idea of the Great Republic will grow from its roots in the Eastern soil, but we simply cannot know whether indeed it will.

3

Redemptive and Democratic
Paradigms in Radical Politics

Ferenc Fehér[1]

Two methodological remarks are necessary by way of introduction. First, while I am going to treat the redemptive paradigm in full, if only in an outline, I will analyse the democratic paradigm, for obvious reasons of length, only in so far as it is related to the alternative under discussion. Secondly, under the heading 'redemptive paradigm in radical politics', I will address both leftist and rightist political theories. However, to avoid confusion, it is to the degree conservatives embrace the redemptive paradigm that I will speak of 'conservative political radicalism', and in no other sense.

I

Redemptive politics was born at the end of the eighteenth century. It entered *theater mundi* in the person of the hero whom Hegel appropriately called *Weltgeist zu Pferde*, and who was undoubtedly Weber's model in elaborating his principle of 'charismatic legitimation', in the person of the First Consul, later the Emperor. It is a historical paradox that the eminently prosaic, even harshly cynical Bonaparte, who despised *idéologues* and who deeply suspected the Incorruptible's ideological politics, became redeemer for his age and many generations to come, yet it is an undeniable fact. There were two sociological factors which prepared the ground for the sudden rise of the redemptive paradigm, as well as constituted its substance. The narrower factor

---

[1] Originally published in English in *Telos* N. 63, Spring 1985.

was the much analysed circumstance that the victorious bourgeoisie, having been emancipated both from its aristocratic and Jacobin enemies, proved incapable of government in five years of lacklustre political rule. The accumulated social contradictions cried out for a redeemer, and the age found it in the person of the paternalist lawgiver, the peremptory absolute prince who was, at the same time, extremely indulgent to what is most human in the bourgeoisie: greed and ambition, and who grew increasingly, in a series of dazzling victories, into an almost mythological god of the battlefields. It has belonged since Napoleon to the essence of the redemptive paradigm that, although it always emerged from the tacit consent of collective forces, it invariably becomes personified; that it is populist (under the Emperor's rule in the sense that everyone carried the proverbial Marshall's baton in his bag), and, finally, that this apparently surprisingly simple, initially seemingly irresistible and rational solution turns out to be the greatest possible, even catastrophic, irrationality in each and every instance. The broader sociological factor was the incomplete secularization of modern society.

The main features of the redemptive paradigm can sufficiently be circumscribed on the basis of the two sociological factors. Such a description will display it as considerably more than a mere personal approach to political affairs, rather it will present it as a genuine paradigm and a competitor to the two further paradigms of modernity in the political domain: the liberal and the radical democratic ones. The first constituent of this characterization is what can be called, in the wake of Luhmann,[2] an overreduction of the inherent complexity of modernity. This means that the collisions within a complex network of social subsystems and regulations which emerge perforce at almost each and every historical juncture are apparently resolved and transcended, if they seem to be insoluble and insurmountable, through a simple medium: the person and the irrational authority of the redeemer (the latter has, of course, claims to a supreme type of rationality). This authority is irrational, firstly, because it does not rest on the conservative rationality of traditions, moreover, it always emerges on the debris of a smashed traditional authority, secondly, because it cancels the Enlightenment project in so far as it is unquestionable. The second constituent is a constantly renewed attempt, successful or unsuccessful, at the homogenization of the intrinsic heterogeneity of complex modernity. All redeemers in a long history of

---

[2] N. Luhmann, *Soziale Systeme, Grundriss einer allgemeinen Theorie*, Frankfurt, Suhrkamp, 1984.

almost two centuries have shown themselves resolute adversaries of the particularistic existence of groups and units (except corporatist social hierarchy), of individual autonomy and of political pluralism. Subjecting civil society to a homogenizing political state has, to a smaller or greater degree, always been the hallmark of the redemptive paradigm, both in its successful and unsuccessful versions. The third constituent is that the redemptive paradigm entails, unlike the liberal and radical democratic ones, no set of rationally predictable institutions. Redemptive institutions vary from redeemer to redeemer. Moreover, such institutions are deduced from the personality, strategy, and often the whims of the redeemer. This circumstance, which is not psychological in nature, underscores the personified character of the redemptive paradigm. Finally, the often repeated critique (or appraisal) of the redemptive paradigm, namely that it is religious or pseudo-religious in nature, stems precisely from the broader factor, incomplete secularization. Where liberalism fails with its 'scientific spirit' to satisfy certain needs emerging from an incomplete secularization, where the radical democratic paradigm has no ethical theory and practice but where traditional religions have lost their cohesive force and appeal, the redemptive paradigm is indeed a substitute for the religious cohesion of the social domain.

The redemptive paradigm died on the battlefield of Waterloo, and its genuine revival, both on the Right and the Left, came on the eve and in the immediate aftermath of World War One. Weber's *Politics as Vocation*[3] was the first emphatic warning about this rising phenomenon and its implicit dangers. The text has become too well-known to be scrutinized from a new angle. Nonetheless, it ought to be revisited for a much less known fact. Weber, in elaborating the key concept of 'the politics of ultimate ends', was directly referring to Georg Lukács, his young and unpredictable friend without mentioning his name, who was then experimenting with setting a 'metaphysical foundation' for Russian revolutionary terrorism and completing a turn to communism. This circumstance will perhaps reveal the deeper implications of Weber's warning. However, Weber only saw the danger and typified the pertinent attitudes but he was apparently unaware of the deeper cause of the new threat (let alone that his solution rested on methodological self-delusion and that it was completely unsatisfactory).

We have to turn to another representative sociologist, Karl Mannheim, to find the social agent of the resurrection of the redemptive

---

[3] Max Weber, *Politics as Vocation*, *From Max Weber: essays in sociology*, transl. and ed. and with an introduction by H. H. Gerth and C. Wright Mills, London/Boston: Routledge and Kegan Paul, 1948.

paradigm. These agents are the celebrated 'free-floating intellectuals'.[4] By the *fin de siècle*, the intelligentsia had a new social status and an adequate novel consciousness. The latter predisposed this stratum for the role of the social agent of the revival of the redemptive paradigm which, this time, included the task of the theoretical formulation of the paradigm itself, a duty not fulfilled when the phenomenon first appeared. In this sense, it can be stated without any attempt at a new kind of demonology that the free-floating intellectuals were profoundly responsible for corrupting social movements with their redemptive paradigm of politics.

The social fact which made the free-floating intellectuals the natural bearers of the redemptive paradigm was their gradually achieved dual situation. On the one hand, the avantgardist intelligentsia was no longer, neither in politics nor in art, a mere appendage to the bourgeoisie. On the other hand, the intellectuals had to pay the price of emancipation in the form of uprootedness and bohemian misery for which, in turn, they were adequately compensated by the equally novel *esprit de corps*. Namely, they shared the proud conviction in common that the intellectuals, not the upper classes, were the repositories of a changing world, a coming redemption. At the same time, uprootedness generated a professional sensitivity and openness in the members of this stratum for new and radical paradigms.

The two complexes to which the free-floating intellectuals, as bearers of the revival of the redemptive paradigm, gave voice when they joined the movements and usurped their leadership, was the fiasco of a self-complacent liberalism and the interrelated re-emergence of the acute awareness of an incomplete secularization at the catastrophic end of the 'scientific century'. The interrelatedness of the two constituents cannot be overemphasized. The nineteenth century was full of liberal noises about 'progress' and 'scientific spirit' which would eliminate dysfunctions and disharmony from social life for good, and this proud expertise managed to trigger World War One, with its hecatombes of casualties, as well as result in the greatest possible miscalculation of instrumental reason: in the suicide of Western Europe as the 'natural' epicentre of world politics. The liberal politicians who never ceased during the 'scientific century' to be condescending towards the intellectuals, for the latter 'only speak but cannot act', proved to be hopeless dilettantes and were appropriately held in utter contempt by the free-floating intellectuals. However, this failure again made what had been suspected, or

---

[4] Karl Mannheim, *Ideology and Utopia*, London/Boston: Routledge and Kegan Paul, 1960.

expressed, by the first generation of romanticism self-evident: namely that at the same time as secularization had remained incomplete, the traditional religious panacea nevertheless remained totally inadequate. Therefore, the hour of a substitute, 'this worldly religion', – or, to use Lukács's aptly coined term, and perhaps self-characterization, that of 'religious atheism' – struck then and there. Both in the case of the Nazis, with the Teutonic cult of the Führer, who called themselves *Gottesgläubige*, in order to be distinguished from Christians while emphasizing their pagan devotion, and the Bolsheviks who raised the Georgian seminarist to the pedestal of a new God, with no less divine prerogatives than those of deified Roman Caesars, free-floating intellectuals or semi-intellectuals, lived up to the exigencies of the historical hour.

It is revealing to cast a glance at the two main motives, commonly shared by rightist and leftist intellectuals, for the revival of the redemptive paradigm. The liberal paradigm was criticized, or rather rejected out of hand, by them as 'banal', 'superficial', 'tedious', and, above all, 'inauthentic', all terms not stemming from an ethics, but from an existentialist metaethics and, above all, an aesthetics. A classic text, *Bolshevism as a Moral Problem*, by Lukács, should stand here as witness. The text was committed to paper a few weeks before the dramatic swap of principles, the author's joining communism in December, 1918. In fact, Lukács aligns himself here with social democracy, as the embodiment of the liberal paradigm as against Bolshevism, for genuinely moral reasons. Bolshevism, he paraphrased a hero of Dostoevsky, is nothing but the actualization of the diabolical maxim: we shall lie ourselves through to truth.[5] However, the choice was made with utter resignation, since this giant of the free-floating intelligentsia was fully aware that he chose the 'joyless' and 'prosaic' task of 'piecemeal engineering'. And resignation over the 'joyless task' could at least also have been co-constitutive of the sudden swap of principles which stunned so many contemporaries. The aesthetic character of the redemptive paradigm, a feature which brings it so close to the conversions of the members of Friedrich Schlegel's generation, a character trait which Lukács otherwise regarded in all matters pertaining to life as outright frivolous, becomes even more conspicuous if we recapitulate the relevant terms. The world has to be 'recreated', and recreated *ex nihilo*, for the ancient gods are, as the prophetic Nietzsche

---

[5]   G. Lukács, *Bolschewismus als moralisches Problem* (Bolshevism as a Moral Problem), in G. Lukács, *Politische Aufsätze I.: Taktik und Ethik (1918–1920)*, Neuwied: Luchterhand, 1976.

put it correctly, indeed dead, the raw material of a disenchanted world contaminated, or, in other terms: cosmos should be created out of chaos. All these terms intimate god and the deified artist with the same breath, and the equally prophetic Friedrich Schlegel remarked ingeniously that the artist's divine egoism is nothing but his own self-deification.[6]

A sketchy morphology of the representative types of the creators and bearers of the redemptive paradigm is appropriate here. Trotsky, as the representative free-floating intellectual, comes first to my mind as perhaps the greatest, and certainly the most colourful personality of the redemptive paradigm, in sharp contrast to Lenin, the man of organization and utilitarian ethics. For Lenin was exactly what he wanted to be: *primus inter pares* in a pragmatic collective dictatorship, but no redeemer. I am quite deliberately not touching upon the hackneyed problem of whether or not, and to what extent Trotsky was the 'genuine' Bolshevik as against the 'perverted' ones, nor upon the other, historically irrelevant one as to what would have happened to Soviet Russia under his leadership. Such a role, I am convinced, had been discarded from the outset, precisely because he was the redemptive intellectual *par excellence*, who could not be entirely domesticated by the organization, who only remained a temporary resident in it. Nothing expresses the fact more eloquently than the famous scene described by Deutscher: *pour épater les bureaucrats*, Trotsky read French novels ostentatiously on the last sessions of the Central Committee in which he participated.[7] Trotsky was indeed everything an intellectual as bearer of the redemptive paradigm ought to be. As an excellent journalist, a great rhetorician, a brilliant popular historian, he was populism incarnate. In his first and third period, he was a religious admirer of the 'crowd', the masses, these mythological agents of another mythological entity, History, with a capital H. As a free-floating intellectual *par excellence*, he refined the professional capacity of his stratum to the point of perfection: the capacity of forecasting events much before the professional politicians could sense it, and that of audaciously changing principles whenever the historical hour struck. He foretold that Russia will be the new epicentre of world revolution when all his colleagues in Russian social democracy still held in awe 'the much more forward Western comrades'. He also fore-

---

[6] Friedrich Schlegel, *Charakteristiken und Kritiken I.* (1796–1801) ed. With an introduction by Hans Eichner, Vienna/Zürich. Munich, Paderborn, Verlag Ferdinand Schöningh – Thomas – Verlag, 1967, pp. 260, 262.

[7] I. Deutscher, *The Prophet Unarmed, Trotsky: 1921–1929*, London: Oxford University Press, 1959, pp. 249–50.

told that the approaching Russian Revolution was mortally endangered by the Russian Jacobin whose best critic he certainly was. He
also sensed when the minute of revolution arrived, and jumped on the
bandwagon of Bolshevism, the only vehicle of practical action he
found, not because of ambition (although he was sufficiently ambitious
and theatrical for this sudden change), but primarily because this was
the hour of redemption and he felt himself the bearer of the redemptive
paradigm. He was therefore perfectly capable of changing principles in
the most radical manner. The arch-enemy of Russian Jacobinism overnight became a Super-Jacobin, and in his polemics against Kautsky, he
gave voice to a contempt for 'the masses', whom he adored before and
after, but now termed a conglomerate of 'lazy animals', to a degree
which made him a contemporary of Mussolini rather than of Lenin.
The latter always preferred the pragmatic work of the terror to verbal
excesses. Luxemburg, with an almost uncanny sensitivity, precisely
captured this aspect of Trotsky's personality when she, in the last
chapter of her lifelong polemics against the process in which Russian
intellectuals expropriated the yield of great revolutions, treated Lenin
with animosity but with respect (for finally he did what he had always
advertised of himself to be his final goal), while she treated Trotsky, the
intellectual parvenu of the terror, with ironical contempt.[8] The only
mistake Luxemburg committed was, as the tone indicates, that in an
oversimplification of character, she attributed the swap of positions to
ambition and opportunism. But the final turn, the decision against the
masters who 'betrayed' and 'perverted' a great revolution, which made
him, with all his future political irrelevance, a moral and political
monument of the redemptive paradigm, Trotsky proved that he always
preferred the work of redemption to ambition and rule.

On the right, we face a wide diapason of the bearers of the redemptive paradigm, a significant number of whom were uprooted, and therefore free-floating, intellectuals. Mussolini was not only the first
champion, but also the conscious creator of the theory of state totalitarianism as a principle of redemption in a chaos void of gods, ideals
and insignia. Croce's sharp eyes had detected the first premonitions of
this role in the young Mussolini much before it was revealed to wider
audiences. When Mussolini was elected into the leadership of the
Italian Socialist Party, Croce commented in an article on the event that
it meant the victory of Sorel and Bergson, rather than that of Marx.[9]

[8] Rosa Luxemburg, *The Russian Revolution, and, Leninism or Marxism*, New introduction
by Bertram D. Wolfe, Ann Arbor: University of Michigan Press, 1961, p. 27.
[9] Quoted in R. DeFelice, *Mussolini il rivoluzionario 1883–1920*, Torino: Einaudi, 1965,
p. 119.

Nor is the term 'creator' used here accidentally in connection with Mussolini. Despite his grand aspirations, he could never be deified to the extent he longed for. So in consolation, he snatched D'Annunzio's invention and turned it upside down. Where the pre-Fascist writer politicized decadent aesthetics, the Fascist Duce aestheticized storm-troop politics. Hence his constructivist–avantgardist architectural predilections, the spirit of which one can decipher from Chirico's magnificent canvasses and his idiosyncratic style of rhetoric. The latter was deeply modernistic: behind the facade of a Hollywood-style presentation, the grotesque, even the clownish always appeared. On its part, German National Socialism was full of second- and third-rate redeemers, almost all failed intellectuals or professionals, all craving for redemption which, however, had to be non-religious in a traditional sense in an age of bankrupt creeds and doctrines. One of the most conspicuous examples of this phenomenon is obviously Goebbels, this strange combination of the nadir of cynicism ever to be produced by capitalist press journalism and a sincere and ruthless fanaticism of a new pagan devotion, with his symbolic intellectual fiasco in the background (Gundolf had turned him down as a prospective Ph.D. student). A similar case is presented by Rosenberg, the dilettantish but strictly doctrinaire philosopher of National Socialism who never achieved the recognition of his academic colleagues whom he admired and from whom he had learned so extensively. But, to climb higher on the rungs of the ladder, let us just glance at the terms in which Adorno described Wagner's character, in order to make comprehensible what he called Wagner's Fascist music: a way of life characterized by a bohemian uprootedness, a person who was never prepared to do any proper work for a living, nor was he familiar with the simplest rules of bourgeois decency, but who was imbued with the haughty spirit of his own predestination coupled with a total contempt for the rest of the world, as well as with a tyrannical inclination to his fellow beings.[10] Is this all not a perfect description of the Supreme Artist, the great adorer of Wagner, who created his Reich *ex nihilo* after he had failed as an ordinary free-floating semi-intellectual utterly and miserably, to send the art work back, in the grandest historical gesture of operatic stage-managing, into *nihil* again?

Several subtypes of the bearers of the redemptive paradigm could be pinpointed here, both on the Right and the Left, but I have to restrict myself to one of them which had deeper and wider theoretical implications. I have in mind the representative intellectual, both on the Right

[10] Theodor W. Adorno, *In Search of Wagner*, transl. by Rodney Livingstone, London: New Left Books, Chapter I: 'Social Character', 1981.

and the Left, who, in a manner of speaking, sensed beforehand the advent of, and the space to be occupied by, the great practical redeemer, who wanted to stand by, and be a counsellor to him, but who, when the redeemer did materialize, felt a bitter disillusionment with his pettiness. Clearly, I am speaking of Lukács, Heidegger and Gentile, with the following qualifications. First, their role as heralds and advertisers of the redeemer was not coextensive with their whole career. Secondly, their self-selected redeemers were not identical as far as value content was concerned. Thirdly and finally, their philosophical *oeuvre*, even if in part not entirely separable from this period and this role, cannot be appraised exclusively, not even overwhelmingly, on the basis of their theoretical advocacy of the redeemer. They came to actualize this role of a counsellor in different but equally tragic or tragicomic ways. Lukács's philosophy first posited a collective redeemer, the world proletariat,[11] and it was only with the low tide of European social revolution that he personified it in the inadequate, which is to say already obsolete, redeemer, Lenin, while he only paid the minimal signs of respect to Stalin. Heidegger first had, in his well-known academic address,[12] an enthusiastic attitude to Hitler which was, in an equally well-known way, followed by disillusionment and the impotent critique of silence and practical adjustment. Neither Lukács nor Heidegger were ever allowed to come close to their personified redeemer, while Gentile was a loyal functionary of Mussolini, even in a period when he could hardly conceal his contempt for the bloodshed and the dilettantish improvisations of the Duce. His death, a result of Quixotic loyalty, is not entirely exempt therefore from certain tragic features. But over and beyond the differences, Lucien Goldmann understood the deeper meaning of this story in common. The representative intellectual of the years following World War One, in quest for the redemptive paradigm, in rejecting traditional religions, but persistently remaining a religious atheist, acted out the satire play of one of the dreams of the Enlightenment: the rule of the wise monarch and amateurish philosopher who is being advised, and tacitly guided, by the professionals.[13]

1945 and 1956 were the years in which the redemptive paradigm seemed to collapse for good. This was the time when the horrific reality

---

[11] G. Lukács, *History and Class Consciousness*, transl. by R. Livingstone, London: Merlin Press, 1971.

[12] Martin Heidegger, 'Die Selbstbehauptung der Universität' (The Self-Affirmation of University) in J.-P. Faye, editor, *M. Heidegger: Discours et Proclamations, Meditations*, Paris: IN. 3,1961, 149.

[13] Lucien Goldmann, *Lukács and Heidegger; towards a new philosophy*, transl. by W. Q. Boelhower, London/Boston: Routledge and Kegan Paul, 1977, p. 19.

behind the operatic facade and the socialist humanist editorials was unmasked; first Hitler's, later Stalin's camps. In addition, they appeared for the theoretically-minded part of a stunned world as a direct result of the Messianic work of amateurish redeemers. For at least two decades, in the West for an even longer period of time, pragmatic political principles seemed to gain the upper hand irresistibly and irrevocably. The theoretically most self-conscious statesman of the *pax americana*, Henry Kissinger, was a self-appointed disciple of a man of sceptical, aristocratic enlightenment turned against the Enlightenment: Metternich. At the same time, he was the incarnation of the pragmatic spirit and the deep problematic of Weber's 'politics of responsibility'. A very similar process took place in Soviet political life under the collective rule of the *nomenklatura* after the fall of Khrushchev. As Victor Zaslavsky pointed out, the ideology-laden slogan of the 'construction of communism' has been gradually replaced under Brezhnev by 'the Soviet way of life' which is nationalist, de-ideologized and pragmatic.[14]

However, the latent social needs for the paradigm of redemptive politics have by no means evaporated. Just recently we have witnessed a deeply problematic new revival of redemptive politics, once again both on the Right and the Left. On the Right, President Reagan's crusading, moralizing and evangelizing politics, as the most visible expression of rightist political movements and their principles, rightly causes consternation in circles far wider than those of the Left *sensu stricto*. A theoretical, not directly political, analysis should not focus on its tangible, practical, actual or potential dangers; it should rather emphasize its roots in American ideological history which, at the same time as they account for its genesis, set the limits of this development. Stanford Lyman and Arthur Vidich have shown, for me convincingly, that American sociological and political thinking has had from its origins a traditionally and religiously grounded, nonetheless messianistic undercurrent, which has partly coloured, partly 'overdetermined' the dominant pragmatic paradigm.[15] In terms of this tradition, American politics has always had to be something more and different than the value-free art (or science) of handling practical exigencies. This undercurrent has sometimes broken through in a liberally benevolent form (under President Wilson), sometimes in an outright venomous way (during McCarthyism), but in both cases it meant the

---

[14] Victor Zaslavsky, *The Neo-Stalinist State*, New York/Brighton: M. E. Sharpe/Harvester Press, 1982, pp. 86–90.

[15] Stanford Lyman and Arthur Vidich, 'Pragmatism and Messianic Trend in American Political Thought', unpublished manuscript.

redemptive principle moved into the forefront of political thinking and acting. In both cases, the practical results were catastrophic. The redemptive zeal of the Reagan period seems to be a new chapter in this apparently long history. On the other hand, precisely this tradition sets certain limitations to the present neo-conservative redemptive ambition. As long as it continues to rest on its own traditional Christian premises, its inherent fundamentalism simply cannot move towards any neo-pagan mythologies with their implicit political consequences. It can restrict and narrow the concept of liberalism to a dangerous degree (for example, one just wonders what Professor Kirkpatrick means by democracy when she endorses authoritarian, as against totalitarian, government). But it cannot eliminate the concept of democracy from its own vocabulary, and this too is a social fact. Nor can it practically eliminate certain fundamental institutions of liberal–conservative regimes. However, this is, needless to say, pointing out the limitation of a position, not its theoretical justification or apology.

On the Left, we witness a similar, although not, or not necessarily, fundamentalist resurrection of the redemptive paradigm. The main tendency in this direction is the evangelizing spirit detectable above all in the environmentalist and anti-nuclear movements whose political message can be characterized as 'negative redemption'. Rescuing 'the environment' or 'human livelihood' as such, or even more ambitiously, humankind itself, is undeniably a redemptive feature. At the same time, it is negative in that it is determined by the adversary, the threatening, personified or impersonal, forces. This leftist resurrection of the redemptive paradigm has a long prehistory which comprises the last two decades. While, in the main, the movements of the sixties were in their overwhelming majority not organized on this principle, rather, they turned sharply against this-worldly redeemers and the idea of redemption, elements of the present revival have been slowly accumulating in the whole period. The first major wave came in the form of the European cult of Mao. Sartre, with his famous and ominous preface to Fanon's book, added his share to the trend. In this preface, the redeemer appeared in an impersonal, abstract form, in the cult of a redeeming violence.[16] Peter Weiss, in *Marat–Sade*, a genuine literary masterpiece, was another promoter of the redemptive paradigm. If a great work of art can be exploited at all to the degree to be used as an ideological document, one can say that *Marat–Sade* represents a lapse behind Büchner's *Danton's Death*. Büchner's great anti-Jacobin and

---

[16] Jean-Paul Sartre, preface to Frantz Fanon, *The Wretched of the Earth*, transl. by Constance Farrington, Harmondsworth: Penguin, 1967.

truly revolutionary drama in the first half of the nineteenth century represented a radical break with the cult of 'Saint Marat', the Redeemer, whereas Weiss's passion play returns to the atmosphere of Jean-Louis David in whose superb painting the dead Marat appears as the dead Christ.

It is relatively easy to grasp the causes of this revival of the redemptive paradigm on the Left and the Right, as well as its menacing implications. I can only hint at the first complex, but I have no space to analyse it. Its constituents are the perhaps longest lasting depression of capitalism, a total fiasco of global politics conjoined with an objective need for global solutions, the loss of an authentic socialist perspective, the further disintegration of party politics, the emergence of marginalized, but socially important, groups, the unemployed youth, the intellectual proletarians driven out of their habitual sphere. All these provide so much 'natural media' for rightist and leftist redemptive politics. The primary political consequences are at hand: on the one hand, the gaining ground of a Cold War atmosphere in the wake of the rightist, on the other hand, re-Stalinization in the wake of the leftist revival of the redemptive paradigm. Both, of course, depend on the interplay of several, equally important, socio-economic conditions. In a theoretical analysis, a new obstacle raised to the progressing secularization of modern society poses the main problem. However, I have to add that, to my mind, the perspectives of secularization have changed drastically since Marx's time. We now see that the abolition of all gods does not necessarily bring freedom and an end to alienation, particularly not if the emancipation takes place in a violent form and in the deification of (individual or collective) messianic forces. Nevertheless, the radical expulsion of this-worldly substitutes for gods and redeemers from politics, this theoretically based, but decidedly immanent form of human action, which reserves free space for beliefs and devotions without the transformation of politics into any kind of pseudo-religion, still belongs to what can, in my view, be called a rational and emancipatory perspective of the progressive secularization of modernity.

II

Two interrelated preconditions established the discovery of the radical democratic paradigm on the Western Left. The first was an understanding of the differences between the liberal and the democratic model, a difference which had to remain hidden as long as the Left regarded democracy as a negligible superstructural phenomenon or even a mere sham. The second *conditio sine qua non* is already spelt out by the last clause: the coming home of the Left to democracy, still an extremely slow and uneven process. Not only a detailed analysis of the models is clearly impossible here, but, in addition, the significantly distinct version of the American and European concepts of liberalism too constitute common knowledge for theoretical observers. But within these limits, a rough outline of what I regard as the democratic paradigm can be given here.

The democratic paradigm departs, in contrast to the liberal dichotomy of the private and public sphere, from the triple status of the person in a new social framework. In the first status, the single person, as a repository of all human and political rights elects its representative political bodies (the parliamentary body in one of its versions). In this status, the person is considered in separation, although it may enter into associations, and it enjoys, beyond the legally and pragmatically uncurtailed rights of voting, the access to all media in which it can articulate, as well as develop, his or her own political opinion and options. In the second status, the person as *political persona* acts as a member of a communal body, and it elects, upholds and modifies certain institutions of a direct democratic system. Eventual conflicts between the two subsystems are not dysfunctions, but the necessary correlate of this conception which accepts social conflict as an inevitable component of all free political establishments. It is, therefore, not a theory of 'guaranteed society'. In the third status, the person acts as member of a social body in which capacity he or she is a unit of collective ownership, a collective proprietor. These three statuses recreate the private and public domain in a specific sense which is thoroughly dissimilar to the liberal dichotomy. The public domain, understood in terms of the first and second status of the person, is divided into two subdomains. They include both the representative and the direct democratic space (institutions, modes of political behaviour, channels of self-articulation). The private domain is equally divided into two subdomains. In the private domain *sensu stricto*, we find the person as co-proprietor of collective ownership as a communitarian but not directly political being. In the second subdomain, the intimate one, we find the person exercizing its duties, acting out its faith and predilections as a family member, as an eventual participant in religious or other social, but not directly political associations. It is precisely this separated, but ultimately integrated and not conflict-free model that I call the democratic, or radical democratic paradigm.

Hannah Arendt's theory of the 'free republic' was perhaps the first audacious theoretical formulation of the radical democratic paradigm. She had an important predecessor, Rosa Luxemburg. This connection, properly understood, presents Arendt's magnificent essay on Luxemburg,[17] a seemingly so unexpected protagonist in her theory, to be much more than a homage to a great tragic personality. Luxemburg was brought up in the Marxist tradition of the withering away of the state and the idea of the dictatorship of the proletariat. But when she pondered, in storms of great revolutions, 'the tasks of the proletariat', she came to the double, although theoretically not sufficiently founded, nonetheless crucial, conclusion that the revolutionary objective must be the combination of parliamentary and extra-parliamentary forms of democracy, instead of the Jacobin confiscation of liberties. Under the heading 'extra-parliamentary' she meant both institutionalized and non-institutionalized forms of democracy (councils and movements alike).

Arendt's theory of the 'free republic', combined with the crucial American tradition, starts exactly at this point. Its main constituents are as follows. Firstly, Arendt is adamant on the necessary demythologization of political theory. One cannot imagine a more convinced enemy of the redemptive paradigm than Arendt. Her famous *aperçu*, which provoked outrage, that 'evil is banal' was conceived precisely in this spirit.[18] So vehement was her passion against redeemers and anti-redeemers (and, ultimately, Christ and anti-Christ belong in the same school of thought) that she simply misread Eichmann. She presented a stupid fellow in lieu of the negative redeemer who was king in Budapest in 1944, a 'purist' in contrast, even in conscious opposition, to his superiors then desperately bargaining with the enemy to save their skins and the loot. But Arendt's warning must be heeded: in this-worldly political action we must have theory and principles, in other words, we have to transcend pragmatism, but we must not tolerate images of 'saviours' and 'demons'. Such images themselves are hotbeds of synthetic saviours and demons to come, therefore potentially dangerous. Only a politics expurgated from these transcendental images can serve actual emancipation. Secondly, Arendt was convinced that the Marxian idea of the abolition of the political sphere, its absorption by what Marx called 'human emancipation' did not simply face insurmountable technical difficulties in modernity, but it is an undesirable

[17] Hannah Arendt, *Men in Dark Times*, New York: Harcourt Brace Jovanovich, 1968.
[18] Hannah Arendt, *Eichmann in Jerusalem: A Report on the Banality of Evil*, London: Faber and Faber, 1963.

objective as well. Continuous political activity is a value in itself, she never ceased to contend, and with this insistence (which, by the way, she shares with Castoriadis),[19] ancient republican virtue, an attitude hostile to, and extremely suspicious of, all 'redeemers', returns into democratic theory in a streamlined version. Finally, she places the direct forms of democracy, from the American township to the French, Russian and Hungarian councils, these revolutionary creations, in the pinnacle of her conception, while she never ceased to grasp the theoretical problems of the party political process.[20]

A second version of the radical democratic paradigm which is now emerging, conceives capitalism, industrialization and the political process towards radical democracy (as socialism) as distinct logics of modernity. For the time being, this version is a promise rather than a complete theory. However, it is without doubt a decidedly immanent theory of politics and it has certain chances of becoming a complete theory. It contains an explicit rejection of all versions of the redemptive paradigm for it recognizes no authority other than the process of rational discourse as the 'just procedure of legislation' (in the sense that Habermas elaborated the concept without extending it to moral legislation proper).[21] In this process, ideally, human beings are authors of all norms and rules which they obey, and they obey no other authorities or rules but the self-created ones, particularly not positive or negative redeemers. Further, this theory implies an at least theoretical and democratic solution, for the transformation of capitalism. It is an heir to the liberal theory which, explicitly or implicitly, maintained that there is no free man without property. However, the radical democratic theory universalizes this postulation which was particularized under the conditions of capitalism. Everyone must become proprietor of the conditions of human social reproduction, if not in all, at least in some respects. From this, an idea of socialism as participatory democracy follows, a utopia in the sense of the Kantian regulative principle which does not tolerate either redeemers or redemption within its domain.

The difficulties about the rejection of the redemptive paradigm are manifold. However, above all, it needs a complete and radical self-criticism by the intellectuals, creators and self-appointed bearers of this project, which is always a painful process. However, recent political history offers some hope in the activity of the KOR, this

---

[19] C. Castoriadis, *L'institution imaginaire de la société*, Paris: Editions du Seuil, 1975, pp. 106–107.

[20] H. Arendt, *On Revolution*, New York: The Viking Press, 1963, pp. 269–277.

[21] J. Habermas, *Moralbewusstsein und kommunikatives Handeln*, Frankfurt: Suhrkamp, 1983, pp. 75–76.

magnificent initiative of Polish intellectuals for half a decade in the seventies, which finally led to the birth of Solidarity. Whatever their actual world-view, the founders and militants of the KOR subscribed to the radical democratic paradigm in that they simply offered their intellectual capacities to Polish workers as a social service, not as a messianic gesture or an attempt at redemption. This heroic but unpretentious deed will, I hope, serve as further inspiration for political philosophy.

4

The Social Character of Khrushchev's Regime

Ferenc Fehér [1]

I IMAGES OF KHRUSHCHEV

Who was Khrushchev? Or in a somewhat more pointed formulation: what was Khrushchev? What did the period hallmarked by his name represent? In order to reply to this question, easier put than answered, we first have to set the time limits of the period that can appropriately be called the Khrushchev era. Speaking accurately, and despite the fact that he was already First Secretary of the Central Committee in 1953 (but, due to a very confused state of post-Stalin affairs, only the fourth man on the *nomenklatura*), the period which can, with many qualifications, be described as his 'rule' certainly did not start earlier than 1955. Its symbolic initiating acts were the fall of his great rival, Malenkov (a fall mainly engineered by Khrushchev, with much cunning and Stalinist demagoguery) in February 1955, and his dramatic appearance on the Belgrade airport to rehabilitate the supposed Gestapo agent Tito and his ideologically newly 'resocialized' Yugoslavia (a most emancipatory deed as far as East European history is concerned) in August 1955. I fully agree with Crankshaw that the never to be repeated peak of Khrushchev's rule and influence came very shortly afterwards, with the 20th Congress of the CPSU, and the world-historic 'Secret Speech'.[2] To indicate the end of the period is a seemingly simple act indeed: apparently, it would suffice to point to the coup in October, 1964. But,

[1] Originally published in English in R. F. Miller, F. Fehér, editors, *Khrushchev and the Communist World*, London, Sydney, Totowa, Croom Helm, Barnes & Noble, 1983.
[2] Edward Crankshaw, *Khrushchev*, London: Collins, 1966, p. 11.

in actual fact, and despite the reality that literally nobody awaited
Khrushchev's demotion (Soviet First Men died, were not demoted, and
since Khrushchev was vigorously alive, he could only have been
murdered, which would have been out of tune with his regime), unmistakable signs on the wall indicating the imminent collapse of the
whole edifice were already visible in 1963. To cut a long story short,
these early signals were his incapacity to restore the order and unity of
the communist world movement under Soviet domination, (the public
break with Albania, and subsequently, and incomparably more
importantly, the public break with China), and his insincere but vulgar
and clamorous attacks against the rebellious Soviet intelligentsia of the
'thaw' which apparently did not convince the apparatus but unmistakably convinced a good many communist reformers in the Soviet
Union and abroad that not much was to be expected of Khrushchev.
The *coup de grace* certainly was Togliatti's famous *Memorandum*, his
testament, an unmistakable withdrawal of a vote of confidence on
behalf of a politician who would have been a natural ally, had Khrushchev really delivered the goods promised at the 20th Congress. All
these events between mid-1962 and early 1964 indicated the slow
agony of a period which can then be characterized as having lasted not
more than 7 to 8 years, in fact, not even the half the time of the
Brezhnev era. Its very brevity indicates rather a transition than a new
phase.

A further puzzle to be resolved is presented by Khrushchev's many
and radically divergent images, the practically total absence of even a
minimal consensus in his assessment, both during his rule and after.
This was not the case with either Lenin or Stalin. Both evoked a
manichean dichotomy: they were either adored or hated; faith in them
or rejection of them was absolute. (Which, of course, does not at all
mean that their adorers had to lionize both of them. As is documented
by the classic case of Trotsky and his followers, an idolatry of Lenin,
not less uncritical as that of the Stalinists, at best, literally more
sophisticated, could still go hand in hand with a hate of Stalin). Furthermore, Brezhnev, to speak of the aftermath, presents a hermeneutically
simple case as well. Firstly, under his reign, with the considerable
assistance of a total lack of personality in this skilful but insignificant
and malevolent *apparatchik*, the 'cult of personality' died peacefully
indeed. There could be really no reason at all to cultify Brezhnev's so-
called personality. What happened around him was just the usual base
court flattery. Secondly, in many respects, the Soviet Union is, for the
first time in its history, fairly transparent at least in one respect: the
post-Khrushchevian state does not inspire any kind of pseudo-

religious beliefs or expectations, it simply attracts certain very pragmatic interests. One made, if one was interested in it, a simple and straightforward deal with the Brezhnevite Soviet Union, one did not invest cultic adoration in it or in its leaders. This, of course, could happen under two conditions: by following Soviet strategical interests, and by importing the Soviet ways of government. All this needed Machiavellian determination (as imitating the Soviet example always did) but no longer elements of enthusiasm. Therefore Brezhnev's image, in marked contrast with that of his historical predecessor, is a matter of a very simple interpretation indeed.

But here I should make very clear what I mean by the term 'image': certainly not the sort of amateurish psychological attempts at decoding an enigma which so many works on Khrushchev, otherwise knowledge-able and interesting, are so ardently preoccupied with. I am in perfect agreement with Dostoevsky's statement that psychology is a stick that has two ends. Every deed, even if it is not wrapped up in veils of deliberate camouflage to the extent that, on the pain of perishing, Khrushchev had always had to camouflage his own, is at least ambi-valent. The term 'image' indicates here a socially relevant ensemble of opinions and assessments of the First Secretary on the part of pertinent human groups which influenced the actions of these groups towards the Soviet Union and communism. Therefore, what these people – so divergent between themselves – believed of the Khrushchev enigma, was an organic part of the Khrushchev era itself, and inseparable from its aftermath, its posterity.

The first representative image of Khrushchev is that of the reformist communist (an image which I myself held, with certain ups and downs, for a long period). As internationally known and acclaimed last Mohicans of this once so numerous type, now so much diminished, one can mention the courageous Medvedev brothers, Roy and Zhores, or that monument of heroism in the face of Nazism and Stalinism, Robert Havemann, inmate of a Hitlerite prison awaiting (and miraculously escaping) his execution, practically under house-arrest for years in the 'real socialism' of Ulbricht's and Honecker's 'German workers' state'. It is appropriate to sum up the reformist communist's image of Khrush-chev with his words (which are a verdict basically identical with that in Zhores Medvedev's book: *Khrushchev – The Years in Power*).[3] 'The disbandment of the Gulag archipelago and the release of its 10 million still-living inmates by Khrushchev was a courageous act worthy of our

---

[3] Zhores Medvedev, *Khrushchev – The Years in Power*, New York: Columbia University Press, 1976.

admiration. Although it was not directed against any external enemy of the Soviet Union, it was directed against its most evil and dangerous enemy in the inside, against the domination of the 'system', against the distortion of socialism and the international discrediting of the communist world movement stemming therefrom. Khrushchev deserves our deepest recognition and respect. It was for the first time after Lenin that with him, a great and courageous revolutionary got on the top of Soviet society.'[4] The main terms of this remarkably dense and comprehensive characterization are the following:

1 On the whole, the Soviet society remained socialist but with remarkable 'distortions' or 'perversions'.
2 These distortions can be repaired by certain (system-immanent) reforms (the abolition of the system of terror, party democracy – whatever the term may mean – and the like).
3 Khrushchev was the actor, or rather the world-historic protagonist of this work of reparation, this is his main claim to glory before history. He was certainly no *chevalier sans reproche* (and both Havemann and the Medvedev brothers criticize him repeatedly): the ineffectual character of his reforms is exemplified by his very downfall, but his policies, if socialism has a future, should be restored to their full rights. (Let me remark here in parenthesis that the reformist communist Khrushchev image is the only one which hopes and predicts a come-back of the First Secretary's allegedly consistent social options.)
4 Finally, and clearly visibly, this logic is circular in that it regards the mass crimes of Stalinism, not a bit less horrendous than those of Hitler, as an atrocity against humanity, but their amendment or compensation as a profit to be put on the account of a reformed communism which is acknowledging, even if with many provisos, a historical continuity with Stalin's period as socialist. While the representatives of this image are rapidly dwindling, they in their entirety constituted some 25 years ago a major social force. For instance, during the preparation of the Hungarian Revolution they were the protagonists of social change *par excellence*.

The opposite pole of the Khrushchev image, that of the militant anti-Communist can again be exemplified by a literary work, by George

---

[4] Robert Havemann, 'Die DDR in den zwanzig Jahren nach Stalins Sturz', in R. Medvedev, R. Havemann, J. Steffen and others, *Entstalinisierung – Der XX. Parteitag der KPdSU und seine Folgen*, Frankfurt Suhrkamp Main: Suhrkamp, 1977, p. 67.

Páloczi-Horváth's *Khrushchev – The Road to Power*.[5] But this exemplification does not at all mean that such an image was the distinguishing feature of certain biased literary circles. For all practical purposes, this was a view widely shared by the policy-making bodies of the Western powers which undoubtedly had good reasons for their aversion; nonetheless, their Khrushchev image was just as one-sided, if not more, than that of the reformist communist. According to this view, Khrushchevism was nothing but a new chapter in the long book of fraudulent Communist strategies, a new Trojan horse. Khrushchev himself was a younger member of the generation of the purgers (which is not only true, but now has been profoundly documented by Crankshaw's excellent biography).[6] His main aspiration to become the new dictator had only been blocked and frustrated by his equally jealous colleagues who dreaded the axe of a new Stalin. The exposition of the crimes (to a great measure: his own crimes) was imposed on him by his colleagues, he only snatched their historical merits to display himself as the liberator.[7] Finally, this view regards Khrushchev as a) a dictator under whom the essence of the regime did not change, and b) as a Soviet imperialist *tout court* against whom the West had to brace itself in exactly the same way as it did against Stalin. (Agnes Heller and I have analysed a blatant example of the results of this short-sighted attitude).[8] The militant conservative took just as extremist a view of the Khrushchev period as the biased reformist communist. While for the former nothing had changed, and Khrushchev's period was not even a transition to something new but a simple continuation of the old, for the latter the system became unperverted socialism again undeniably with certain minor blemishes, at least for the time of the rule of Khrushchev.

The liberal image of Khrushchev represented by such journalists and historians as Crankshaw or historical protagonists as Sakharov, have a far more objective and differentiated view of our hero than any partisans of the former two positions. No doubt, Khrushchev epitomized a social force totally alien for them, but within its limits the First

---

[5] London, Secker and Warburg, 1960.

[6] See n. 2. above.

[7] To cut a matter of Party history as short as possible, let me quote Crankshaw's most convincing remarks: 'Nothing was ever said about a speech which Khrushchev made in Sofia on his way back from Belgrade in June [1955]. Here, it was later discovered, only ten days after he had invited Tito to join him in blaming everything on Beria, he for the first time attacked Stalin openly . . .': *Khrushchev*, p. 211. Apart from the fact that this is a practically irrefutable proof of Khrushchev's intentions, the position biased in hostility against him cannot account for the actors who had allegedly imposed their reformist will on him. Who were they? Perhaps Kaganovich or Molotov?

[8] F. Fehér and A. Heller, *Hungary, 1956 Revisited*, London: Allen and Unwin, 1982.

Secretary had two immense merits. The first was the moderation and
relative tolerance of his regime as compared with that of Stalin; the
second its capacity for occasional (not overall and regular) rational
bárgaining and discussion. If I gave earlier the summary of the
reformist communist's image of Khrushchev by one of its morally outstanding adherents, it is only fair to proceed in a similar manner on the
liberal side and listen to the testimony to the both scientifically and
politically representative personality of Sakharov. His list of 'Khrushchev's contributions' to a more liberal turn of Russian history is remarkably (and let us add: deservedly) lacking in enthusiasm or even
sympathy, which only enhances its value of objectivity. 'His contributions include the release of the prisoners of Stalin's times, increased pay
for the kolkhoz peasants, a remarkable rise in pensions, a growing
proportion spent on housing, a quest for new methods in international
relations, attempts at improving the style of leadership, attempts at
restricting the prerogatives of the *nomenklatura* and at reducing the
enormous military budget. The last two ventures were the main reasons
for Khrushchev's fall eleven years ago'.[9] The main terms of the liberal
assessment are the following:

1   While Khrushchev's regime had obviously never questioned the
    principles of the Leninist dictatorship, it was an incomparably
    more humane edition of it than the phases under both Lenin's and
    Stalin's rule. (The liberal analysis is visibly uninterested in the
    problem, fundamental to Khrushchev's self-understanding
    whether and to what extent Khrushchevism was dependent on its
    historical predecessors.)
2   The liberals also emphasize the relatively more peaceful character
    of the Khrushchev era, primarily in terms of a reduced military
    budget.
3   All this adds up to the verdict that Khrushchevism was a short
    period in Soviet history which, alas, turned out to be only a
    transition towards a more rigid and conservative, also much more
    expansionist rule of a leadership from which it has to be distin-
    guished. Whether or not Khrushchev's policies can return, and if
    so, in an unchanged form, the liberals mostly do not care to
    predict.

A distinct and outright hostile image of Khrushchev appears in the
Chinese view of his leadership. For all consecutive Chinese leader-

---

[9]   Quoted in Medvedev et al., *Enstalinisierung*, p. 308.

ships, however divergent, Khrushchev and his policies inaugurated in the Secret Speech appear as a 'Thermidor' (even if they do not use the terminology), as a treason against the 'correct proletarian line' whose patron saint was Stalin, the loyal continuer of Lenin's work. In this regard, not even the Chinese version of Khrushchevism, Deng's rule, relinquished the unmitigated hostility against the Khrushchevite 'revisionism'. The explanatory value of these theories is necessarily very limited. First of all, and for good reasons, the official Chinese theorists who hatched together the idea of the 'Khrushchevite Thermidor', have never taken up the question of the cause of such a traitorous turn. They particularly did not touch upon the responsibility of their adored Stalin's mass murders for triggering a response in the form of a liberalizing turn. The Chinese propagandists are equally hesitant to step on another minefield discussing whether the Soviet Union has remained, under Khrushchev's and his successors' traitorous rule (the latter are no better for them in this respect than Khrushchev was) a 'socialist' country or whether capitalism, pure and simple, has been restored there. Theory for the Chinese Party theorists (except for the time of Chén Po-ta who was a genuinely fanatical, Babuvian–egalitarian theorist and the creator of the Mao Tse-tung idea) is a matter of purely pragmatical considerations, just as it is for their Soviet colleagues, and they are not foolish enough, by declaring the Soviet Union capitalist, to walk into the trap Yugoslavia presented for Soviet propagandists in the Forties, as this might prove embarrassing later. Therefore the more verbose their 'theory' is, the more it hints in the direction that Khrushchevism is a distinct and fatal new phase in Soviet history, the less actual explanatory value it has.

Finally, a certain image of Khrushchev on the New Left has to be briefly scrutinized here, actually a somewhat arbitrary merger of several theories from the sixties. On the whole, none of the new leftist trends was infatuated with Khrushchev and his regime, and of course the lack of affection was absolutely mutual. The Soviet observers found the new leftist at best superfluous (if they were new editions of a pro-Soviet policy, why did they not join the communist parties, the observers logically asked), and if not, then their evaluation ranged in Soviet files and articles from a characterization as 'muddle-headed' (*sputannik*) to one as agents of the class enemy. The aversion of the average new leftist to Khrushchev mostly had a twofold motivation. On the one hand, they found his regime still too oppressive for their liking, and on the other hand, very conservative, which reproduced bourgeois prejudices mobilized against them at home on a much higher and a far more intolerant level. The terms of this – mostly negative – evaluation displayed a certain affinity with the Chinese polemics, even in the case of non-Maoist interpreters, and since the New Left had a far greater theoretical freedom than the Chinese theoretical apparatus, it evinced an incomparably wider and more convincing explanatory value. First of all, most new leftist observers grasped the causal nexus between the excesses (errors, distortions and the like) of Stalin era and the emergence of Khrushchevism. Further, they have perceived at least one fundamental aspect of Khrushchev's period, its involuntary 'Bukharinism', the (limited) rehabilitation of the consumer in the Soviet citizen, and, since they also grasped the deeper implication, the partial rehabilitation of market relations, they condemned it. (They had to do so as they were the opposition of the so-called 'affluent society' and blamed everything on market economy.) Finally, the whole idea of 'peaceful coexistence' was a most suspicious sign for a generation inspired by Guevara's 'hundred Vietnams'. This seemed to be an outright betrayal of the revolutionary impetus, especially as implemented by the First Secretary during the Tonkin Gulf Crisis. In final summary, they believed Khrushchevism to be a transition which could be superseded, at least for most of them, not by any relapse to Stalinism but by the 'healthy regenerative forces' resurrecting 'proletarian democracy'. Needless to say, here we have arrived at the main weakness of all new leftist theories of the sixties: their verbal vehemence on behalf of a non-existent proletarian democracy turned into a most ambiguous and half-hearted discourse when they had to answer the main question: whether or not the Soviet Union represented socialism for them.

Were these many interpretations, in irreconcilable variance with one another, simple instances of misunderstanding but for one? If so, which is the one I choose? My answer to this question runs as follows: none of them was a total misunderstanding, even if they obviously do not represent an equal explanatory value for me. An even superficial glance at Khrushchev's memoirs,[10] at this amazingly inconsistent and, at the same time, dramatically revealing document, will find smaller or larger chunks of evidence for each standpoint. Was our hero then a hopelessly confused man, a dilettantish, accidental protagonist who just stumbled upon the stage of a world-historic drama mixing in his policies the most contradicting options of great juncture? My answer is decidedly in the negative: Khrushchev was undeniably one of the great statesmen of modern Russia, ineffacable from its annals but at the same

---

[10] *Khrushchev Remembers*. Introduction, commentary and notes by Edward Crankshaw. Translated and edited by Strobe Talbott, Boston: Little, Brown and Co., 1970.

time the reservoir of all the options facing the war-ridden and Stalin-ridden country after the despot's death. He frantically strove for a unified and coherent policy of his own which, in conflict with colliding and resisting forces from both the top and from the bottom, would have put an end to a long martyrology of his people. It was the 'fault', if one may state this in a unhistorical way, of these forces to the same extent as it was Khrushchev's if he could not forge a coherent policy and remained the repository of many conflicting options. To understand this unique situation, we have to cast a cursory glance on the options the Soviet Union faced in 1953 to 1955, when Khrushchevism was *in statu nascendi*.[11]

Here I will only briefly mention, not analyse, the three options which, partly in reality, partly in the conjectures of such observers as Isaac Deutscher and many others, presented themselves for any historical actor having an influence on Soviet and world history, and which were all hostile to Khrushchev's intentions. The first was looming large over all surviving members of Stalin's Old Guard in the form of Beria's personal dictatorship which was to be implemented through empty but popular gestures, such as the very limited release of Gulag prisoners[12] exposing the 'illegal methods' employed by investigators in the Doctors' Plot, introduced by Yezhov and Beria but this time put to use against the latter, and the like. It is more than just another of his usual hackneyed *Pravda* phrases when Khrush-chev's remarks in his memoirs that he would have worried about the 'achievements of October', had Beria ascended to supreme power. Since to all testimonies Beria was the only one from a murderous bunch of political fanatics who seemed to have no convictions at all, one of the Gestapo-Müller types, his reign could easily have ended – after a bloody rule of terror without political programme – in general anarchy and the disintegration of the Soviet state. The second option was a military takeover which I deem for reasons not to be analysed here in detail, only a logical, not an actual sociological possibility. (And whatever one's position on Castoriadis's interesting book *Devant la guerre*,[13] which describes the Soviet Union now as a society under the clandestine domination of the military, military rule was certainly only a logical option then.) The third option, the return to Stalinism pure and simple, which had influential partisans in the

---

[11] For a more detailed analysis of these options see Fehér and Heller, *Hungary, 1956 Revisited*.

[12] Roy A. Medvedev and Zhores A. Medvedev, *Khrushchev: The Years in Power*, New York: Columbia University Press, 1976, p. 9.

[13] C. Castoriadis, *Devant la guerre*, Paris: Fayard, 1981.

Presidium (Molotov and Kaganovich above all) and in a considerable part of the apparatus, was not only contrary to Khrushchev's expectations, but also highly unpopular, to say the least, both on the top and on the bottom. On the top it was a nightmare because of the unavoidable collateral purges: the purgers did not want to accept the liturgical act of a 'revolutionary self-sacrifice'. And if one takes Zhores and Roy Medvedev's remarks seriously, that in the first post-Stalin years the tide had already turned, and it was the countryside that needed manpower from industry and not vice versa, one can see that the necessary social space for Stalinism, inextricably bound up with expansive industrialization, was no longer there.[14]

The only remaining and valid option was then consolidation including the more or less open admission that under Stalin's rule (or at least: after a certain period of Stalin's rule) 'Lenin's work' had undergone a crisis inside and outside the Soviet Union. Khrushchev was decidedly the man for the job as for him only three versions of consolidation were outright excluded from the start: a total abrogation of the Party's primogeniture, its prerogatives to steer and control social life; the continuation of the government by methods of mass terror; and military dictatorship. But, plastic and 'poliphonic' as he was, he was open to the following courses of consolidation. Firstly, as a man of authoritarian habits, he was most favourably inclined towards a simple swap of Stalin's terroristic totalitarianism for a non-terroristic but autocratic and repressively conservative paternalism. Such a social state of affairs would have needed a leader with great authority, a wide power of command without glorification and the physical elimination of the *Neinsager*; and such a position would have suited him fine. But, secondly, a situation characterized by 'Party democracy', in other words, a repressive liberalism in the methods of Party administration, a complete recognition of the rights to increased consumption of the Soviet citizen without the slightest recognition of his or her rights to free political action would have also been acceptable for him. Thirdly, under certain circumstances (to which I will return later), even a gigantic edition of the Yugoslav alternative version would not have been impossible. The leading role for the 'emancipating upper stratum' would have been preserved but, instead of favours, actual and legally stipulated concessions to the populace would have been granted while the satellite states would have been granted the status of 'Finlandization'. To that end, it would, of course, have been necessary not to crush the Hungarian Revolution but to negotiate with its leaders along the

[14] R. and Zh. Medvedev, *Khrushchev*, p. 149.

lines of the many drafts of compromise, in principle highly acceptable
for the Soviet Union, worked out by Hungarian politicians. Having
missed this historical bus, they missed, or rather miscarried, important
internal Soviet social options as well. But, given the official myth of the
regime (the famous 'return to Leninism'), given the still expansive
agricultural policy, given the general hatred against the material
prerogatives of the *nomenklatura* (one of the greatest gaps between
rich and poor in all the world, easily exploitable by demagoguery),
given, finally, the doctrinaire streak in Khrushchev himself (for
instance his dogmatic and really stupid atheism), one cannot exclude
from the strategies open to him a policy called by the Chinese leadership the 'mass line' – quick and often mob-like mobilization of masses
with highly arbitrary policy objectives and a collateral, dangerously
adventurous foreign policy. As far as the latter component is concerned, he had indeed repeatedly experimented with such, starting
from the Soviet note to Britain during the Suez crisis, simply threatening nuclear world war, or his apocalyptic histrionics during the Berlin
crisis in 1962 or, finally and most spectacularly, his attitude before and
during the Cuban missile crisis.

It is no puzzle for the expert, and perhaps not even for the un-
professional but incisive observer, why an oligarchic conservative
paternalism became the winning option after Khrushchev's fall. Therefore I mention the causes very briefly. Firstly, the regime had an
apparatus not only with an iron hold over the whole societal life but
also with a self-confidence of half a century's rule and a great victory in
war. Secondly, the fact that they had passed through a period of forced
and expansive industrialization demanded different options to those
both of Stalin and Mao. Thirdly, Khrushchev himself, although open to
some other options as well, was personally a product of the apparatus
whose sincere feeling was instinctive mistrust, sometimes outright
hatred, against the Polish and Hungarian rebels and those 'traitorous'
communists like Imre Nagy who had sided with them. But, finally, a
factor has to be mentioned which very rarely appears in the list of
reasons: the Soviet masses themselves. It is trendy to make retrospective reproaches to certain leaders on the grounds that they, as subjects,
had their freedom to act otherwise and did not. But masses, these
anonymous entities equally have different options and a freedom to
choose between them for the simple reason that they are constituted by
individuals. And had the millions of petitioners mentioned by Zhores
Medvedev, on first hearing of the Secret Speech and anticipating the
rehabilitations, taken to the streets and demanded, instead of suppli-
cated, the release and the rehabilitation of the inmates of the Gulag,

together with the publication of the Secret Speech, Soviet history might have taken a different turn. I emphasize: it might have, and it was far from excluded that Khrushchev would have put down the rebellion by armed forces. But, polyphonic as he was, other options were equally not impossible for him. And since he was polyphonic, Khrushchev's many images all describe, even if not with an equal explanatory value, options inherent in his personality and politics. Whereby I have answered the question put in my title: his regime was a transitory period, not a lasting new phase in Soviet history and had to be because of several colliding options. What future his promises have for coming Soviet history, if any, will be answered in the conclusion of this paper.

II THE SECRET SPEECH AS THE HERMENEUTICAL CLUE FOR UNDERSTANDING KHRUSHCHEV'S REGIME

Khrushchev's Secret Speech to the 20th Congress of the CPSU was actually delivered under mysterious circumstances after the Congress had completed its formal duties. The genesis and instigation of the speech are wrapped in legend and enigma. Intended to be secret but leaked immediately to the world press, it is one of the most important documents of our century. It became a source of inspiration for my generation of reformist communists (but even George Lukács remarked that under the spell of the speech, he expected a *Blitzkrieg*-like self-purification of socialism). It became an object of hatred and fear by the ruling apparatus, as for many doctrinaire communists outside the apparatus who never forgave Khrushchev this 'traitorous act'. In the West, perhaps with the exception of the most important recipient, the US State Department, it was generally taken as the sign possibly of a new Soviet Union in the making. There are in the main three versions of its genesis, and if I touch upon them only briefly, it is not with the intention of solving the riddles, a task which I cannot perform (nor can anyone, for that matter) but rather to argue against the accidental and occasional character of the genesis and to put it firmly into the general context of the Khrushchevite strategy. The first version has already been mentioned: this is Pálóczi-Horváth's militantly anti-Khrushchevite explanation which attributes the speech to mysterious and, I think, unidentifiable, protagonists who allegedly coerced Khrushchev to read under duress.[15] Apart from Crankshaw's important evidence to the contrary (see above), one simply has to remark: even had it happened so, which is almost impossible and contradicts the whole body of knowledge about the period, the fact still remains that the mask grew on Khrushchev's face and from then on he has been the man of the Secret Speech. But let me mention a piece of additional and, in my view, cardinal evidence since it comes from a man of irreproachable character, Imre Nagy. This later victim of Khrushchev's 'legality', then still a favourite of all 'consolidators' in Moscow, mentioned in his memoirs that Khrushchev complained to him (on 1 January 1954!) that in Hungary the work of rehabilitation could not even be started because of the sabotage of Rákosi and his apparatus.[16] This certainly displays the author of the Secret Speech, not its enemy. The second version appears in Medvedev's book on Khrushchev and describes the speech as a *coup de théâtre* improvised by the First Secretary sensing the general anti-Stalin tide on the Congress after Mikoyan's stormily applauded attack.[17] This is an improbable version, given the whole character of the text of the speech, which shows unmistakable signs that its authors explored the archives, schemed shrewdly and assessed the possible limits. The final version of the speech's genesis is one of Khrushchev's typical self-apologetic lies in his memoirs. According to this story, even if the Pospelov committee, which actually gathered the material and in all probability wrote the main draft of the speech, had the text completed before the Congress, there was no decision to address the delegates on a secret session, and he, Khrushchev, in a way foisted this option on the reluctant members of the Presidium. Whatever the truth may have been, one thing seemed to be undeniable: beyond any reasonable doubt Khrushchev was the initiator of the whole report and the text offers the best clue to understanding his politics; it contains certainly the strongest version, even if not the only one, of his social experiments.

After the first shock of consternation or relief, the speech was generally mistreated, as far as both its intellectual and moral level and emancipatory content are concerned. There were four objections made against it (not counting the fifth which regarded it as material evidence of Khrushchev's treason). The first was the charge of

---

[15] Pálóczi-Horváth: *Khrushchev – The Road to Power*, London: Secker and Warburg, 1960. p. 160.

[16] Imre Nagy, quoted in F. A. Váli, *Rift and Revolt in Hungary*, Cambridge, Mass.: Harvard University Press, 1961, p. 129.

[17] Z. Medvedev, *Khrushchev*, p. 20. *Khrushchev Remembers*, p. 311.

shallowness and superficiality. What sort of social explanatory category is the 'cult of personality', many people asked? What does it explain of all the horrors which happened in a society, in what way does it account for their structural causes? The adherents of the second position simply called Khrushchev a cheat and a liar who pretended in the speech to be a democrat and immediately after the Congress oppressed all voices opting for actual social changes. The third remarked, with understandable moral contempt, that after a holocaust which has its only match in Hitler's deeds, the First Secretary only mentioned the communist (and from among them, overwhelmingly the Stalinist) victims and most atrociously, gave the number of not even 8,000 people having been rehabilitated up to the time of convening the 20th Congress. Finally, other observers remarked that the speech displayed a cynical morality since it distinguished between necessary and unnecessary murders and it condemned Stalin only for having committed some of the latter type.

To some extent, all these critics are justified, even if not to the same degree, except the ones who termed Khrushchev's position fraudulent. The remarkable feature of the Secret Speech in Khrushchev's career so full of lies and tricks is that it was 'strictly Weberian' in the sense that Khrushchev (who had obviously never heard the name of Max Weber) clearly identified his leading values and stuck to them. He never called himself in the speech a democrat. If my textual inventory is correct, he made only one, and even then a very perfunctory, reference to inner-party democracy by which he meant that leaders should preferably not be butchered if they disagreed on the priority of winter or spring wheat. This is not an exaggerated conception of democracy. But gallows humour aside, he unrepentingly and very sincerely identifies with Lenin's system of terror when and where such 'harsh measures' are necessary (by which he clearly meant: when and where the leaders deemed it to be inevitable and useful). As in his memoirs (except for one remark where quite unexpectedly he sets a question mark against Stalin's horrendous collectivization) he approved retroactively not only the terror practiced in the Civil War but all those wars of extermination against wide strata of the population (mostly during the fatal years of 1929–32 in the countryside) which led to the consolidation of Lenin's shaky edifice. For him, negative history starts *ab urbe condita*: when the 'socialist' bases were already solid since cemented by the blood of millions, but when Stalin's fury turned against the builders. Roughly then, it started with the symbolic act of Kirov's assassination and with the 'Lex Kirov', the dreaded formula of terror whose last applier (against Beria, Bagirov et al.) was Khrushchev himself. This is a cynical and in many respects a brutal view of history indeed, but certainly not a fraudulent one.[18]

But the obverse side of the coin, Khrushchev's great excuse before History for all eternity, has to be mentioned here in all fairness: while he spoke of thousands, he immediately released millions. (According to Medvedev, Havemann and other sources some 10 to 12 millions were released.) This was not only an act of humanity and audacity of the first order which will always shield his personality against even just charges, it meant a general moral turn in a world which was on the brink of losing all moral norms whatsoever and sinking into that social situation which Marx predicted under the remarkable name: relapse into barbarism. I fully agree with Mlynář's assessment (and will later come back to expand on it): 'Khrushchev's critique may have been more primitive on a national scale, but it did highlight, whether intentionally or not, the question of guilt and responsibility of the individual'.[19]

The deep inherent ambiguity of the Secret Speech, its most 'ideological feature' (in the sense of a 'false consciousness') is not to be found in its alleged democratic promises. No such promises were made; as a result all those who left the historical scene with disillusionment, should have blamed it on themselves in the first place. The ideological, and therefore false, claim in the speech is the main slogan: back to Lenin. It is sociologically impossible to return to Lenin because Lenin was and is dead in the simple sense that his unconsolidated Jacobin dictatorship, whose many options did not even totally exclude a return to political democracy (and thereby the withdrawal of the relevance of the very period of dictatorship), was consolidated through Stalin by the cataclysmic exclusion of practically all its earlier options. Lenin had indeed introduced the system of 'la permanence de la guillotine' but, together with his party, was most reluctant to admit its permanence and regarded his rule as an emergency government – a most Jacobin feature indeed.[20] Stalin had here no scruples whatsoever.

---

[18] I would like explicitly to avoid calling the interpretation of Khrushchev's text as democratic a misinterpretation. It was a social project of one representative social actor: the reformist communist who read Khrushchev's mind in this way and who succeeded in imposing this way of reading on a wide audience spreading their later disillusionment to equally wide spheres of reception.

[19] Z. Mlynář, *Night Frost in Prague*, London: Hurst and Co., 1980, p. 31.

[20] In my *The Frozen Revolution* (manuscript) I have analysed the social character of Jacobinism. In *The Dictatorship over Needs*, Oxford: Basil Blackwell, 1983. G. Markus and I have analysed how and in what respects Stalin was indeed the 'continuator of Lenin's work', how Stalin alone, the man, dreaded by Lenin himself, was the only possible safeguard of his regime. And when I mention names, I certainly mean social tendencies.

His famous formula of the 'necessarily sharpening class struggle in socialism' parallel to the progress of 'constructing socialism' heralded precisely this permanence of the terror without much ideological disguise. After Stalin, the 'historical innocence' of Lenin's government (which can, of course, be stated *cum grano salis* of a government of systematic terror) is no longer possible. Anyone with moral responsibility who intends to establish a Jacobin regime based on the actual permanence and the illusory short-term use of the terror, must (as for instance, the original Cuban Jacobins, Castro, Guevara and others did initially but with an adequate historical consciousness) be perfectly aware of one fact. That fact is that the actual permanence will remain and the illusions evaporate, leaving after them a hangover of cynicism and a greed for power.

But why did Khrushchev need the myth of 'return to Lenin'? Was it simply paying lip-service to the ideological continuity of the regime or did it reveal its incapability of thinking a theoretical problem through to the end, certainly a character trait of the First Secretary, a great statesman and a simpleton in all cultural and ideological question in one person? The insistence on ideological continuity certainly played some role in this decision but it, equally certainly, does not account for the central, maniacally repeated role of the slogan: return to Lenin. As to the second explanation, intellectual simplicity is no answer here given that a thinker like Lukács who had no match in his culture since the death of Karl Marx hatched the same universal panacea in his capacity as the representative theorist of the Khrushchev period. Khrushchev, as all reformist communists, was caught up in an inextricable dilemma. On the one hand, he wanted to preserve untouched the whole structural network of the Stalinist regime (one-party dictatorship, command economy, totalitarian homogenization of society) remaining totally uncritical towards its essence and at the same time he wanted to eliminate Stalin (in other words: regularly practised mass terror) as it became dangerously dysfunctional: Stalin, through whom alone the regime had achieved its final shape and had become consolidated. This impossible task could only be fulfilled under a twofold condition. Firstly, it had to be declared that Lenin's period had elaborated the 'correct' solution to all problems of 'socialist construction' which were later 'to some extent distorted' by Stalin (to what extent, it always remained a mystery, not only with Khrushchev but also with Lukács). Secondly, it was necessary to raise a scholastic and totally misleading pseudo-dilemma: granted that all this was true, to what extent was Stalin 'necessary' or 'only accidental' in Soviet and world history? The first statement is the greatest ideological lie of the whole Khrushchev period. Lenin's regime was, after the moment the Civil War was won, absolutely confused and undecided regarding its own options; the leaders were without the faintest idea whither to go. As a first aspect of this very complex situation, it has to be mentioned that this mythical entity, 'History', meted out a just punishment to 'Maximilien Lenin', the Jacobin who during the bitter struggles of a quarter of a century had forged a social force capable of 'snatching' from triumphant revolutionary crowds the fruit of their own deed, a free and victorious revolution itself, and had preached uninterruptedly that there is one single revolutionary duty and problem: seizing state power. It had finally achieved its goal through a system of unprecedented terror whereby it had found itself in a historical and social vacuum without the elementary social options. The diapason of Lenin's choices covered no smaller social territory than the one ranging from the abolition of money and the introduction of direct exchange (at least in principle in the system of war communism) to a restoration of market relations and the principle of '*enrichissez-vous*' (in the system of NEP) – a remarkable distance to travel even in fantasy. Contrary to historical legends, under Lenin there was no system of planning, not even any central idea of how and in what forms it ought to be introduced: even a general socio-economic strategy was absent. Lenin's lamentations about a single sentence which ought to have been passed down by the 'classics' to their unhappy grandchildren but which they had failed to do, his self-contradicting ideas to cure bureaucratism through new super-bureaucratic institutions, the platitudes and inner confusion of his so-called testament relaying only one message, namely that the revolution had been frozen, might have aroused an understandable contempt towards him in Stalin who must have increasingly seen in Lenin a mummy better put in his mausoleum rather than the leader and paradigm he publicly mourned.

Secondly, Lenin's inability to himself opt for the permanence of the terror, under any theoretical justification he might have chosen to that end, must have appeared for Stalin, and justly so, a very inconsistent and a very dangerous brand of politics. It was inconsistent because Lenin had earlier most generously administered mass terror against whole social groups and this is a type of activity, as Stalin knew all too well, which cannot be stopped until terror is internalized; as we all know, it is easier to mount the tiger than to get off it. It was a very dangerous inconsistency as well: as long as the populace only sensed that there was not an iron determination on the part of the terroristic authorities to go to literally any lengths in preserving their power, not short of measures of the magnitude of demographic catastrophes, the spirit of rebellion is never quelled. People understand that the murder of their father, mother, children and brother was the 'necessary by-product' of a beneficiary world-historical necessity only if the simple inner doubt and the slightest external sign of it implies a similar fate on their part as well.

Therefore, thirdly, Stalin, whose intellectual capacities, as a comprehensible reaction to his earlier Byzantine cult, are now systematically underestimated, conceived correctly that Lenin's emphatic advice given to Rykov when he first thought he might be dying: 'Let no blood flow among you', was a false piece of advice. More precisely, it was a classic instance of false learning from history: the representative Russian Jacobin wanted to avoid at least one spectacular fiasco of the original. It was his inner imperative that the Russian Revolution must not devour its children. But Stalin grasped correctly that this was a formalistic learning from history (obviously without consulting Michelet who proved why, for similar reasons, it was a practical necessity for Robespierre to embark on the gradual extermination of exactly his own faithful but much too independent and critical *Montagne*). Stalin was determined that blood should be let – precisely in the ruling apparatus – and – from the viewpoint of the survival of the regime which was a joint venture with Lenin – he was far more consistent than 'Ilyitch'. The Bolshevik Old Guard, seemingly a barracks under military discipline for European socialists, was a much too freedom-loving, strifing, innerly dependent lot to implement a totalitarian system within which the spirit of terror is so deeply entrenched that all other options vanish from the membrane of social imagination and resistance itself becomes self-censored. There is no need to point to the Trotskyites' half-hearted demonstration in 1927: they were anyhow an alien body in the Party, barely tolerated. It was not even necessary to think of Zinoviev and Kamenev's letter before October, it was enough if one had in mind no one else but Lenin himself who, as is well known, threatened to leave the Central Committee and agitate against it publicly during the Brest–Litovsk debate. Stalin understood quite correctly that a Party where behaviour like Lenin's can occur, where, in other words, the Leader is the head of a dictatorship but not a personal dictator, a despot, is itself no tool for a totalitarian dictatorship to realize its mission. Stalin was, therefore, adamant on two points. Firstly, the Party must be subjected to the iron will of one leader, cost this in human lives what it may; and this despotic leader of a dictatorship which now became aware of its permanence was, of course, he himself, Stalin. The second point related to the 'general line': collectivization and industrialization. It was too often emphasized that Stalin snatched, as it were, these ideas from the so-called leftist opposition. In actual fact, this was mentioned so often that in the heat of the copyright debate people tended to forget that Stalin did not and could not steal any random programme. For the purposes of his regime, Bukharin's policy was totally inadequate because only militarily enforced collectivization plus a military order in the factories (complemented by the more than 10 million slave labourers of the Gulag) guaranteed the total control of the society he aimed at.

This is also an answer to the pseudo-philosophical problem of Stalin's 'necessity' or 'contingency' in history.[21] If we start from the above analysis, the whole sophistry can indeed be reduced to the following simple propositions. For all those who wanted to transform Lenin's system of Jacobin terror into something permanent which could not happen but through the self-conscious permanency of Stalin's dictatorship with the adequate – anticapitalist but non-socialist – institutions, Stalin was a logical conclusion of Lenin's premises; in that sense, Stalin was a necessity. For all those who wanted to revise the very initial idea of a Jacobin dictatorship, Stalin represented a causally well-established but unacceptable and monstrous as well as eliminable system. Stalin was certainly not contingent but he was not necessary either. But Nikita Sergeyevich Khrushchev certainly was not among those who wanted to revise the Jacobin idea in this way. He was not one of those who became critical of Lenin's overture to the slightest degree but was one of those who understood that Stalin performed, in terms of Leninism, something 'very positive' but which had already outlived its 'stimulative phase'. Since he wanted to keep the results without admitting the necessity of the methods leading to it, he needed a new historical mythology. This was the widely accepted idea of 'return to Lenin', to the legendary but never existing 'perfected' institutions and solutions of the Lenin period. Needless to say, the Soviets never again enjoyed even those miserable remnants of their freedom of action Lenin most reluctantly had to temporarily grant them. The adherents of this legend also referred to the non-existent 'Leninist norms of

---

[21] I term it pseudo-problem because there is no reasonable answer to it, especially not in terms of the theories of those who raised the very question. If one deems Stalin's emergence necessary, one has to, first, account for the nature of this generative necessity which is, philosophically speaking, practically always an impossible task and, secondly, if Stalin was a necessity how does the de-Stalinizer know that he is no longer? And if he still is, the de-Stalinizer commits a crime against 'historical necessity' which, in the form of Stalin, metes out very harsh punishments. Should, however, Stalin be declared a 'contingency', a sizeable and most palpable contingency indeed, then the whole view of history of the observer collapses immediately and no phase of the Soviet development can be explained any longer.

legality'. Lenin's legality had one single principle, a very doubtful one when left standing alone without penal code, formalized procedures of law enforcement, rights of the dependent, an at least formal independence of the court; this was the Roman maxim: *salus rei publicae suprema lex est*. There is only one respect in which the Khrushchevite mythology of the return to Lenin proved to be a realistic description of the state of affairs: he and his colleagues really renounced bloodshed in their own circles. This is, of course, a statement which needs a certain qualification. The moment a Bolshevik was ready to go so far as to relinquish the primogeniture of the Party, to abrogate the usurped prerogatives on behalf of the much mentioned but totally discarded masses, as Imre Nagy did, the principle of 'no bloodletting' was no longer applicable.

But the fact that Stalin's system outlived its usefulness could not be restricted to the leading stratum. It was, first of all, a problem of wide masses, outside the Soviet Union in the East European countries often in the form of open rebellion, inside the Soviet Union (and often within it: inside the Gulag) in fermenting discontent, in a state of gathering storm. The only solution could be, and it was Khrushchev's political genius to have understood this without ever having formulated it, the closure of the period of destructive 'revolutions from above'.[22] In this sense, the Chinese theorists were wrong in picking their simile. It was not the analogy of a Thermidor but of a Brumaire that could be, with the necessary vagueness and inexactitude of all historical analogies, applied to Khrushchev.

It could not be emphasized too strongly here that as elsewhere, history cannot be 'inferred' from the psychological make-up of a representative protagonist. In the given case, Khrushchev was anything but a peaceful man, a fan of methodical and liberal government. He was of a violent and cruel, even if not sadistic, nature, a born improviser, a statesman of authoritarian leanings. Here is the vivid description given by Crankshaw of his work-style during his first spectacular action, the construction of the Moscow Metro in his charge as Moscow Party Secretary in the early thirties: 'The task of tunnelling was a job after Khrushchev's heart: it called for boldness amounting to recklessness, sacrificial toil, vast operations based on insufficient forethought, a standing disregard of the limitations of human flesh and blood and the facts of nature. Speed was of the essence. Immense risks had to be

---

[22] Stalin's Trotskyite enemies tend to forget that Stalin also snatched the idea of the permanent revolution: the Soviet Union, from the late twenties until his death, did live in such a permanence.

taken to keep up to schedule: nobody knows how many died as a consequence of the inevitable catastrophes.'[23] As a viceroy of the Ukraine for 13 years not only did he mete out more than the usual share of terror and oppression delivered by Stalin's emissaries everywhere in the gigantic country: his was the privilege to perform the round-up and mass deportation of more than a million Poles from the 'liberated' West Ukraine under the methodical guidance of his crony, the later hangman of Hungary in 1956, General Serov, who was just a 'jolly good fellow' for Nikita Sergeyevich. As visible from his memoirs, written after being driven out of office and when, to hear Khrushchev, he might have invented democracy, he did not feel the slightest remorse of conscience concerning this not particularly brilliant episode of his curriculum. His much discussed figment of a particularly feverish Stalinist voluntarist fantasy, the plan for agrotowns – which would have transformed a much too dispersed Soviet kolkhoz peasantry into city-dwelling agricultural wage-labourer, and that preferably overnight, also testifies to a man of violent and irrationalist impromptus. Quite irrespective of the theoretical merits or demerits of such a plan, the war-ridden Soviet Union was lacking in just about everything such a new 'transformation of social nature' needed.

And yet he was the only one in a leadership – probably during Stalin's last years but certainly immediately subsequent to his death – who understood the imperative of the historical hour: to close the revolutions from above. All those who describe him as just another ambitious politico ruthlessly jockeying for supreme power or remind us of the unsophisticated character of his 'sociological' descriptions of his adversaries' positions (Stalin's pathological mistrust and vanity or the attempts of the 'anti-Party group' at avoiding the admission of their responsibility) miss the important point. In marked contrast to 30 years of Soviet history, Khrushchev at least tried to give explanations instead of the usual labels: wrecker, the enemy of the people. Initially, in his fight against Malenkov, he did resort to the old technique of referring to 'the belching-up of Bukharinite–Rykovite rightist deviationism'; and, whenever he had antagonists he could not cope with, he immediately relapsed into Stalin's vocabulary: Imre Nagy's entourage was for him 'Nagy's gang' as it was earlier his *de dernier cri* to speak of 'Tito's gang'. But he did try to account for what had happened to 'Lenin's work' to provide a rationale of his, and the Party's future plans as best he could, enclosed, of course, in the Procrustean bed of his neo-Leninist mythology and the ensuing, often meaningless

[23] Crankshaw, *Khrushchev*, p. 90.

and always doctrinaire, vocabulary. He was also impeded by his own ineptness at genuine theoretical thinking.

The theoretical formulation of the exigencies of the 'Brumaire period' of the Soviet Union started with a discussion to which practically all Western observers (who generally consider everything expressed in Marxist vocabulary just so much rubbish) attributed only a factional and personal importance: with forcing Molotov to recant his 'erroneous statement' that the Soviet Union had not yet accomplished the phase of constructing socialism. Molotov had to admit that the Soviet Union did accomplish this phase and was then 'constructing communism'.[24]

But there was much more to this than an empty exercise in the Stalinist blend of Marxism–Leninism. Given that, for a quarter of a century socialism in Stalin's authoritative interpretation was still a phase in which there was class struggle, and this class struggle had perforce to constantly sharpen, and given that the constantly sharpening class struggle was but the code name of the permanence of the terror, this sterile debate meant (and the shrewd Molotov understood it perfectly well) that an end must be put, not only tacitly but also publicly, to the reign of terror. The second step was made immediately afterwards. In his anti-Stalin campaign at the 20th Congress, Khrushchev declared erroneous the principle of constantly sharpening class struggle in socialism; this meant the abrogation of the objective of mass terror and the undermining of Stalin's theoretical authority *in uno actu*. The third and parallel step was wrapped up in the fairly meaningless demand of the transition from Stalin's cult of personality to 'collective leadership'. This meant the important step of the closure of the wars of extermination from above against the leading apparatus. Behind the facade of an infantile psychology as presented in the Secret Speech and the hackneyed phrases of *Pravda* editorials, this was equivalent to a return to the Lenin recipe: no blood should flow between you. Khrushchev, who in his truly polyphonic memoirs finds a good word even in defence of the Stalinist purges of the late thirties, which he so emphatically condemned in the Secret Speech (true, in the form of a recollection of his position then but without having the slightest guilt feeling for it), was fully aware of the fact that the purges in the leading stratum were no longer needed. Now no one would have the crazy idea Lenin had during the Brest–Litovsk crisis: to leave the

---

[24] Needless to say, at a certain level all this is so much rubbish for me as well. The Soviet society is not socialism and the theoretical hair-splitting about the differences between socialism and communism have always served the purposes of the dirtiest pragmatism.

Central Committee and take to the streets to agitate publicly against Party resolutions. There is no stronger proof of this than Khrushchev himself who accepted without hesitation his post-coup confinement to a polite form of house-arrest and prudently did not say one single word about the colleagues who had ousted him from office.

Two subsequent steps in terminating the period of revolutions from above are closely interconnected: these are the 'restoration of the Leninist norms of legality' and announcing the advent of the 'all-people state' instead of the dictatorship of proletariat. Of the first, we have seen that there are simply no such norms; of the second, it must be stated that it is one of the phoniest formulations of the Khrushchev period, because the First Secretary certainly did not intend to renounce the Party prerogatives, in other words: the one-party dictatorship. Nonetheless, behind the ideological double-talk, these words had a definite and circumscribable meaning. They contained the firm, and in the main kept, promise of Khrushchev's Brumaire government: a) not to launch again any campaign of mass extermination like the collectivization (and the concommitant mass execution and mass starvation to death of millions) b) not to use one stratum of the population as a weapon against the other, as, for instance, during the collectivization when the alleged interests of the working class were mobilized against 'greedy kulaks' and well-off middle-holders. This theoretical declaration was complemented by the already mentioned, truly historical deed, the disbandment of the empire of Gulag which, apart from its obvious and primary humanitarian aspect, had a general practical economic importance as well. I do not accept the so widely circulating theories (especially in German leftist discourse) on which Stalin's regime was – by virtue of the ten million or more regular slave workers of the Gulag – an 'Asiatic mode of production'. But it is undeniably true that during the whole Stalin period there had always been a sufficient number of slave workers at the disposal of the 'planners' to realize any lunatic or at least unnecessarily costly project. And, at least in principle, the number of slave workers could easily be made up, even increased, at any given moment. It is very important therefore to emphasize that the system of mass terror did not only serve directly political purposes, but was a vigorous reinforcement of the total and uncontrolled economic voluntarism of the system. The moment Khrushchev put an end to this state within a state, to this separated but immense realm of a slave workforce, he reduced the socio-economic space of total irrationality.

A further step was the announcement of the era of peaceful coexistence. Whatever the truth and sincerity behind the declaration, whatever the merit of the principle for a radical global strategy, one salutary effect was imminent: the power centres lost their legitimation for stepping up terror by reference to the 'encirclement of the Soviet Union' by world capitalism, a constant excuse for any action of mass terror touched off for any reason. The encirclement theory was, of course, untenable in the whole postwar period of the Stalin leadership despite the short time span in which the United States had, and the Soviet Union did not yet possess, nuclear weapons. But it was for good reasons that Stalin remained silent on this subject. He did not want to relinquish this comfortable principle of justification for any action of mass round-up. An important aspect of the Secret Speech related to this is a general laughing-stock of both Khrushchev's Stalinist and liberal critics: his description of Stalin's methods of war leadership. The story may abound in childish elements (even though the most dramatic part, the tragic collapse in the fateful years of 1941, is wholly sub-stantiated by Nekrich's excellent and important book),[25] but it had two important social consequences, both pertaining to the closure of the revolutions from above. One of them was the collective rehabilitation of all Soviet soldiers and officers who were prisoners of war on account of Stalin's lunatic and criminal unpreparedness for war. These were people who were reluctant to commit collective harakiri for the greater glory of the *Vozhd*, over whom, even if they were not deported to Siberia, the Damoclean sword constantly hung. A second constituent was the rehabilitation of whole nations, the 'punished nations' which Stalin, on the basis of a truly Fascist principle, namely collective punishment for collective crime, sent into deportation because of alleged or actual collaboration with the Nazis by some groups within them. Even if Khrushchev did not keep his word and these nations could not return to their proper domicile (Medvedev gives quite a credible account of this: the Volga Germans, especially, were an excellent agricultural workforce needed for the virgin land pro-gramme), the verdict of their innocence was an important and remain-ing deed.

Two additional gestures – theoretical and practical – completed the programme of closing the revolutions from above. The first was the well-known (and much ridiculed) slogan of 'overtaking America in per capita production' and the second the 'scientific thesis' that the Soviet Union and the brother countries would simultaneously enter the phase of communism around 1980. Now, and this is true in spite of the

---

[25] A. M. Nekrick, *June 22, 1941 – Soviet Historians and the German Invasion* (compiled by Vladimir Petrov), Columbia: University of South Carolina Press, 1968.

capitalist world crisis, a quick comparison between Moscow and any Western shops will encourage a sardonic view of the predictive value of the first statement, and just a look at Polish shop windows will inspire a much grimmer view of the second. And yet, they were not so much balderdash but, once again, two positive promises of Khrushchev's government, which he at least honestly intended to keep. Ironically enough for such an ardent anti-Bukharinist, Khrushchev drew ever closer to the original project of the designer of the NEP and while he did not have the slightest intention of creating a politically free citizenry (at best, he could have been pushed into Yugoslav concessions), he certainly wanted to respect the consumer in the Soviet man. Since his 'gulash communism' became the stumbling block of the Chinese theorists and the New Left but was scorned even by those liberals who have nothing against consumerism in their own society, it simply has to be stated that Khrushchev's consumerism, shabby as its result had turned out to be, was a deed with beneficial effects in a country whose populace had systematically been ravaged by artificially created famines and had been lacking in elementary consumer goods for decades. As to the second promise, and even if we disregard the Marxist–Leninist 'wisdoms' inherent in all the discussions whether East European countries had already built up socialism or only its foundations, the Khrushchevian slogan contained a promise to them which also had a reasonable content. It is a debatable point whether or not the Soviet and East European economic interrelationships during Stalin's lifetime were based on a simple exploitation of the latter by the former but this much is beyond any doubt: an economic system and strategy was imposed on these countries which was disadvantageous for them economically and advantageous for the Soviet Union, at least politically (by making them dependent on Soviet demands, energy sources and the like). Now one of the possible shades of interpretation of the Khrushchevian dictum of arriving simultaneously at the promised land was precisely the intention of abolishing this economic dependence of Eastern Europe on the Soviet Union and replacing it by a mutually profitable 'cooperation'. At least certain countries, as different from each other in their general policies as Rumania and East Germany, interpreted it in this manner and got away with it. What the real face of these allegedly so harmonious relationships was, both under Khrushchev and his successors is another question. But the very promise formed an integral part of the Khrushchevite Brumaire: the policy of closing the period of revolutions from above.

Up until now, I have constantly pointed out the inconsistencies of this policy and I could easily add other important aspects. Khrushchev

solemnly promised to restore the Leninist norm of collective leadership but constantly tried to impose, if necessary by breach of his
promises and dirty tricks, his arbitrary will on his colleagues; this is why
his downfall became a necessity for them. He also promised, even if
indirectly, to respect the inner peace of the *nomenklatura* but by
constant and deliberate reorganizations which were aimed at weaken-
ing the power of the bureaucracy, he made their life hell, and, more
importantly, he disrupted social bonds between them which were
simply necessary for the functioning of that particular society, with its
irrational command economy. Even if no formal promises were made
to relinquish the policy of population transfer, as we have seen, it very
logically followed from his whole general line. Nevertheless, there can
hardly be any doubt that the majority of these 500,000 who were
mobilized for the cultivation of the virgin lands did not leave their
domicile and accustomed milieu voluntarily. On the one hand, he consolidated Stalin's work through the mythology of returning to Lenin,
eliminating at the same time the gravest horrors and the genuine dysfunctions, but he thus provoked the appearance of a come-back of
'Soviet democracy' which did not belong to his objectives but which
appeared as a logical conclusion of his own exposing of the Stalinist
horrors. And the list of inconsistencies could be further expanded.

However, the really important question is the following: should a
closure of revolutions from above be assessed positively or negatively?
There are only two clear-cut answers. One comes from the conservative who estimates terminating any revolution as a beneficial deed in
the main; it was this conservative audience that was ready to applaud
Khrushchev during his visits abroad. Without a theoretical framework
for understanding Soviet affairs, they sensed, as it were, the protagonist
of a Soviet Brumaire in Stalin's successor. The other unambiguous, and
unambiguously negative, answer to the question comes from the
Maoist for whom the crux of the matter was precisely this closure of
revolutions. The Maoists regarded Khrushchev as a traitor precisely in
that they no longer regarded Khrushchevite Russia as a revolutionary
country. Here I do not have either space or time to criticize the
mythological elements of the Maoist conception of revolutions based
on 'contradictions within the people', therefore a simple statement of
the fact of condemnation will suffice.

To speak for myself, I have an ambivalent attitude to the Khrushchevite Brumaire, one I think that all democratic but radical socialists
should adopt. On the one hand, he was indeed a liberator of his own
people from the unmitigated pestilence of the Stalinist mass terror, an
unavoidable corollary feature of all revolutions from above. Here once

again, I have to emphasize, against shallow interpreters of a complex historical development, that Stalin, one of the most horrible phenomena ever in human history, was not a lunatic half-wit but the evil genius, the designer and realizer of one of the most important social projects: a society living in permanent revolution. I have to repeat that both collectivization and forced industrialization were means, not ends, for him: partly, but not overwhelmingly, they were means to defend his revolutionary Russia from the adversary, a task which he very incompletely fulfilled, and overwhelmingly they were means to keep society under total control and constant military mobilization. The latter two features were for Stalin identical with 'revolution', these were his genuine policy objectives. It is a very hard task to speak of the unwittingly positive yields of such a horrendous period. Nonetheless, so much has to be said in summary that Stalin's period put a world-historical end to the delirium of enthusiasm, that halo of magnificence surrounding the very word 'revolution' since 1789 (or more precisely, since 1793) on the Left. The results of a sobering, a state of mind which accepts revolution as a last resort against tyrannical regimes but is most suspicious of the working of the instrument, are dawning upon us, of course, very slowly. But this undeniably happens, and the somnambulist but energetic push with which Khrushchev drove his country beyond the orgy and mythology of permanent revolution was an emancipatory deed precisely in this sense.

On the other hand, the work has remained uncompleted, and when one looks at his successors, the Brezhnevite Soviet Union with its threatening military might, expansionism, unbroken and ever-expanding inner oppression, the total silence of graveyards which replaces the Khrushchevite promises of a cultural renaissance, the unquestioned and haughty rule of an ignorant, brutal and oppressive apparatus, one should say: the First Secretary did not have Mao's resolution (nor did his followers who, in a good Russian manner, invested their hopes in authority and did nothing for themselves) to launch a revolution from above. Undoubtedly, it could not have been a democratic revolution: no revolution from above is democratic. But, somewhere in the middle of the road it might have met social forces released by the impetus from above which had genuinely democratic intentions. In this sense, and irrespective of the mostly psychological question to what extent it belonged to the potentialities of his personal make-up, Khrushchev's renunciation of revolution from above has a negative final balance sheet.

5

Forms of Equality

Ferenc Fehér and Agnes Heller [1]

I

A spectre haunts the industrialized world – the spectre of egalitarianism. Demands to equalize the first and third worlds or to reduce needs to bring about social equality are articulated by movements and theories which keep 'social equality' on the agenda. But, as we will try to show, a consistently implemented egalitarianism is a myth. All attempts to realize it as a general principle of social organization in a context of even minimal industrialization lead to a decline of wealth. Yet, recurring egalitarian tendencies constitute an indispensable social monitoring system. They always point to concrete inequalities that threaten to become permanent and therefore must be opposed. That is why theories and movements that point out inequality and seek to eliminate it must be recognized as socially valuable.

To characterize egalitarianism as a social movement incorporating specific principles, it is necessary to study the main types of human equality. These fall into two basic types: equality with respect to ownership of property and equality in the evaluation of men as individuals.

Equality in ownership

One interpretation of this calls for the equal distribution of social goods – that is, an 'equal share' of property, an equal distribution of the

[1] Originally published in English in abbreviated form in *Telos* No. 32 (Summer 1977) (Saint Louis), pp. 6–27; reprinted in E. Kamenka, ed., *Justice*, London: Edward Arnold, 1980; published in full in German as 'Formen der Gleichheit' in *Diktatur über die Bedürfnisse*, Hamburg: VSA 1980; in Italian as *Le Forme dell' Uguaglianza*, Milan: Edizioni Aut-Aut 1980; in French as 'Les formes d'égalité', in *Marxisme et Démocratie-Au-delà du socialisme réel*, Paris: Maspero 1981. *'Equality Reconsidered'*, (postscript) published in *Thesis Eleven*, Melbourne, 1981.

land, or equal ownership of the means of production. This view is generally connected with obsolescent conditions of production or agrarian societies, especially if the equal distribution of social goods also means equal division. But this concept of equality can also refer to equality of needs or to an equal level of the satisfaction of needs. Usually, when this demand claims to be a general principle of social organization, it is tied to a plea for the simultaneous redistribution of property. But when it is directed only at small groups, it may refer solely to consumption. Lastly, this conception can mean equality in the allocation and control of social goods. This can mean that all have control over their own, equally apportioned, property, or that all have an equal say in matters of politics, management and so on.[2]

But the demand for equal property is never made where the economy has not yet developed into an independent sphere, that is, where reciprocity is subordinate to kinship or social custom, where the latter serves as the 'natural means' for the equalization of goods, and where redistribution is carried out through personal, face-to-face relations which guarantee equality. In short, this demand can never arise where redistribution and reciprocity remain on the level of a quasi-natural homeostasis.[3] Rather, this demand appears only in a limited form under conditions of undeveloped commodity production, where the goal of relative equality of wealth is to create and preserve the material basis for equality in making political decisions.

In general, the concept of and demand for equal ownership are responses to the generalization of commodity production and the independence of the economy from other social areas. These demands thus appear when the system of redistribution through kinship bonds and social customs breaks down. Equal exchange in the self-regulating market then becomes the sole form of reciprocity or symmetry in the economic sphere, that is, when the main task of new, profit-oriented production and redistribution is to conserve existing inequalities resulting from the market and to create new inequalities. Thus, with developed commodity production, economic inequality becomes the

---

[2] This latter programme holds that, simply because their property is equal, all individuals should have an equal vote in social matters. This sort of egalitarianism stems from the particular equilibrium of agricultural societies, based as they are on community property or land already divided into separate parcels. Consequently, this programme was the one most closely connected with movements aiming to equalize property ownership. But today, in the midst of hyper-industrialization, we are witnessing the revival of such demands for equal disposition over property – even in regard to its use.

[3] We have borrowed the concepts 'reciprocity' and 'redistribution' from Karl Polanyi. But we use them in a specific sense relating to conditions of developed commodity production and industrializaton.

basis of general social inequality. This results in a divergence between constantly developing needs – growing in both quantity and quality – and their satisfaction, and growing antagonisms between the 'haves' and 'have-nots'. The classical form here is the relation between bourgeoisie and proletariat in nineteenth-century *laissez-faire* capitalism. Egalitarianism thus appears as a universal ideology wherever inequality becomes a recognized and accepted social condition (in other words, where there is inequality in property ownership, the satisfaction of needs, or the ability to make decisions).[4]

Equality of men as individuals

This concept of equality arose with the concept of humanity. In its original formulation, it is perhaps only the blurred reflex of the process

[4] Here Polanyi and Sahlins do not mean by 'reciprocity', 'redistribution' and 'market mechanism' the different forms of economic transactions, but three basic types of economic organization. According to Sahlins: 'Pooling is socially a *within* relation, the collective action of a group. Reciprocity is a *between* relation, the action and reaction of two parties. Thus pooling is the complement of social unity and, in Polanyi's term, 'centricity'; whereas reciprocity is a social duality and 'symmetry'. Pooling stipulates a social centre where goods meet and hence flow outwards, and a social boundary too, within which persons (or subgroups) are cooperatively related. But reciprocity stipulates two sides, two distinct social-economic interests.' Sahlins, *Stone Age Economics*, Chicago and New York: Aldine Athertone 1972, pp. 188–9. According to Polanyi and Sahlins, societies can be regarded as organized on the basis of reciprocity if their economic, social and moral spheres are not fully differentiated, and if exchange is not based on market relations.

Of course, there are 'pure' economic systems – that is, built exclusively on reciprocity or redistribution – which exclude the competitive, price regulating market of buyers and sellers. But larger economic integrations cannot be pure: they entail economic transactions such as redistribution. Polanyi concurs with this: it is demonstrated precisely by him that the self-regulating market was only an economic utopia of the nineteenth century. Moreover, in the same work, his preference is given to a society in which market economy ceases to exist without the abolition of the market: 'Also the end of market society means in no way the absence of markets. These continue, in various fashions, to ensure the freedom of the consumer, to indicate the shifting of demand, to influence producer's income and to serve as an instrument of accounting, while ceasing altogether to be an organ of economic self-regulation.' *The Great Transformation*, Boston: Beacon Press 1967, p. 252. It is in this sense that we introduce the concept of redistribution into our argument as one of the regulative channels, but by no means the only one.

There is, however, a crucial similarity between the reciprocity of economic anthropology and the market mechanisms of buyers and sellers: both presuppose symmetrical relations (in contrast to redistribution), and include symmetrical, dual transactions. These relations always have an economic function, since they are social channels for the satisfaction of needs (primarily material ones). No modern, dynamic society is possible without symmetrical economic relations: they cannot be replaced by redistribution. Thus, we call all symmetrical economic transactions 'reciprocity', in contrast with asymmetrical redistribution, or 'centrality'. Only a social balance – albeit a conflict-laden – of symmetrical and asymmetrical economic transactions can guarantee the functioning of an optimal economic decision-making model that satisfies the needs of individuals in modern society.

by which mankind attains self-consciousness. In essence, it holds that we are all human beings and as such are equals. This idea first appeared in Christianity and was perfected with the proclamation of equality before the law. The basic principle here (never fully realized, but also never in principle denied) is the abstraction of person and deed from property and from social rank (from the place occupied in the division of labour).

II

Ever since the revolutions of the eighteenth and nineteenth centuries seeking *liberté, égalité*, almost all social systems regard equality in some sense as a positive value. But there are two opposing models. One considers equality as a partial principle within prevailing inequality, while the other seeks to generalize equality as the basic social principle. The first model is characterized by the possibility of unlimited acquisition of property and the conscious acceptance of inequality. Supporters of this model see exchange in the self-regulating market as the only conceivable form of reciprocity, entailing inequality in needs and consumption and in the social hierarchy. Of course, various groups most affected by inequality and whose needs are least satisfied demand a more equitable distribution. Thus, today the ideologies of inequality increasingly employ a social game theory to investigate the role of such pressure groups within the model. Here, however, a more equitable redistribution is possible only in the area of consumption. Decision-making is not redistributed, and the 'will of all' has nothing to say about this. At best, it only chooses those who will.

Within this model of inequality, two forms of equality are generally recognized. First there is equality before the law, which has never been more than an ideal inasmuch as it is in constant conflict with the inequality of property. To remedy this contradiction, the independence of judicial power is usually built into the model as a partial guarantee. Ideally, the judicial arm is independent of the executive or legislative arm, but it can never avoid the underlying principle of inequality. Although within this model all constitutions guarantee men's equal rights, these rights can be realized only negatively – by forbidding certain actions. Anatole France's *aperçu* is more profound than first appears: equality negatively defined only increases actual inequality. Furthermore, all those eighteenth- and nineteenth-century liberal utopias that sought to complement the negative code of law with a positive and rewarding part turned out to be naive and unfulfillable because they lacked a supporting social mechanism.

The second type of equality within the capitalist model is that of equal opportunity. This is a relatively recent development and is connected with the increasing influence of pressure groups. This principle abstracts from the place occupied in the division of labour as well as from other factors, such as sex, race or religion. A prime example of this is the demand for equal opportunities for men and women. As a widespread social postulate – a kind of social 'domino theory' according to which the prevalent system of inequality can be broken at any point – the principle of equal opportunity is an excellent substitute for genuine equality. Although its role cannot be under-estimated in as far as it challenges centuries-old inequalities, it is far more illusory than the idea of equality before the law, since it is posi-tively formulated and as such contradicts the basic principle of property ownership and power influence. Its latent function, in fact, is to assure the optimal 'distribution' of individuals in the social hierarchy. The constant struggle between this principle of equal oppor-tunity and the underlying inequality is part of the model and con-tributes to its functioning (for example, in the form of constant struggles for educational reforms, social and political opportunities and so on).

The second basic model, that of egalitarianism, is opposed to the capitalist model and always comes about in response to it. Marx called this 'primitive communism', the 'negative abolition of private property'. According to him, communism is

In its first form only a *generalization* and *consummation* of this relation-ship [i.e. private property]. As such it appears in a twofold form: on the one hand, the dominion of *material* property bulks so large that it wants to destroy everything which is not capable of being possessed by all as *private property*. It wants to do away *by force* with talent, etc. For it the sole purpose of life and existence is direct, physical *possession*. The task of the *labourer* is not done away with, but extended to all men. The relationship of private property persists as the relationship of the community to the world of things . . . In negating the *personality* of man in every sphere, this type of communism is really nothing but the logical expression of private property, which is its negation. General *envy* constituting itself as a power is the disguise in which *greed* re-establishes itself and satisfies itself, openly in *another* way. The thought of every piece of private property – inherent in each piece as such – is *at least* turned against all *wealthier* private property in the form of envy and the urge to reduce things to a common level, so that this envy and urge even constitute the essence of competition. Crude communism is only the culmination of this envy, of this levelling-down proceeding from the *preconceived* minimum. It has a *definite, limited* standard. How little this annulment of private property is really an appropriation is in fact proved by the abstract negation of the entire world of culture and civilization, the regression to the *unnatural* simplicity of the *poor and undemanding* man who has not only failed to go beyond private property, but in fact has not yet even reached it.[5]

The first model is distinctly capitalist. Property as ownership is the source and at the same time the limit of appropriation, in other words, appropriation is subsumed to ownership. This fusion is also accepted in the second model, that of primitive communism, as the 'negative abolition of private property'. The difference between the two models is not that unequal ownership is regarded by the latter as the source of unequal appropriation, but that it regards theoretically equal ownership as the source of likewise equal appropriation. As Marx described it, ownership as the essential expresson of private property is 'universalized' and 'developed' in primitive communism.

Thus, the second model is characterized by the following traits: first, strong limitations on ownership. One way to do this is to divide a society's material forces into 'equal portions'. Today, however, this is purely utopian and, even in principle, incoherent (for example, how can raw materials and energy be divided into 'equal portions'?). Another way is through the state's confiscation of all property. As Marx concludes, the model of 'primitive communism' in its pure form can be either democratic (and thus mixed with self-deception), or despotic (as in the latter case).

The second characteristic of the primitive communism model is the equalization of needs. Since modern individuals are violently outraged by egalitarian conceptions (public opinion is so strong here that people are seldom candid on this subject), to evaluate this proposal, we must turn to the classics. In *Conspiration pour l'Égalité*, Bounarotti – one of the main historians of the Babeuf movement – speaks with naive candour:

> The natural equality that we envisage is this unity of *needs and feelings*
> which are born with us or developed by the first use we make of our

---

[5] Karl Marx, *The Economic and Philosophic Manuscripts of 1844*, ed. with an introduction by Dirk J. Struik, trans. Martin Miligan, New York: International Publishers 1964, pp. 132–4.

senses and organs. The need to eat and reproduce; self-love; pity, the ability to feel, think, desire, communicate one's ideas and understand those of our fellow men, and to conform our actions to the rule; hatred of constraint and love of liberty exist *to about the same degree* among all healthy and well constituted men. *Such is the law of nature*, from which the same natural rights emanate for all men.[6]

The naiveté of this passage reveals social intentions more clearly than the scholarly epigone's complicated mental constructions. When Buonarotti – and, in retrospect, Babeuf – speak of the uniformity of needs and feelings (for example, 'to about the same degree'), it is clear that they apply purely quantitative criteria to essentially unquantifiable human expressions. Thus, the result is a social movement as impractical as it is radical. Instead of reviving the system of social inequality, it suggests that we ignore the heterogeneity of all our feelings and needs, and sacrifice personality – one of the most significant developments of human culture.

Ideologies of this type contrapose 'natural' to 'artificial' needs.[7] This polarity is inevitable in all egalitarian ideologies that call for a levelling of needs, since, in order to bring about a levelling of needs the 'right' structure of needs has to be determined. The reason is evident: where reciprocity and redistribution balance out in an almost natural fashion, there are no right or wrong needs, since there is no alternative to the status quo. The problem arises only with the generalization of commodity production, where the inequality of needs and consumption is already a fact, that is, wherever the prevalent structure can and should be confronted with an alternative.

Thus the two recurrent features of ideologies calling for the levelling of needs are, first, the 'right' structure of needs is always determined in contrast to something, and thus narrows the world of human wealth. Furthermore, this demand is always authoritarian since it abstracts from what people regard as their own needs, or else regards them as 'delusions' to be eliminated. Of course, a critique of the predominant structure of needs based on chosen values is by no means impossible *ipso facto* authoritarian. But the levelling of all needs to a single exclu-

---

[6] Buonarotti, *Conspiration pour l'Égalité*, reprinted Paris: Éditions Sociales 1957, I, p. 29. Italics added.

[7] This polarity can take on quite different forms, according to various ideological points of departure: real needs versus those that are only imagined or which are aimed at prestige, natural needs versus luxuries, etc. Yet, they all lump cultural needs (especially those indispensable for creation and reception of avanced culture) into the category of imagined needs, luxuries, etc. As Marx put it, primitive communism 'wants to do away *by force* with talent, etc.', and is 'the abstract negation of the entire world of culture and civilization'.

sive model is inevitably tyrannical. What, then, are the functions of the egalitarian model and what are its chances of success?

The democratic model of egalitarianism, which seeks to divide ownership into 'equal parts', is utopian not only for industrial societies, but furthermore in all societies where redistribution centres cannot function independently of world commerce. Moreover, it is a regressive utopia since it would reduce and undermine the material resources of society. All redistribution centres would break down, together with mechanisms that regulate commodity exchange. It would bring about a system of haphazard exchange whose only real redistribution would be the redistribution of poverty. Again, this utopia is condemned as regressive from the viewpoint of our value preference based on Marx, from the preference of man rich in needs.

Before going further, it is necessary to establish whether Marx's man rich in needs is identical with *homo oeconomicus*, that is, whether his enrichment can be distinguished from the all-consuming, all-repressive development of human needs in bourgeois society. As an empirical historical product, *homo oeconomicus* arises along with man rich in needs as the promise of a free species. The growth of needs of *homo oeconomicus* is based on universal quantification. Its perfection is industrial production hypostasized to infinity. Its faith is in the transcendence of technological progress, in the 'future', in industrial production 'yet to be achieved'. Man rich in needs also opts for social dynamism, but for him it does not consist just in the increase of quantifiable needs. Although he sides with industrial development (accepting the continued development of the domination of nature, the growth in world trade, and so on), man rich in needs still subjugates the economic sphere to ecological limits and to the recognition that the birth of new, qualitative needs is also a new enrichment – one, moreover, that is opposed to linear growth.

The 'despotic model' of egalitarianism is enforced by the state as the 'representative of public interests'. It carries out the confiscation of the private ownership of everything simply by defining private property, or by setting the quantitative upper limit on ownership. Of course, it can always redefine these limits either in an authoritarian way or under the influence of pressure groups. In this model, all decisions are centralized in the state, which is not only the most important executive organ of redistribution but also its only centre. This is further guaranteed by the fact that the state not only has unlimited power to redistribute material goods and energy resources, but can also redistribute the work force. Symmetrical market relations vanish for the simple reason that the state has no partner. At the same time, the state regards all free activities as dysfunctional and eliminates them. Therefore, the elimination of symmetrical market mechanisms cannot be supplanted by the revival of reciprocity in the form of 'gifts', which is the form assumed by the redistribution carried out by the state. In this way, the authoritative character of the 'equalizing' centre is further strengthened.

This model – 'despotic' in the Marxian sense – is an illusion and at the same time a destructive character trait in regard to our value preference. It is illusory in its belief that equality can be attained by fixing an upper limit on ownership. Since to achieve the reduction of needs the model requires an authoritarian state, over-centralization of redistribution, and the degradation of symmetrical mechanisms, a new inequality comes to permeate all of social life, in other words, that between those who distribute and those who are distributed. Marx has already indicated the destructive nature of this new inequality: it is the complete negation of personality by the 'representatives of the common interests' and the negation of the entire world of civilization and culture. While this model does not absolutely exclude dynamism, it does preclude qualitative needs of personalities and a plurality of life styles. Furthermore, even though this central determination of needs cannot bring about uniformity (for the simple reason that not all needs are quantifiable), it nonetheless brings about the impoverishment of the permitted life styles.

But even the embittered confrontation between the capitalist and primitive communist models cannot transcend the bourgeois era. Both subordinate appropriation to ownership or else incorporate the former into the latter. The first model represents the world of private property, while the other model represents the world of universalized private property, to use Marx's terms. In the former, ownership is both the source and the limit of the origin and satisfaction of needs and participation in decisions. In the latter, ownership is by allocation: a centrally determined amount of goods is 'allocated' for the disposition of individuals as consumers.

Both models seek to further the 'common interest', but in different ways. Marx's statement, that 'the general interest is precisely the generality of self-seeking interests',[8] applies to the first model. The 'general interest' is thus constituted in the struggle of particular forces and is nothing but the generalization of the strongest particular interest operating 'behind men's backs'. In the second model, if the general interest is centrally determined, those other interests and needs that crop up at various social points are denounced as particular (that is,

---

[8] Karl Marx, *Grundrisse*, trans. Martin Nicolaus, Harmondsworth: Penguin 1973, p. 245.

excludable and negligible) when compared with the centrally determined ones. The majority of individuals does not participate in real
decision-making processes in either model. Reified forces decide on
personal needs and possible actions. Thus, both models become reified
and alienated structures, though in different ways and for different
reasons.

III

Is there an alternative, third model? Is it possible to transcend the first
model by a non-egalitarian one which takes egalitarianism into account
as a 'social monitoring system' and incorporates into its structure its
'negatively valid' truths? These are real questions which, like all
theoretically responsible questions, are at the same time postulates.
More precisely, the question is: can the two factors of property –
ownership and appropriation – be separated in modern society? In
other words, can the process of abolishing alienation begin in modern
society while preserving social dynamism, considering the relativity of
wealth and the constant recurrence of 'scarcity'?

A solution to this is possible only by clearing up two further
questions. First of all, why and under what conditions do we, following
Marx, regard ownership and appropriation as two different aspects of
property? Second, why do we regard their separation and simultaneous social 'encounter' as the starting point for the abolition of
alienation?[9]

As to the first question, we equate ownership with possession. As an
abstraction, this means the ownership of one, or the ownership of some
people, where all others are excluded from its use, from the satisfaction
derived from it and from the disposition over it. Of course, this is only a
theoretical abstraction, since the particular, exclusive satisfaction of
needs, just as the exclusive disposition over them, goes beyond ownership in the direction of appropriation. Furthermore, it is abstract
inasmuch as modern society creates a duality among all working
people: they are both producers and consumers. Only in an abstract
model can one picture a producer who completely satisfies his needs

---

[9] Our analysis of the various aspects of property parallels Andras Hegedüs's study,
'Adalékok a tulajdonviszonyok szociológiai elemzéséhez' (Contributions to the Sociological Investigation of Property Relations), *Magyar Filozófiai Szemle* 6 (1969).

from what he exclusively owns (even though he might share this ownership with several others). Lastly, it is an abstraction since 'exclusive
ownership' cannot be understood in the sense of one's omnipotence
over property: in simple terms, the more complicated a society is, the
more regulations it has and the less the individual can do as he wishes
with what he owns. But whenever he can do something, he alone can do
it, and not someone else. For this reason, ownership is exclusive.

Appropriation, the other aspect of property, entails the satisfaction
of needs connected with production, a hand in decisions pertaining to
production, distribution and consumption, and the determination of
their preconditions. Two groups of production-related needs must be
distinguished. First, there is the need for activity, in other words, the
need to express and realize one's personality, the development of one's
abilities through work and socially vital activities. Secondly, there are
the requirements for consumption of immediately produced goods, be
they material or non-material (for example, cultural products, medical
services,) whose precondition is production.

By definition, there can be no ownership without appropriation, for
the very purpose of ownership is in appropriation. I only want to own
something – and at the same time exclude others from this ownership –
when the property secures a particular field of appropriation for me.
But this does not mean that one's ownership is the source of all that one
appropriates. On the contrary, the process of appropriation always
goes beyond ownership.

The distinctive feature of capitalist society is that in it, the amount of
goods appropriated is completely determined by ownership, while the
'location' of the goods appropriated, when compared with previous
societies, is least of all one's ownership. The specific feature of
bourgeois private property is the unity of the contradiction between
social production and individual expropriation. The limit to satisfaction of needs is determined by ownership; the more one owns, the
more one can satisfy needs of activity and consumption. Furthermore,
participation in decision-making also grows in direct proportion to
ownership. You are what you have. Human conditions appear as
conditions of things. At the same time, the need-satisfying quality of
ownership is subordinated to social production; only at the point of
possession can it be the source of need satisfaction. Thus, appropriation is a category of the conditions of property; and ownership and
appropriation are separate aspects, even though their object is the
same: that is, they are reciprocal determinations.

The answer to the second question, then, is that capitalism is the
exemplary alienated society. In its fully developed forms, ownership

not only determines the limit of appropriation, but also strives for its universal subjugation. This condition is enhanced by the fact that capitalism is a universal money society, 'free' of the bonds of caste or kinship systems. Consequently, the means exist for universal quantification – hence, the dominant striving to compare what is incommensurable and to reduce qualitative needs to quantitative ones. But the limit on ownership – that is, that it can only strive for universal subjugation of appropriation – is important[10] The complete homogenization of the two basic aspects of property is thus revealed to be a myth believed by the supporters as well as the staunchest detractors of liberal capitalism.

Despite all these qualifications, the analyses of ownership are accurate: one is what one has and the needs that can be satisfied or the social conditions one can dispose over depend purely on wealth. Ownership dominated the appropriation process by transforming its entire environment into the universe of quantifiable needs, and by establishing ownership as the exclusive standard for disposition – again a quantitative principle. The simultaneous development of these two aspects creates the world of bourgeois private property.

The positive abolition of private property is not identical with the simple 'abolition of all ownership'. This socially nonsensical objective cannot be seriously entertained, even in its most extreme egalitarian form. Moreover, the development of man rich in needs presupposes the expansion of ownership of things used to satisfy needs, and the directions that this expansion may take can be blocked or rechannelled only as a result of a consensus reached through discussions and social conflicts.

The positive abolition of private property means that ownership will no longer be the focus of social dynamics; that appropriation gradually will be freed from the ownership that suppresses it; and that essential human forces will increasingly be realized in the process of appropriation as the origin and satisfaction of new, qualitative needs and as

---

[10] Two examples suffice to show the limits of homogenization. One is the revolt of the propertyless against the injustices of appropriation, from the Luddites to the labour union movements at the end of the nineteenth century. However one labels them – 'anarchist' or 'reformist' – it is difficult to deny that these movements have influenced the appropriation of surplus value since they have reduced the 'extension' of capitalist ownershp, even when they did not question its 'propriety'. In so doing, however, they demonstrated the practical possibility of separating the two aspects right in the midst of the supposed universal homogenization. The second example, which was repeatedly analysed by Marx, is that, even at the height of *laissez-faire* capitalism, the bourgeoisie had to delegate a considerable degree of control, in part because the administration of ownership and the regulation of the process of appropriation seldom could be carried out by one person: the complete surveillance of the process of appropriation by the owner was usually only an ideal.

disposition over its objective preconditions and results or, in broader terms, appropriation as the mastery of the world's objective wealth. Thus, this process can be the real sphere of the human appropriation of the world, that is, of the positive abolition of private property, because here 'taking possession' is not necessarily an exclusive act but presupposes a similar activity by other men. Our model thus presupposes two parallel series: the increase in the amount of delimited, separate property (the expansion of needs), even though certain directions of expansion may be blocked, and the gradual 'emancipation' of appropriation from the domination of ownership. These two tendencies comprise the process of the positive abolition of private property. But is this model practical? In other words, is a responsible experiment to realize it in a modern, dynamic world possible? To answer this, we must re-examine the meaning of reciprocity and redistribution.

Modern society is a commodity-producing society; thus, the point of departure for a model purporting to be a 'third way' is the recognition of the existence of commodity exchange as an economic necessity. Commodity exchange, that is, the market, is the only form of symmetrical economic relations in existence.[11] It functions on the basis of calculation for all stable industrialized societies, in a twofold sense: first, it is this basis that provides the terms to assess social wealth. Its rival could only be a system of entirely arbitrary central decisions or a 'simulated market', a totally superfluous detour either to the market or to the above-mentioned subjectivist model. Further, it is the market that allows a society to calculate scarcity and shortages where scarcity means the finiteness of natural energy resources at a given historical moment and the finiteness of working time available in a concrete social context. This means that it is impossible to abolish property as ownership in a concrete social dimension. The property holder appears in the market as an 'owner', the subject of reciprocity in exchange relation. All sorts of property can enter into symmetrical market relations – private, exclusively owned property, collective property (owned by a group of stock holders, or a worker-owned factory), nationalized enterprises with independent economic authority, and so on. In our model, the predominant place will be occupied by the property held by democratic groups and by state property authorized to take independent economic initiative. Although we presuppose a society where these two forms of collective ownership prevail, we are still operating within a world of symmetrical

---

[11]   Much of what follows is derived from the unpublished manuscript of György Bence, János Kis and György Márkus, *Is a Critical Economy Possible?*

market relations, since the market remains as the basis of economic calculation.

Thus, ownership cannot cease to be a factor in determining appropriation. The positive value of ownership in a social model is based on two factors which have proven to be lasting achievements of mankind, transcending the pre-capitalist and capitalist periods: the rational administration of property as the source of the rational satisfaction of needs, and the direct relation of decision-making to ownership. This applies not only in economics, such as the planning of personal accumulation and consumptions, or in the affairs of a small community (for instance, the family), but also to 'personal life strategies'. It is easy to see how significant this is for the growth of all people and how far it extends beyond the sphere of ownership. The control learned in the disposition of ownership develops the abilities for rationally sharing in the process of appropriation as it becomes emancipated from ownership.

Appropriation is freed from ownership in yet another decisive respect, that is, in redistribution. The existence of need structures pointing beyond the scope of ownership is the precondition for appropriation as more than mere 'appropriation' of whatever consumer goods one may own. Here appropriation as redistribution is not only the redistribution of socially produced goods, but also the determination of overall social strategy – a constant redistribution of all of society's material and spiritual resources through a general consensus. The precondition for this is the equal possibility of deciding on redistribution for all. This is one constituent of the process of appropriation not connected with ownership or with symmetrical market relations. Equal participation in redistribution is not just the only rational significance of the equal opportunity to articulate needs emancipated from ownership, but is also the essential reinterpretation of the concept of property. What remains of the concept of ownership is the basic act of personal satisfaction of needs and the social basis of calculation constituted in the act of exchange.

As the process of appropriation (presupposing a new structure of needs) becomes predominant, the world's objective wealth, which is in principle appropriated by all in order to develop, becomes human property. But this can be achieved primarily by communal acts which, by definition, have no exclusive character.

What, then, is required so that redistribution becomes increasingly determined by appropriation and decreasingly by ownership? As already mentioned, the increased expansion of ownership – as the enrichment of needs – does not rule out limiting some possible

directions of expansion. On a broad social level, this means placing
limitations on those private groups and collective properties which,
because of their monopoly situation, can disproportionately influence
redistribution, thus subverting equality in decision-making. Thus, the
old call for socialization and nationalization reappears within this
model. But this call today is not followed by the traditional argument of
planning versus anarchy. It is ridiculous to think that the liquidation of
the basis for calculation carried out in the elimination of symmetrical
market relations would in any way promote the cause of purposive
rationality. Thus, two limits must be set on the realization of these
preconditions. First, from the standpoint of purposive rationality,
nationalization becomes mystified only when the amount of property
has reached or exceeded the point where a centralized administration
is the only viable economic alternative. The secod limit is dictated by
two principles of rationality: one, there should be no income without
work as a constant basis of self-preservation and two, the state's
control of ownership must never become such that it would tend to
destroy values in the previously described manner.

The second precondition for democratic redistribution is just the
reformulation of the previous one in a different way. The development
of a broad scale of ownership by groups, communities and the state
which makes possible symmetrical market relations creates a situation
where the state can and should be the administrative organ of redistribution, while still not extending over all social life. The state will be the
'representative of general interest' and not 'generality' itself. This
model strives only for a dynamic equilibrium, in other words, the
model does not know or recognize a panacea for every possible
dysfunction. Yet, even assuming the purely democratic character of
ownership groups, there is always the danger that the symmetrical
market relations once again become dominant and the state loses influence as the administrative organ of redistribution.

Another precondition for equality in redistribution is equality in
decision-making. But what does this mean?[12] First of all, subjects
should have a growing competence in all areas (that is, all areas should
equally be areas of decision). Second, individuals should have the
opportunity to participate equally in decision-making. Within such a
framework the idea of 'equal opportunity' is no substitute for equality,

---

[12] Here we need to mention recent untenable views of egalitarianism developed during the
great social conflicts of the last decade. They can be briefly summarized as follows: since
all men are equally competent to make the most varied decisions, hierarchic orders are
conscious mystifications that can be abolished by the revolution. This disregard of the
division of labour creates illusions that are still with us today.

but is a real mechanism in equalization. To decide, one must have the ability and competence to decide. This can never be the equal competence of all men in every single question, but all men are competent in some socially relevant question. Moreover, an individual's competence can grow. But for this to take place, individuals must be assured equal opportunity, which means equality of the unequal. While original differences in abilities can and should be diminished, they can never be completely eliminated.

Finally, there is the question of equality of income. Today, those who accept the egalitarian standpoint are concerned with the principle of equal income. At first, this idea seems so plausible that all other interpretations seem artificial or insincere. Why, then, do we reject it?

The idea of equality of income is popular because it is plausible; it offers a quantifiable and clear criterion and fully corresponds to the spirit of bourgeois society, which measures only in terms of ownership. Thus, it does not correspond to our model.

To clarify this point, it is helpful to discuss the relation of ownership and income in the previous two models. In the case of the first model, the relation of income to ownership is clear. Income either stems from ownership (as revenue) or from the sale of labour power (as wage). In the despotic model of egalitarianism, however, the central authority allots an equal income to the whole population on the basis of its estimate of social wealth. When ownership is distinguished from appropriation, however, it becomes evident that both models separate property from income. In the first model, no wage worker can ever directly influence the process of social appropriation, while in the second case the central authority converts the whole society into an ensemble of wage workers. Even if a perfectly equal distribution could be achieved, with the representatives of the central authority receiving only as much as wage workers, a new inequality would still result between those who determine income and those whose incomes are determined. Only those completely imbued with the bourgeois spirit can consider this inequality to be secondary with regard to income equality.

In our model, wage labour is abolished and collective owners themselves decide their income. Of course, there would be upper and lower income limits reached through free discussion and social decisions made by those concerned. The lower limit must enable the satisfaction of all needs within the given cultural context so as to allow individuals to participate freely in the appropriation process. By this participation, he also satisfies a whole series of other needs not expressible in quantitative terms. The upper limit on income would prevent any one person from gaining power over others, especially over entire groups of people.

At the same time, efforts to equalize income must not disregard the actual plurality of needs. It is argued that, if needs are allowed to develop unchecked, men will always want more, thus leading to extremes of wealth and poverty. Therefore, a central authority is necessary, since the fact that one person possesses more than another is already a cause of alienation. Despotic egalitarianism, which adheres proudly to the materialist standpoint, in fact represents the materialism of bourgeois society since it can think only in terms of quantitative needs: given a finite amount of goods, one person's needs can be satisfied only at the expense of another's. Despite the oppositional attitude, the spirit of ownership or of universalized private property prevails here, and the resulting alienation is the morality of collective envy. But if we envisage the future as a world where the free process of appropriation is the collective form of satisfying qualitatively different needs, and if we regard the qualitative needs that can be satisfied only collectively as fundamental from the viewpoint of the freely developing personality, then we must recognize the plurality of needs. The ethic of alienation should then itself be alienating for us as the spirit of collective envy, which we want to leave behind.

It is especially important to recognize the plurality of needs in work. Our model regards one's work as the basis for satisfying quantifiable needs and condemns parasitism. Moreover, the reproduction of social life always requires a certain amount of human labour which individuals must somehow divide among themselves. But here also we reject the pattern of despotic egalitarianism where not only is the same income ideally allotted to all members of society as wage-labourers, but the quantity and quality of work are centrally determined as well. Labour becomes compulsory with no chance for an individual to select his or her life strategy. In this model, decisions are not the personal expression of free, communal individuals concerning their destiny, but are external and alien powers opposed to them. Of course, there will always be possible conflict so long as some have 'more' while others have 'less'. But the awareness of these conflicts and efforts to solve them are natural parts of the process of human self-liberation.

As the central question of industrialized society, the extension of decision-making in the area of production – that is, 'workers' democracy' or 'self-management' is extremely important. Although in the industrial world everyone is affected by wrong directions in technological development, the warning signs for this and the need to redirect it can first be articulated by those closest to it. Of course, such a redirection has limits, but human control of technology is an integral part of the process of appropriation.

The form of participation in determinig society's overall strategy of redistribution is, to use Habermas's terminology, 'undistorted communication'. Its regulative principle, the 'ideal speech situation' – that is, the open public character that plays so important a role in our model – is described by Habermas as follows:

> An interchangeability of dialogue-roles is possible, and not just in principle. Furthermore, there is also an effective equality of opportunity in the perception of these roles, i.e., in the choice and performance of speech acts . . . In the ideal speech situation, the only genuine speakers are those who have *equal opportunities to act* or to make use of representatives; for only reciprocal coordination in individual expression . . . guarantees that subjects are candid with each other concerning what they really do and mean and, if necessary, can translate their extra-verbal expressions into verbal ones. This mutuality of unimpaired self-depiction implies, further, a reciprocity of behaviour-expectations and excludes privileges in the sense of onesidedly binding norms of action.[13]

The public sphere analysed by Habermas arfd presupposed by our model is more than a formal principle. It speaks not only of the 'interchangeability of dialogue-roles', but also of the equality of the 'speakers' as active people and excludes 'onesidedly binding norms'. This principle of public life corresponds to our process of appropriation, which includes the free possibility of formal 'verbal acts', but which does not remain on the level of this formality, inasmuch as it is embodied in both institutionalized and spontaneous forms.

The last precondition for our model is that total social learning process become an organic part of the process of appropriation. Today education is caught between those who see it essentially as the hierarchic training of specialists, and those who regard the whole hierarchy of technical knowledge as mere mystification created by the division of labour. Both approaches identify education and instruction with the accumulation of knowledge and they see schools as the only place where this can be done. We reject both. The concept of instruction as

---

[13] Jürgen Habermas, 'Vorbereitende Bemerkungen zu einer Theorie der kommunikativen Kompetenz', in Jürgen Habermas and Niklas Luhmann, *Theorie der Gesellschaft oder Sozialtechnologie*, Frankfurt: Suhrkamp 1971, pp. 137–8. Here Habermas speaks of 'reciprocity' and 'symmetry' in reference to equality attained as a result of communication. This appears to contradict our account where communication is regarded as the underlying determination of the process of redistribution, detached from reciprocity. But the contradiction is only apparent, as will become clear later.

the training of specialists is functional, but it ultimately cripples men. Yet, to deny the need for technical knowledge and all social differences that this implies is illusory. The competence to make decisions is necessary for the expansion and equalization of the decision-making process. Consequently, education is not merely a preparation for social activities, but is achieved in the actual carrying out of these activities, in the very process of making decisions. Without this, the new model of redistribution is impossible. Instruction is not merely the acquisition of knowledge, but prepares people to make decisions: school cannot be its only setting.

To guarantee appropriation, culture should gradually be withdrawn from the context of reciprocity underlying commodity exchange. Of course, it is impossible to be more specific than this: it is the task of undistorted value-building communication of the public sphere to decide what the community 'can' and 'wants' to provide for culture. But, at the same time, this is inadequate. Certainly, the infrastructure must also be withdrawn from market controls in order to create a 'cultured environment'. The gradual rollback of market regulation in the area of culture entails that, in determining the proportion of resources allocated to cultural development, no market interest can constitute the predominant viewpoint. Rather, only the promotion of a new type of appropriation process is relevant (that is, the development of man rich in needs). Within a framework of this type of redistribution, the proportion allocated to culture cannot be a function of ownership (in other words, all individuals must have 'equal opportunity').

The appropriation process outlined here does not call for the abolition of the market, but for the separation of its functions that *laissez-faire* capitalism sought to homogenize. We have already described the first of these functions (the market as the basis of calculation): its existence is necessary for society's purposive rationality, and it does not make sense to speak either of its expansion or contraction. As to the second function, we agree with Polanyi: the market as a general reference system will gradually recede, the autocracy of 'having' will be abolished, and Marx's great postulate – the subjugation of the economic sphere to the totality of the social life process – will be realized. Equality in this model gradually becomes identical with the equality of decision-making possibilities both in reference to ownership and in the sense of gradual separation of appropriation from ownership.

While we reject any guarantees for our model, we still must take into consideration the question of its possibilities for realization. In our model, conflict is no evil, but one of the principles that makes the system workable – so long as it does not reach the point where it destroys the ability of the model to reproduce itself. The most important conflicts are between ownership and appropriation; between the 'solvent needs' articulated on the basis of calculation and the need-correcting principle of the public sphere in the decision-making process (a conflict that results either in the attempt to subject fundamental areas of the appropriation process to a narrow profit-centredness or in the threat posed by exalted utopian plans for 'undistorted communication' to the functioning of the calculation basis); and between institutionalized and non-institutionalized forms of the public sphere concerning limitations of property and investments. All these conflicts are reminders that our model is not overly optimistic.

The possibilities for the model can be located, first of all, in a social need (in the form of dysfunction, conflicts, and so on) that the model addresses. Yet at the moment, there are social forces moving in just this direction. The best chance for our proposal, however, lies in the fact that, while it takes account of the existence of nation states, it has mankind as its reference system. The universalization of the first model implies that the 'weak' are downtrodden by the 'strong', while the universalization of the second model means that the sphere of need determination is turned over to a world government, a chimera that eliminates all particular interest groups, need structures, and national cultural traditions: in short, it eliminates reciprocity and forcibly quantifies qualitative difference of needs.

Mankind as the frame of reference for our model is determined by a basic necessity: for economic planning to work, it requires that all of mankind's energy resources and means at its dispossal be considered, at least if we want to preserve the dynamism of needs and production. From this stems the very possibility of our model.

All this shows that, with respect to the broadest degree of openness of mankind, the dynamics of the self-regulating market cannot be a universal reference system. Thus, the outlined model is no naive wish, but stems from real needs. Of course, we do not intend to formulate new economic fantasies: the world's energy sources and supplies are a fact that must be accepted. Consequently, symmetrical market relations will remain in force. But since the universalization of the market's self-regulation into a universal reference system threatens to break down and thus make all calculation impossible, another form of reciprocity will appear more and more frequently – gift-reciprocity. This will not be detached completely from symmetrical market relations since its limits are determined by interests embodied in the basis of calculation and because the continued existence of world trade is also an 'interest'. It can be easily imagined that a gift-reciprocity implemented in the interest of the 'stronger' party's expansion of following the goals of a new 'need-determining' world centre is degraded into a pseudo-gift.

But if gift-reciprocity develops true to form and becomes a main channel for world trade, it would bring about a situation independent of property ownership, and determined by the above-described appropriation process. Thus, a new type of redistribution would be the precondition of gift-reciprocity and at the same time would be confirmed by it. For gift-reciprocity is a form of redistribution *sui generis*: it entails a redistribution of forces and wealth and, if the gift is not to degenerate into a pseudo-gift, such a question can only be decided in the 'ideal speech situation', that is, through the equal disposition over it by groups of people.

IV

So far, we have considered primarily the first form of the principle of equality – that related to property. This form, as the exchange of equal values elaborated in the Marx quotation, plays an important role in symmetrical market relations, but not the only one. Gift-reciprocity between the integrations is not equal, because it does not follow the principle of symmetrical market relations. A 'gift' that promotes the development of backward areas or that seeks to avoid ecological disaster is 'reciprocal' in the most elementary meaning of the word, since the recipient responds to this gift by participating in world trade or by being smoothly integrated in production processes, and so on – although this 'return service' cannot be quantitatively regulated. Here, for the first time, we encounter the social meaning of the concept 'incommensurability', while at the same time a rationally comprehensible meaning of equality develops in the area of disposition (decision-making). In the process of appropriation, only equality of decision has social significance.

The second form of the principle was characterized by its abstraction from ownership. This form is prevalent in the model of equality before the law. In the model we are proposing, the idea of legal equality retains absolutely its validity as the social scale of judgement. Nothing can replace its social function. Even so, there have been attempts to revise it or to replace it by a system of *ad hoc* decisions dictated by 'general interests' from whose viewpoint this model is too inflexible. Or else it has been seen as excessively formal compared with the multi-dimensional wealth and totality of human individuality, thus requiring replacement by an uncodifiable moral propriety. But these two principles, often interwoven, would only produce arbitariness and consequently the violation of human equality. Whenever a social structure endorses a formal principle of equality, the standard of equality before the law is inevitable and irreplaceable. Hence, violations of the formal principle of equality before the law in the name of some *raison d'état* cannot be condoned, especially in our model, where the state is not the exclusive embodiment of the 'general interest' but merely its executive organ.

There is a growing network of communities based on the principle of equality abstracted from property – a network that creates a series of symmetrical reciprocal mechanisms, preserves equality, but also transcends it in the direction of incommensurability. These communities can grow out of radical needs generated in the production process, or out of new needs of those 'drop-outs' who turn their backs on production. Of course, this is not to say that there are no problems with these movements. One objection frequently raised against the 'drop-outs' seems to be particularly justified: the criticism that they deceive themselves in thinking that they have stepped outside industrial civilization, while vegetating in its midst and allowing themselves to be nourished by it, that they oppose industrialization, while using its technical advantages. Their anti-work theory and practice is especially dangerous, since it seeks to replace productive life and self-realization (including objectification) with an artificially induced permanent euphoria. Yet, despite these deformations, without the broad development of such movements (and the gradual eradication of the parasitical, destructive ideologies of some of them) it would be impossible to realize either the subject of our appropriation process or the subject of worldwide gift-reciprocity. Thus, it is not the generalizable (and pluralistic) new subject of these communities who is utopian, but the rigidly rationalist idea that dares to hypostasize a world condition out of the mere insight of people living private and isolated lives. This transformation presents a number of psychological dilemmas. But it is no more impossible than it was for the free citizen of antiquity to regard slaves or barbarians as his equals in the eyes of God, or no more impossible than the idea of universal equality before the law for men of feudal epochs. While historical analogies have limited value for future-oriented models, there is little doubt that the *new* regulation of human production can develop only in conjunction with the subordination of the economic sphere to the totality of social life process and the development of new life styles.

What are the advantages of such a network of pluralistically developed communal life styles? Their pluralistic nature is determined by the various qualitative structures of needs and by the different relations which produced them. The basic principle of such communal life styles is suited from the start to developing many reciprocal – symmetrical situations that can encompass the whole of everyday life. Thus, it is unimportant whether these communities may be transitory and constitute only an educational phase or may turn out to be permanent life styles for certain groups of individuals; whether they grow out of the needs generated by the appropriation process or represent a transitory opposition to the world of production; whether they form 'ideal communities' or encompass the greatest part of vital activities. Even the community as an end in itself points beyond itself, precisely by its situation oriented away from interests that create gift-reciprocity. Furthermore, these communities are the best means of education for the ideal speech situation as the form of public life necessary for the new model of redistribution. A worldwide network of communal life styles is the precondition for public communication where rational discussion is the accepted norm. The development of the entire spectrum of qualitative radical needs is thinkable only in communities of this type, not because these communities suppress quantitative needs, but because the pillars of this community – the associated individuals – will develop their personalities and the 'gifts' themselves will become fundamental qualitative needs.

These reciprocal – symmetrical communities differ from those resulting from the restructuring of life styles during previous historical periods, where it was undertaken as a society-constitutive endeavour in the direct sense of the word. It suffices here to refer to the role of friendship in the Greek *polis* or to the function of the intimate family circle in bourgeois public life as analysed by Habermas. Because of the complicated nature of modern society, these communities are not state-constitutive but citizen-constitutive. They contain one of the most important nuances of meaning for the principle of equality – the equality of personal contacts embodied in 'face-to-face' relations abstracted from property.

The last question in our model is this: if we expect the future to bring about this incommensurability based on equality but transcending it, have we really abstracted from property?

The answer is yes. The realization of incommensurability in the network of personal contacts is based on this abstraction. In a broader sense, however, this abstraction can always be only relative. The precondition for our model is the emancipation of appropriation from ownership. Therefore, it is more than a moral utopia.

But the process of the abolition of alienation is essentially a Kantian 'regulative practical idea', presupposing an infinite progression – in other words, a process whose limits we cannot conceive, owing to contemporary industrial civilization and our own value assumptions. The concept of infinite progression is consciously contrasted with Hegel's conception of the 'return of the world spirit', because the 'moment of returning home' as the clear and final ending of alienation is a crypto-theological concept – not for philosophical, but for sociological reasons. Our model is based on the ever-possible conflict between ownership and appropriation, between reciprocity and redistribution. It recognizes no cure-all in the form of ideal institutional configurations and takes into account recurrent inequalities and the constant process of equalizing them in the gradual (and practically infinite) task of achieving equality in decision-making.

The aim of our model, then, is not equality, but constant equalization always restructured in social movements and institutions in response to concrete inequalities; not the abolition of ownership, but its purposive, value-rational restriction and the gradual emancipation of appropriation from ownership; not the reduction of needs nor the constant growth of the needs of *homo oeconomicus*, but the creation of a human being rich in needs whose needs-dynamic is not only or even primarily limited by scarcity, but who is directed to other, heterogeneous qualitative needs, to needs oriented towards the wealth of human contacts. No longer will the role of purposive rationality be autocratically dominant and monopolistic, but purposive rationality will be acceptable only together with informal, non-quantifiable principles of value rationality.

EQUALITY RECONSIDERED
(POSTSCRIPT, 1981, TO 'FORMS OF EQUALITY')

What makes a reinvestigation of equality necessary within the framework of a theory which takes Karl Marx as a point of departure, or, if one intends to glue a fancier label to our position: in a neo-Marxist theory? The reason is simple: the status of equality was, to say the least, dubious within Marx's thought. Every interpretation of a text is, of course, a personal reconstruction and as such equally vulnerable, but we would challenge all attempts which try, without violating the relevant passages, to attach centrality (or even an unproblematic existence) to this concept in Marx. It goes without saying that our statement cannot be pushed to the other extreme: Karl Marx could not choose inequality for a value. He, like all his radical contemporaries, was so deeply and indelibly influenced by the Great Revolution that *liberté, égalité, fraternité* as fundamental guiding principles of the modern body politic could not possibly be discredited for him. But their relative importance, their historical validity and their inter-relationships could – and as Marx was convinced – should, be reassessed. As a result, freedom (with such collateral notions as human dignity) had constantly been, in all phases of his activity, central to his thinking. Friends and (impartial) foes alike have often pointed out that Marx's theory was a philosophy of freedom. On the other hand, fraternity played a subordinate role in his vision. Even if he never made a general statement against it, this haughty spirit and individualist philosopher of collectivity could hardly make head nor tail of it. His Feuerbachian contemporaries with their emphasis – for Marx: *ad nauseam* – on the 'socialism of love' rendered *this* shade of the inter-pretation empty and unacceptable for him. On the other hand, as a regulative principle of international contacts, Marx did not need it. His theory never bothered explaining the ways in which a supranational human community will work. More complex was, however, his relation-ship to equality.

The problem has to be approached through the category which has traditionally been connected with equality: justice. In our firm convic-tion, all those who infer from Marx's overt hostility to law and legal regulation an absence of the concept of justice in him, disregard the crucial passages of *The Critique of the Gotha Programme*. But as we interpret this celebrated text, it allows for two conceptions of equality, both supervised and rejected by his sense of justice. One of them stems from the liberal tradition and is nothing but the simple acceptance of the principle of equality before the law without any further addition. For Marx, the lawyer, it was a truism that, as long as law exists, there can be no other guiding principle of a non-tyrannical legal system but equality before the law. However, it is precisely the emphasis that counts. Since Marx's central idea was the withering away of the state, with it of law and legal regulation, he was also convinced that the legal principle of equality, reasonable as it is in itself and necessarily opera-tive during the first period of socialism, will disappear as unjust (as compared to the collective morality which takes into account the incommensurability of every individual) when the new society comes to full maturity. Even if he cannot be made responsible for the total neglect, nay contempt that his disciples displayed towards all kinds of legal equality and justice already at the beginnings of their so-called socialism, he undoubtedly undermined the centrality of a millennial category within his (and his followers') system of thought. The second conception was that of economic equality, and in this respect justice was a counter-concept for Marx of all attempts at economic, substantive equality. He was convinced that, given the ineradicable heterogenity of human needs, there are only two channels, both unjust, of their quantitative homogenization which is the necessary methodological precondition of the application of quantitative equality to the variegated and many-faceted cosmos of articulate human needs. One is the logic of market, his main enemy, a dynamic through which equal values are, at least in principle, exchanged but through which social inequality of all kinds is daily reproduced. The second alternative has also appeared in his vision – and this should be noted by those who make him co-responsible for Gulags of any type – as an inherent danger of modern industrial civilization: the despotic regulation of economy, and with it, a tyrannical government of man.

But Marx's negative attitude provides us with a dilemma rather than with an answer. The real question is: why was it so? There are two reasons, one historical, the other immanently theoretical. The historical reason had been created by the very period which pushed the category of equality to the forefront: by the age of preparations, rule and aftermath of the Jacobin dictatorship in which all social actors (at least those who were outspoken enough to admit it) experienced freedom and equality as colliding, not complementary categories. In 'Forms of Equality' we have already referred to the fact that for a liberal genius like Vergniaud, any other interpretation of equality but that before the law was an attempt against the exclusive notion of private property, and as such, an atrocity against civilization. But an equally consistent, even if at that time less conspicuous, thinker formulated the adversary principle: Babeuf, the greatest theorist of *égalité de fait*. Even if we avoid superfluous historical detours, Babeuf's highly interesting anabasis to the concept and social role of communism based on a political dictatorship has to be mentioned here. He first revolted in an angry and nearly open protest against Robespierre's tyranny. For a short historical moment, his choleric temperature drove him to the point of becoming a leading journalist of the Thermidor. But he made inventory of the social results of this genuine emancipation from political terror in terms of substantive inequality, and precisely because equality carried for him an incomparably greater weight than freedom, he gradually returned to the idea of the necessity of terror, as allegedly an implementor of social equality, and he paid with his head for it. The following quotation from his famous letter to Bodson will fully demonstrate the above characterization. It contains nearly all the negative elements which induced Marx (and later all democratic socialists) to reject 'crude' or 'despotic' communism: a superior contempt for the life of the allegedly necessary victims among whom, it should be noted, only Hébert et al., the far leftist victims, are listed as those whose fate is worthy being considered at all; the quasi-religious social transcendence embodied in the future happiness of others, of the 'majority' as a claim to legitimize the terror in the present; the principle of the charismatic leader who has prerogatives different from the rights we ordinary mortals have. One very rarely sees such a full programme of total disenlightenment in concentrated form formulated in the name of 'democracy' (as contrasted with liberalism) as here. Needless to say, democracy was, according to the radical fashion of using the term in that period, identical with the Republic of 'égalite de fait'. The quotation reads as follows.

I freely confess today that I am vexed with myself for having formerly taken an unfavourable view of the Revolutionary Government, Robespierre and Saint-Just. I believe that these men alone were worth more than all the revolutionaries put together, and their dictatorial government was a devilish good idea . . . I do not at all agree with you that they committed great crimes and caused the death of many republicans. Not so very many, I think! I will not enter into an enquiry as to whether Hébert and Chaumette were innocent. Even if that were the case, I should still justify Robespierre, for it was he who might justly pride himself upon being the only man capable of guiding the chariot of the Revolution to its true goal . . . this man who must have been conscious that he was the only capable leader, must have seen that all these ridiculous rivals, however good their attentions may have been, would trammel and spoil everything. I suppose him to have said:'Let us cast all these intrusive triflers under the extinguisher, good intentions and all'; and to my mind he was right. The salvation of 25,000,000 men cannot be weighed in the balance against consideration for a few shady individuals. A regenerator should take broad views. He must mow down all that impedes him, all that cumbers his path, all that might hinder his safe arrival at the goal he has set before him. Knaves or fools, presumptuous or greedy for fame, it is all the same thing, and so much the worse for them! What are they doing there? Robespierre knew all this, and it is partly this which makes me admire him. This is what makes me see in him the genius in whom resided truly regenerative ideas ... Robespierreism is democracy; and these two words are absolutely identical.[14]

Marx, we think, understood perfectly the hidden meaning of the Babeuf tragedy, precisely in its antinomic character, which his radical contemporaries and heirs mostly tried to eliminate with the aid of pseudo-solutions and empty reconciliatory formulas. Babeuf was the first martyr for him in the communist calendar and as such, a highly respected memory but also an example to be avoided in further radical practices. Since Marx clearly drew the consequences from the 'Babeuf story' that all substantive conceptions of equality are, in their capacity as the main principle of social regulation, particularly the ones which aim at a forcible homogenization of needs, by definition tyrannical, this principle had to be overruled in his theory by freedom and 'man rich in needs' the latter as the protagonist of a non-alienated future.

The immanent theoretical difficulties regarding the concept of equality in Marx's thought are also well known for those who are familiar at least to some extent with the criticism made against Marx 'from within'. There were namely two considerations in Marx's doctrine which rendered the problem of equality practically superfluous. Apart from political inequality, in regard of which we have mentioned Marx's emphasis on legal and political equality up until the time of full communism, equality appears in connection with scarcity, usually as an option to cure the social ills caused by it, and with the qualitative difference between the various types of work mostly felt as degradation and suffering, particularly on the part of manual labour. For Marx, scarcity was no problem at all, except in terms of the ever-available amount of work time, given the finitude of workforce regarding age, working energies and number. His whole idea of the society of associated producers was based on an elimination of the dilemma of scarcity. As to the qualitative differences between the types of actually performed work, it was easy for Marx to conceive of a communist future without lifelong compulsory roles binding the individual to one type of work activity, since he believed it to be an incipient present tendency of capitalism to simplify every type of human work activity into accountable elements of homogeneous and interchangeable 'simple labour'. Had it been true, it would have made human multiversality an unproblematic and objective socio-economic fact of the present. Clearly, within this orbit there was no need to attribute a

---

[14] Quoted in A. Mathiez, *The Fall of Robespierre and Other Essays*, New York: A. M. Kelley 1927, pp. 246–8.

central role, or perhaps any role at all, to equality, even if its opposite could not be chosen for a value.

. As far as the Russian Revolution was concerned, the story is short and simple. For its leaders the whole case would rest where it had been left theoretically by Marx: in limbo. Lenin was neutral in this respect; he only insisted on a 'modest' way of life on the part of the apparatus. Stalin was, however, already an outright enemy of 'uravnilovka', which is a sneering translation of equalizing in Russian. Solzhenytsin read Stalin's mind correctly in the tyrant's *monologue intérieure* in *First Circle*. Here Stalin, 30 years later, recalls his (imaginary) debate with 'Ilyich'. 'It was a lot of nonsense, of course, giving them all secondary education and sending all these cooks' sons to university. This had all been Lenin's fault . . . "Any cook should be able to run the country" . . . What had Lenin actually meant by this? A cook is a cook and his job is to get the dinner ready, whereas telling other people what to do is a highly skilled business; it can only be done by specially trained personnel who have been toughened by years of experience . . .' Equality was definitely not a popular idea among the communists who unjustly appeared in the vulgar image of their enemies as equalizers.

For a variety of reasons, most of which can only be touched upon here, in the sixties, in different places, the phoenix of equality rose from its ashes. The first place of its rebirth was obviously China in the stormy period of her 'proletarian cultural revolution'. We would not venture even to try and outline the complex social character of this crucial event. We simply note that all accounts of it are, in our view, though at various levels of expertise, wholly unsatisfactory in answering the questions, solving the riddles they themselves raise and formulate. For us, the cultural revolution appears as a coincidence and a partly accidental combination of three separate events. The first of the three factors was a general abhorrence both at the top and the bottom in society of the Russian way of industrialization with the concomitant expropriation of huge peasant masses (in China this would have been incomparably greater than in the Russian case). Secondly, it was fuelled by, and gave new impetus to, long-time factional strife in the 'heavens' of Chinese political life, certain contingents of which identified themselves with the anti-industrializing dissatisfaction of the bottom and provided them with leadership and a channel of self-articulation, the only available one in a communist dictatorship. Finally, at a certain point, the cultural revolution became an actual battlefield between the armed forces of the ruling apparatus and various rebellious masses of urban and rural population which hated the whole apparatus as their oppressor. But whatever its causes, in the joint emergence of these elements the cultural revolution reproduced the famous antinomy of 'freedom versus equality' for the first time since 1793–4, in an even more marked way. For these elements – so disparate between themselves – simply could not be articulated with the aid of the category of freedom, only with that of equality as contrasted with 'bourgeois' freedom. This was so for a historical, a sociological and conceptual reason. The historical reason is the Chinese option for Stalin, against Khrushchev, a choice which was not due to 'Oriental backwardness' or to a simple misunderstanding. If historical analogies are of any assistance, in (at least a certain type of) the leading Chinese communist's social imagination – perhaps only in one faction, perhaps transfactionally – Khrushchev was Thermidor and Brumaire in one person. Here space does not allow for the analysis of the problem. Therefore we simply state that for us this is not the whole story, and even when we agree with statements of fact, we totally differ in our evaluation from the Chinese assessment of that period. Khrushchev represented Thermidor in the Chinese view in so far as he put an end to the reign of terror and showed a minimum amount of tolerance towards the consumer in man. He also launched the slogan of *enrichissez-vous* on a very modest scale. He represented Brumaire for the Chinese communist leader, with his abolition of the thesis of sharpening class struggle in socialism and with his 'all-people's state' in that he seemed to close the period of 'revolutions from above'. But at that time China lived through a period in which both rank-and-file militants and political leaders embarked on a powerful new revolution from below and from above in which they were ready for excessive bloodletting in order to achieve their most heterogeneous objectives. Therefore, the enthusiastic and often uncritically liberal emphasis of East European masses on civic liberties and the small concessions made to these demands on the part of the ruling apparatus, appeared to both Chinese protagonists as so many signs of 'embourgeoisement'. The second – sociological – reason is simple: in every society near the edge of subsistence – and China was certainly one of them – the expropriation of general freedom by a ruling elite appears first and foremost as inequality in the amount of goods consumed by the elite. Finally, conceptual difficulties consisted in the fact that freedom perhaps could be a banner for the third component of the combination of disparate aspects but equality was an easy and homogenizing framework for all of them.

The egalitarianism of the Chinese proletarian cultural revolution was absolutist, in other words, the central, nay the exclusive category of social regulation, reductionist in that it energetically gave voice to its opposition to a trend of increasing industrialization of both Western and Soviet types and tyrannical in that it regarded the simple existence of different needs – and even more the libertarian aspirations for their recognition – as suspicious signs of bourgeois infiltration and contamination. It dealt with them accordingly. In this triple capacity the process bound up with the name of Mao was the first authentic Babuvian communist revolution. There is evidence gathering that it even had a secret protagonist, Chèn Po-ta, a frail and broken 76-year-old charged in the trial of various 'conspirators', a former political secretary to Mao who seems to have been fully conscious of both the egalitarian and the tyrannical aspects of the new revolution, and who made a eulogy of it precisely in this double character.[15] There is also good reason to assume that this tendency strongly influenced the Khmer Rouge leaders in whose murderous rule this conception reached conclusions and assumed dimensions which did not belong to Chèn Po-ta's explicit aims but in which he does not seem to be, at least theoretically, innocent.

The second locus of the rise of the phoenix was to be found in the leading capitalist countries of Western Europe and, to a lesser extent, of North America. The 'China example' served here as a triggering effect, but only as an ideology or rather as a figure of speech, as an incentive, not as a cause. All the harsh, sometimes horrendous, features now so widely publicized by the Chinese press itself and which to some extent could have been known even then, disappeared from the rosy idyll drawn up by West European Maoism. What remained was a factually inaccurate but ideologically important pathos of 'Seid umschlungen, Millionen', the portrait of a fraternal community in which people voluntarily share and work, allegedly without the line of demarcation between the manual and intellectual types of labour. The question is not whether there was a drop of bad faith in the mythology of the Paris mandarins who lived in the middle of an overrefined culture and sang eulogies of a social condition which realized Marx's prediction to a frightening extent: the rule of absolute equality which appeared as a tyrannical reign of envy incompatible with culture. There was obviously much more than a drop of bad faith in this attitude and it had to be followed by the mardi gras of new philosophy. The element which needs and deserves analysis is that, because of specific conditions it was only through the rebirth of the concept of fraternity that West European egalitarianism could become articulate.[16]

---

[15] See R. F. Wylie, *The Emergence of Maoism, (Mao Tse-tung, Chèn Po-ta and the Search for Chinese Theory, 1933–1945*, Stanford: Stanford University Press, 1980.

[16] The great exception, here as elsewhere, is the lonely but increasingly influential figure of Cornelius Castoriadis. He is a partisan of an absolute equality, obviously without thinking

The social reasons for the predominance of the category of fraternity – in which equality was contained as everyone's sharing everything voluntarily, everyone's developing all human capacities – can be found in the particular character of the new opposition. For the New Left that which is (and always has been) the most discussed point and the fundamental weakness of Marx's economic conception, namely the absence of scarcity from the theory, was, in a strange way an axiomatic collective – practical social experience. As members of a generation which was brought up during the longest and most spectacular boom in the history of capitalism, in a dynamic of increase which seemed to be unstoppable, they dismissed the whole issue of limited economic resources and potentialities with a gesture of emotional radicalism. In a way, contrary to all traditional leftism, communist or labour, they blamed all social ills partly on affluence, partly on the division of labour. The critique of the division of labour in the form of an incisive morphology and romantic suggestions played a central role in the new radicalism. This proves the important function equality – and the 'China experience' – fulfilled in the ideology centred on fraternity, since, as we mentioned, the line of demarcation between manual and physical labour is one of the main targets of all types of egalitarianism. As a result, in their world-view, the opposite of the 'haves' was not the 'have-nots'; 'having' was contrasted with 'being'. It was due to this need that the young Marx of the *Paris Manuscripts* was revived so vehemently. The main social objectives were formulated in terms of immediacy, communal–collective life style, sharing, creativity. But this egalitarianism of fraternity had a very limited interest in questions of income, taking for granted that incomes will grow in the future generally – and for revolutionary potential – dangerously. 'Equality through fraternity' was a principle hostile to increased consumption, the main goal of Khrushchevite Russia and Eastern Europe. Nonetheless the New Left did not want to replace it by a forcible reduction of needs as the militants in China had done, although they were otherwise exalted by it. The target was self-creativity. The New Left was critical of overindustrialization and increasingly ecologist, but it was urban-based and its partisans thought in terms of a 'cultural' abolition of the division of labour rather than in those of destructon of the cities which

---

its implications for freedom, which – as 'autonomy' – is a central category for him as well, to the end. Precisely for that same reason, he is a zealot of the absolute predominance of the political over all other social activities and an admirer of the egalitarianism of *sans-culotte* masses in the Great Revolution.

reached so nightmarish a realization in Cambodia. In brief, an anti-industrial, romantic and collectivistic–communal concept of equality became popular in the New Left through the mediation of fraternity. But it had definitely no absolutistic or tyrannical character, despite the gradual political re-Stalinization through Maoism of several new leftist groups.

The third and the least important locus of the rebirth of equality was Eastern Europe in its Khrushchevite and post-Khrushchevite periods. The reason for its being the least important cannot primarily be accounted for by the undeniable Khrushchevite consumerism which always generates 'differentialist' rather than equalizing tendencies. The reason is rather the absolute predominance of the category of freedom in this area. As in all tyrannical societies, in East European Soviet regimes as well, all social ills were and still are articulated in terms of the absence of freedom, and everything else was derived only from this single major want. Nevertheless, the social differences between the standards of life of the ruling apparatus and the hard lot of the toiling majority were so blatant that this constellation partly provoked the critical activity of writers and sociologists (mainly in Hungary and Poland), partly the spontaneous activity of dissident militants from particularly poverty-stricken areas, minority groups and the like, all of which revived to a limited extent the importance of the concept of equality.

In the seventies we lived different experiences in every respect. The Chinese absolutistic, tyrannical attempt at achieving equality of the Babuvian communism had become more and more discredited among its supporters (whom the leaders, in a good old Stalinist fashion, repeatedly betrayed and sacrificed), and finally the egalitarian faction was crushed in a palace coup. True enough, the so-called trial in which the indomesticably courageous personality of Jiang impressively represented the *élan*, at the same time the misanthropic cruelty of the egalitarian revolution, was not a total defeat precisely because of certain protagonists' resolute stand. But the revelation of the Chinese press (and this time one can safely believe the enemy's – relative – objectivity) gathered enough material to discourage morally any new experiments with absolute equality, at least in the near future. In Western Europe, the capitalist depression energetically put an end to the period in which social ills were blamed on affluence. The category of scarcity has now been fully rehabilitated. More importantly, on the one hand several deep social inequalities, always guessed but never proven, have been exposed behind the affluent facade of liberal conservatism. On the other hand, a new trend has surfaced in recent years, the monetarist economic doctrine and philosophy which, in a general offensive against the welfare state, overtly declares socio-economic inequality a precondition of liberal freedom, which is meant only or mostly as 'freedom to choose', especially in the case of doctrinaire monetarists who can build Pinochet into their concept of freedom. All this has the result that while equality (with certain remarkable exceptions, such as Castoriadis or Rossana Rossanda) has ceased to be the central category of social organizations where there is a critically thinking left, the problem of equality in a relativized sense has increased in its importance and not only on the Left. It became indeed a general test of whether social actors referring to freedom mean business or their aim is only the monetarist free market of the Pinochetian brand.

Even though we came from the turmoil of the Eastern European scene (where equality has remained to date a secondary category) and lived in it up to our neck, it was this social need we tried to cater for in 'Forms of Equality' in 1975. Living since then in a Western context it became clear to us that the problem is constantly increasing in importance and that our original essay, which was a sketch not a detailed analysis, needs further qualifying remarks.

The first is self-critical. Even if we reject any conception of equality which puts questions of income and income distribution in the pinnacle of its system, no consistent, even if relative, egalitarianism can exist without an economic strategy in the long run, and we have none. The general situation on the Left is that either the torn vestiges of a Marxist orthodoxy survive (in Sweezey, Mandel and others) which explain absolutely nothing of the specifically new situation, but only repeat old theses of a dubious value, or pragmatism reigns supreme. It is a very moderate consolation for us that this decade has witnessed an equal humiliation of the once so haughty club of liberal–conservative economic theorists. Our suggestions regarding other questions might be vague, but we do have suggestions. Here, however, we are just as nonplussed vis à vis the new situation as everyone else. The main problem, as far as we can see it, consists in the following. Economic regulations are always bipolar structures: they consist of primarily economic actors, and institutions not necessarily of economic character which delimit, channel, regulate their activities. With the usual crudeness of too large sketches, and without entering into world-historical detours, the following typology of this relation in the last 200 years can be made. In the *laissez-faire* period it was mostly a reshuffle of old institutions created by the economic actors themselves, together with generating new ones which ensured the economic functioning of the system. This took place through the gradual demolition of guilds, the legalization and expansion of the stock-market and the bank-credit system, and later through the gradual recognition of the official status of trade unions. All this together meant the institutional framework in which a 'liberal free market' existed and regulated the unlimited appetite of *homo oeconomicus*. Even if, as we know from Polanyi and others, it was not true that the state had no role in economic processes (there has never been a time in modern development in which not only municipal but also state legislation of a kind regarding economic transactions did not exist), but the role of the state was initially undoubtedly limited .

The second period, generally called Keynesian, that of state inter-vention, has been characterized by a changed relation of economic actors to non-economic institutions. The latter, and first of all the state, became a constitutive element in all transactions and this is not only true of welfare liberalism, but of rightist totalitarianism as well. Norman Stone has recently remarked wittily that Hitler's economic survival – expected by no one – was simply due to his 'stumbling upon public spending'.[17] But it has to be mentioned here that 'leftist' totali-tarian states are excluded from this typology: in them the state does not intervene, it creates and fully commands economic conditions. These states obviously differed widely regarding the chances of a meaningful life (sometimes simply regarding the chance of survival) but there was one element in common in them. Even if economic activity consider-ably transcended the national limits (some of them were centres of vast empires), it could be checked and regulated to a reasonable extent by the nation state.

The third period is, however, that of global economy *sui generis*. Apart from the traditional ones, even the most influential economic actors, the multinational trusts are no longer national in character. This makes controlling even tax evasion a very complex duty. Further, there is no longer a country which possesses sufficient resources for an industrializing strategy within its national borderlines. Therefore, at least to some extent, every country is dependent on every other (or at least: on many others). The consequences of present-day technology (e.g. nuclear wastes) hit whole areas inhabited by nations other than those setting this technology in motion. In a world of superpowers the simple technique of dreadnought diplomacy has become obsolete: the possible victim of one superpower seeks and finds refuge with the other. All these and several other factors have created in the last decade a scene of truly global economic activity without adequate insti-

---

[17] Norman Stone, *Hitler*, Boston-Toronto: Little, Brown and Co., 1980, pp. 53–54.

tutions, even without the hope of such institutions (because there is no 'world state' and cannot possibly be). In our firm view, it is this, and not the social theorists' insufficient acumen that creates a general confusion in economic theory.

Our only, necessarily very vague, suggestion can be, and it has already been made in 'Forms of Equality', that equality in the form of reciprocal redistribution at an international level realized by domination-free discussion of whole human groups and not by force, has to play a central role in the global, interstate regulation of economic affairs. But it must be repeated emphatically: not even this form of equality can be absolutist and tyrannical. This is perhaps somewhat more than theoretical hairsplitting. Frantz Fanon, the leftist doctor and ideologist, in his famous *Wretched of the Earth*[18] formulated the postulate of total, immediate and, if need be, forcible, economic equalization between the first and the third world in terms of an imperative moral duty (obligatory recompensation) on the part of Western civilization. He would hardly be glad, were he alive, if he knew that it is the Ghadaffis of the world who in fact have set out to realize his programme. (The Ghadaffis who would have sent him to torture cells and prisons, if not in front of an execution squad for his fancy *marxisant* ideas and 'infidel' contacts). But every social strategy deserves its adequate subject. All suggestions of blackmailing Western industrial civilization into an immediate and forced equalization, workers and capitalists alike (because this is what the programme boils down to in practice), instead of forcing, for so much force is admissible, an egoistic partner into a situation of discussion over priorities of need satisfaction, disregards the existence of the qualitatively heterogeneous vast universe of Western needs, among them, working-class needs, which must not, and cannot, be forcibly reduced. (And it equally disregards the vital interests of many countries of that same area in the name of which such a politics of extortion allegedly speaks: it was Indhira Gandhi who stated that Arab oil policy pushes third-world countries without oil resources to the brink of destruction). And if attempts are made at 'meting out punishment to the decadent West' – as in fact happened between the United States and Iran where the Fanon programme tacitly resurfaced – instead of legitimately reclaiming disposition over the ways in which national wealth is being put to use, the Western working class and all lower social strata and groups will support policies which are far from implementing their interests. They will occasionally even support policies which are ready to push

---

[18] Frantz Fanon, *Wretched of the Earth*, Harmondsworth: Penguin 1967.

through radical inequality in the most violent form: wars. Thus a strategy of simply depriving the 'haves' (of very moderate richness, as far as the working class is concerned) can only lead to a tragic deadlock, to the conservation (or even sharpening) of the existing inequalities.

The next qualificatory remark is the following: our theoretical proposal as it is expressed in 'Forms of Equality' is fairly Aristotelian in character.[19] As generally known, Aristotle distinguished three levels of equality. At each level, the category has a different meaning and a different extension. At the first level, that of *politeia*, in modern words, the political sphere, everyone (meaning every male and free inhabitant of the city-state) is equally free. In this respect equality is absolute. At the second level, the level of economy (which is in Aristotle's view crucial for the preservation of political equality) equality is relative. The extension of (primarily landed) property cannot (or must not) be totally equalized for a number of reasons (physical obstacles, the tyrannical character of the undertaking and the like) but its unlimited growth and expansion similarly cannot be tolerated in order to preserve the other, for Aristotle fundamental, equality in the political sphere. Finally, at the level of the individual it is either meaningless or absolutely tyrannical to speak of any kind of equality at all. Our natural differences are at the same time guarantees of our individual freedom, and equalizing in this respect is a dangerous and tyrannical undertaking.

We have three reasons for reaching far back to the Aristotelian legacy. The first is that the Aristotelian notion is, in contrast with nearly all other concepts of equality, highly differentiated. It takes into account that all undifferentiated use of equality will conclude in tyranny and thus in the self-abolition of equality itself. The second reason is simply a paraphrase of the former: the Aristotelian notion is not an absolutist, even if it is a cardinal category of social organization. It leaves room in its differentiated character for other social principles. The final reason is that, as an internally differentiated notion, it reconciles the antimony of 'freedom versus equality'.

We have preserved all three levels of equality in differentiation. It was at the first level that we performed the most minimal alteration on the original Aristotelian conception. Political equality is absolute for us

---

[19] The fact that the proposal is Aristotelian does not contradict the other fact that we take Marx as a point of departure. Even though we have very little interest in questions of orthodoxy and in solving the riddle of up to what point is the ship of Theseus Theseus' ship, if we replace a fair (and always increasing) amount of its components by others, so much should be remarked here that Marx himself was Aristotelian enough to legitimize such attempts.

to the same extent as it was for Aristotle: it means the equal freedom for all citizens without discrimination, in all respects of political life. The general counter-argument in modern radical thought, that such an absolute political equality is only formal given that the actors' potential to use their respective weight is far from being equal because of their unequal respective socio-economic situation, need not have bothered Aristotle since he only counted with free (and male) citizens of relatively equal economic standing. There is no reason for us to be concerned with the problem either and in what follows we are going to explain why. But it is all-important to stress, because of the many (fundamentalist, neo-Babuvian and other) adherents of a tyrannically introduced equality, that any conception of equality which does not posit itself politically as an absolute freedom of equals is not only self-contradicting but also self-destructive: neither equality, nor freedom remains at the end of the road.

At the second level, certain modifications have to be introduced into the original Aristotelian conception. Clearly, any 'partitioning' of a collectively owned property into approximately 'equal portions' in an industrial society makes no sense at all given the character of the requirements of modern technology whereas it is, at least in principle, not nonsensical as far as landed property is concerned, and such a state of affairs has constantly been a dream of agrarian communism. In an industrial society (whose critical adherents we are) the problem of equalizing property relations can only be raised consistently in three ways. The absolutely and overtly negative attitude to equalizing regards private property in its exclusive character (as one's unmolested *ius fruendi, utendi et abutendi* extended to the main forces of production) as the prime civic liberty and is ready to counterpose it to all others, so that it coexists with civic liberties if possible but sacrifices them without sentimentality on the altar of the first if necessary. This is the position adopted by liberal conservatism. In the second approach, the solution of the dilemma of inequality of property is achieved through a general confiscation (called nationalization) of all properties. The sterile discussions about the distinction between 'private' and 'personal' property simply derive from the extent of such expropriations. In Cambodia, it went to the point of the nationalization of the toothbrush and the confiscation of life. This is the position of all elites seeking a dictatorship over needs, even if not always with such a nightmarish consistency. In contrast with liberal conservatism, which is a self-conscious principle of 'substantive inequality', but only in relation to it, the position of the partisans of confiscation of property is in this respect an equalizing one, with the inevitable Orwellian proviso: everyone is equal, but the elite, in its capacity as the custodian of all properties, is more equal. The third consistent suggestion is, and this is what we accept, self-managed society. This implies a relative concept of economic equality in a triple sense. Firstly it presupposes that everyone is a proprietor (it is only thus that our suggestion can be a principle of economic equality) but it cannot presuppose, as things now are, that everyone is equally a proprietor. Or else we would deny the fact of the division of labour which, as far as its present structure is concerned, can, even should, be modified in a slow process but which undeniably exists. Secondly, this principle does not imply formal equalization of the extension, the relative economic strength, of the collective units of property, as this would be an absurdity in modern industrial dynamics. Thirdly and finally, as we indicated in 'Forms of Equality', there should be two limits of income difference although we explicitly reject a total equalization of all incomes.

It is at the third level that we perform the most drastic transformation of the Aristotelian principle. While we do not deny for a moment that all attempts at homogenizing individual differences is a totalitarian nightmare, the Aristotelian formulation is merely negative, therefore insufficient. We try to replace it by the following: all needs (except the ones which are aimed at using others as mere means, or in other words, except the alienated needs) should be recognized as equally legitimate ones even if they can never be satisfied in their entirety in any given particular moment.[20] As a recognition of all needs, this is a principle of equality. As it does not even try to homogenize human needs, it is an antitotalitarian principle of equality. Moreover, it is not a relative principle but a principle of incommensurability. But it is a positive concept in that it creates a social problem, a social sphere and a social task by the postulate of the recognition (even if not the simultaneous total satisfaction) of all human needs, together with the preserved validity of the restrictive formula.

Generally there are two objections to this. The first is that our principle is a simple reinvention of liberalism. The second objection is that the principle is empty and its social consequences are irrelevant, and the critics ask of what use it is for people if their needs are 'recognized' with the immediate proviso that they will never be satisfied in their entirety. Is recognition under such circumstances any more than a verbal exercise only satisfying the conscience of the

---

[20] See this, in detail in Agnes Heller, 'Can "True" and "False" Needs Be Posited?' in Katrin Lederer, ed., *Human Needs, A Contribution to the Current Debate*, Cambridge, Mass.: Oelgeschlager, Gunn and Hain, Publishers 1980, pp. 213–27.

intellectual who formulated it, while those whose needs are recognized but not wholly satisfied remain in an unaltered state of dissatisfaction?

It is relatively easy to answer the first question because it is related to so-called facts. For example, it will suffice to read E. P. Thompson's grandiose reconstruction of the 'making of the English working class' to see that liberalism, in all consecutive phases of its political development, was very far from recognizing all needs of the so-called 'lower classes' or even the majority of them. For social recognition of human needs is not identical with the fact that there is no direct censorship over the articulation of certain needs, in other words, that there are civic liberties of speech and opinion. (Even though every radical history of the modern industrial classes will show how much the latter had to fight even under liberal rule for their right to the free expression of their 'incendiary' views and how late was their achievement of formally unimpeded expression.) But, let us repeat, the social recognition of needs is more than simple tolerance towards their expression. It means concerted and deliberate collective social action for their satisfaction to the extent of the exploitable social resources, in constant debate regarding priorities. The only major change in this respect in the history of liberalism is the introduction of welfare mechanisms in certain highly industrialized liberal countries. But even so, it was only a particular cluster of needs (mostly embracing ones directed at physical self-reproduction and, to a lesser extent, education) which have become socially recognized. In general, one can say that no profit-regulated society recognizes human needs in their totality for the perfectly simple reason that a great variety of eminently human and non-alienated needs are not profitable. There is another reason as well. While representative constitutions and declarations of human rights fully recognize everyone's needs for political and legal equality and everyone's human dignity in his/her capacity as a rational being, no liberal system has ever recognized human beings in their full human dignity. There are two reasons for this. Firstly, it is only *ratio* in us that deserves general and equal recognition by liberal theory and practice. All other human faculties and passions, and the needs stemming from them, have a subordinate status. Secondly, it is only in the form of the rationality of the political male that human dignity and the collateral needs are recognized. In our capacity as female, alien, belonging to minority groups and the like, our full human dignity has never been recognized in a socially active sense. Therefore we reassert our conviction that the active social recognition of all human needs is a radical socialist principle which transcends the liberal tradition.

It is more difficult to answer the second objection. In order to provide a relevant, not verbal, answer we have to make a detour and give a sketchy typology of scarcity and abundance. Logically speaking, there are two types of scarcity, absolute and relative, and two types of abundance, similarly absolute and relative. Absolute scarcity means a social condition in which whole groups, strata of a given community, or communities themselves vegetate on the level of near-subsistence. This has been quite a usual feature in the early history of human species, and in Africa and Asia it recurs even now, to the greater glory of our civilization. Of course, absolute scarcity, except for war situations, natural catastrophes and periods of tyrannical delusions of totalitarian systems, has vanished from industrial civilization. Relative scarcity means a social condition in which there are more socially articulated needs than commodities to satisfy them with and (this is a proviso most important for us) this situation appears as an unbridgeable gap in the sense that there are no existing social mechanisms to mediate between unsatisfied needs and the production of commodities. Rather the contrary, the leading mechanism of society, a profit-centred market regulation is only interested in solvent demands. Absolute abundance logically means a situation in which the commodities and services available are always in a greater quantity and on a wider range than the simultaneously expressed human needs. This is a practical impossibility, a situation which never existed and never will. It has only appeared in certain social dreams and fantasies (the German term *Schlaraffenland* expresses exactly this state of affairs). It has a polemical edge against indigence and social dissatisfaction but no relevance as a social programme. Finally, relative abundance means a (dynamic) social situation in which there are more expressed needs than commodities and social services to satisfy them simultaneously but in which all human needs are recognized in the above active sense of the world. As a result, a) even those whose needs in their totality will not be satisfied here and now, can participate in the decisions regarding the priorities of satisfaction which is a social status radically different from simply being a mere object of the political decision regarding need satisfaction, b) every one can at least feel that he or she has a chance, in a socially relevant sense, of the future satisfaction of several of his or her presently unsatisfied needs.

The only relevant contrast through which the real meaning of the category of recognition of all human needs will become clear is that between relative scarcity and relative abundance. Both can cover social conditions in which the actually produced quota of available material goods are not necessarily crucially different but the principles of social organization are.[21] The crucial social difference is precisely the sphere created by the recognition of all human needs as opposed to mere profit regulation. (Here, for obvious reasons, we are not going to mention the dictatorship over needs.) This sphere consists of three constituents. The first is an ongoing public debate about the priorities of need satisfaction, the ways and modalities of a possible shortening of the duration of unsatisfied needs in order that satisfaction should fall within a generation's lifetime and not be postponed to any social 'transcendence'. This will develop its new institutional forms and general and social regulations which will not destroy markets but which will overrule the exclusively profit-regulated principles of market economies. The second constituent is a new collective social conscience in which everyone feels it a loss, not a gain, if his or her needs are satisfied but those of others are not. Obviously we are not speaking about any collective social altruism, but of a new motivation of collective social activity. This is one of the most important social movements and mechanisms (if not the most important one) which, while denying the blackmail strategy, will be ready to discuss need priorities unselfishly on a global scale, in order to gradually equalize the blatant inequalities between 'centre' and 'periphery'. Finally, it consists of solidly based individual hopes regarding the future satisfiability of now unsatisfied needs which can cure the main disease of 'therapeutic society': general frustration. In this sense, the recognition of all non-alienated human needs fulfils Collingwood's norm of progress: it is gain without losses.

---

[21] At this point, the problem of poverty should be raised. Apart from societies of absolute scarcity, emergency situations in societies of relative scarcity (such as post-war destruction of the economic foundations of a defeated country and the like) the problem of poverty, as all sociologists know perfectly well, is not simply that of insufficient natural and social resources even though the latter always is part of it. But as a relative category, it consists in the following constituents. Firstly, in the indifference of the majority of society and of the pertinent authorities in acknowledging the fact that social groups exist in a blatantly disadvantageous situation which – in totalitarian and non-totalitarian societies alike – regularly develops into an outright denial of this fact. Secondly, the elimination of poverty is often not the question of the amount of the goods produced but the non-recognition of certain needs, therefore, the strategy of production (which, of course, touches upon the central regulative principles of the particular society). Thirdly, welfare activities and regulations introduced gradually from the great depression onwards, only stabilize poverty on a subsistence level. Organized charity is a principle incapable of eliminating poverty. Finally, there are inherent cultural, political, socio-psychological, racial, linguistic factors in the poverty-stricken group and its relation to the rest of society which are absolutely fundamental in creating and preserving poverty. These factors will, of necessity, be preserved in an intact form in all societies of relative scarcity but can, in principle, be eliminated in a society of relative abundance even if the difference between the two in terms of material wealth is not significant.

6

Freedom as a Value Idea and the Interpretation of Human Rights

Agnes Heller[1]

The theory of natural law and natural rights, rejected and ridiculed throughout the nineteenth century, has been resurrected by the bloodshed of the twentieth, both in philosophy and in political documents. The revitalization of this ancient concept is not restricted to any particular world-view. It would suffice to refer to the Marxist Ernst Bloch on the one hand, and to the liberal Gilbert Ryle on the other in order to get an idea of this 'general resurrection'. Bloch wrote a book in which he argues for the reacceptance of the theory of natural law.[2] D'Entrèves refers to Ryle's understanding of 'laws' as 'warrants' as a theoretical proposal 'which will make the old natural law theorists rejoice in their graves'. As far as the political application of the theory is concerned, we have one of the earliest examples in the Atlantic Charter; later, the category of 'crimes against humankind', accepted and legally enforced in the Nuremberg Trials, was based on natural law. The Universal Declaration of Human Rights, adopted and proclaimed by the General Assembly at the United Nations in 1948 (referred to below as the Universal Declaration) as a 'common standard of achievement for all peoples and all nations' posits in its first article that 'All human beings are born free and equal in dignity and rights. They are endowed with reason and conscience ...' In other words, the Universal Declaration restates the natural law in an axiomatic way. Of course, there have always been scholars who utterly disagreed with the resuscitation of a theory they considered obsolete

---

[1] Originally published in English in A. E. S. Tay, ed., *Teaching Human Rights*, Canberra: Australian Government Publishing Service, 1981.
[2] Ernst Bloch, *Naturrecht und menschliche Würde*, E. Bloch Gesamtausgabe, Vol. 16, Frankfurt, Suhrkamp, 1961.

and irrelevant. For example, Croce described the first draft of the Universal Declaration as ridiculous and obsolete, and warned the authors against getting entangled in philosophical fallacies. It is beyond doubt that the basic notions of natural law theories need to be reinterpreted by modern philosophy. It is, however, equally certain that, their restoration being an exigency of our times as a conclusion of the last 70 years, they should not be rejected out of hand. In order to propose a theoretical reinterpretation of both 'natural law' and 'natural rights', I want to start with a less ambitious enterprise, namely a brief analysis of the various and heterogeneous rights considered to be 'universally human'.

Most criticism of the Universal Declaration of Human Rights challenged the relevance of certain particular items occurring in the catalogue of these rights and did not question the relevance of the mere enumeration of these rights. The main controversial issue was the differentiation between political rights on the one hand, and social, economic and cultural rights, on the other. Some scholars, such as Maurice Cranston,[3] suggested that social, economic and cultural rights should have been completely omitted from the Universal Declaration since their presence harmed the 'purity' of the catalogue, on the grounds that while political rights are moral obligations in the sense of the Kantian categorical imperative, so-called social, economic and cultural rights are not. This standpoint has been generally rejected as extremist, without denying, however, that two types of right are of a different provenance. It was suggested that political rights should be defined as rights proper, and socio-economic and cultural rights as claims; for liberties to be defined as 'rights for action' and welfare rights as 'rights to receive'; or the former as rights against (versus) the state and the latter as rights claimed from the state; or the former as immediately applicable rights, the latter as progressively implemented rights; and so on. If, however, we glance at the catalogue in question, we see immediately that some of the rights enumerated cannot be fitted into either of the clusters mentioned, nor into another common cluster; to be more precise, the cluster they may be fitted into depends on how they are interpreted. Of course, there are certain unambiguous cases such as freedom of conscience on the one hand and the right to paid annual leave on the other, but these are extreme cases.

---

[3] Maurice Cranston, 'Human Rights, Real and Supposed' in: David Daiches Raphael, ed., *Political Theory and the Rights of Man*, London/Bloomington: Macmillan/Indiana University Press, 1967. Chapter IV, pp. 43–93.

At a further glance, it becomes equally clear that both clusters encompass heterogeneous types of rights or claims. For example, the right to elect and to be elected belongs to the first cluster: it is a right to act but not a right against the state. Freedom of assembly belongs to the same cluster: it is also a right to act, but at the same time a right against the state. The right to asylum which belongs again to the same cluster, is at once a right to receive and a right against the state. The right to life (one of the basic rights of the first cluster) is immediately applicable in its capacity as protection against homicide or against state terror, but it can only be progressively implemented (or at least we hope it can) in international conflicts.

In spite of all this confusion, the distinction makes sense from the standpoint of political choice. The first cluster without the second vaguely encompasses the principles of a liberal state. The second cluster without the first vaguely encompasses the principles of a paternalistic, despotic state. In what follows I am going to argue that these are not the only possible options. But even if they were, they could not be based on a logical or structural analysis of different rights and their subdivision carried out on this basis, since such attempts are never conclusive.

If we look at the test of the Universal Declaration, it becomes entirely understandable why the advocates of liberal states had to subdivide rights according to their allegedly different structure. In so doing, we have to compare it with the famous declarations of the eighteenth century, especially the United States' Declaration of Independence and the French Déclaration des droits de l'homme of 1789. Natural law and natural rights (even though the two are clearly and properly distinguished only in the Declaration of Independence) serve in all three cases as axioms. But axioms for what? In these two eighteenth-century declarations, natural laws and rights function as axioms for action. They figure as assertions of a conclusion which is an action. The action results from the acceptance of the laws of nature and natural rights as self-evident in character. The Crown violated them, hence the United Colonies constituted themselves as the United States – so runs the logic of the argument of the Declaration of Independence. As a consequence, it is natural law which legitimates an action otherwise illegitimate in this case. The French declaration states that the 'misfortunes' and 'corruption' of governments are due to the neglect of 'inalienable' natural rights, hence the new constitution must be in harmony with them. The enumeration of rights serves as the foundation of positive laws based on popular pluralism. This is why the declaration not only proclaims the rights of man but also those of the citizen.

If the axiom of natural laws and rights justifies an action taken, the action in question determines how many rights and which ones have to be enumerated. In order to declare independence, three rights sufficed, but in order to found a new constitution, they were not sufficient. In both cases, natural law and natural rights serve as universal political principles. It is presupposed that since the concrete action taken is in harmony with the principles, all actions taken should be in harmony with them, they should not contradict them. The principles become the measures of the legitimacy of all political actions. If we return to the case of the Universal Declaration, it becomes clear that its basic problem does not lie in the heterogeneity of the rights enumerated in it, but in its not being a declaration proper. Although natural rights and laws are taken as axioms in it, no conclusion is drawn from the axioms and no action is taken in accordance with them. Thus it cannot implicitly contain the following imperative: since this fundamental action was taken in harmony with the above laws and rights, all actions should be taken also in harmony with them. The axioms of natural law and natural rights do not function as universal political principles of action. From this standpoint, we have to ignore the particular political situation in which the document was formulated and the compromises which this meant. The problem has to be analysed from a purely theoretical standpoint. In the eighteenth-century declarations, a nation took an action as a 'functioning' social entity. But it is quite unlikely that all nations could take any common action according to universal political principles in our times. Does it follow from all this that axioms of natural law and natural rights cannot be applied as universal principles in our time at all? Do we have to state again with resignation that a catalogue of heterogeneous rights and claims has nothing to offer since these rights, called 'liberties', are violated every day by a majority of existing governments, and since the sum total of the enumerated rights is nowhere guaranteed?

As mentioned, Cranston suggested, in a discussion about the heterogeneous character of the rights enumerated in the Universal Declaration, that political or liberal rights (liberties) should be understood as moral rights. I agree with the assertion that liberal rights have a moral implication equally as much. Moreover, if rights do not serve as foundations for common action taken – as they did in the classic declaration of the eighteenth century – they cannot function as universal political principles, and represent nothing but moral imperatives, moral standards for possible or impossible political actions. Something is, however, left unclear by mere enumeration, namely that the moral implications of various rights varies, as do those of so-called liberties. Rights stand in a hierarchical relation to each other; there are basic ones and inferred ones and only the highest have an absolute moral claim. To my knowledge, the only document which made this hierarchical relation perfectly clear was the United States 'Declaration of Independence' since it distinguished between natural law and natural rights and inferred the latter from the former. The manner of reasoning of the Declaration of Independence is that since men are born free and they are equally endowed with reason, they have Life, Liberty and the Pursuit of Happiness as their inalienable rights. The axiom described as 'self-evident' is the statement about natural law: all human rights have to be related to it in order to be justified as inalienable ones. In the forthcoming analysis of 'natural law' I shall refer to this axiom as the axiom of freedom since practical reason is a constituent of freedom whereas instrumental reason has nothing to do with human rights and can be ignored in this respect.

Here the philosophical fallacy involved in the acceptance of natural law, the one referred to by Croce, has to be considered. It is far from necessary to accept eighteenth century theory of natural law philosophically in order to start from freedom as the axiom of all human rights. The statement that men are born free and equally endowed with reason is only an expression of the historical consciousness of modern time: it is not an ontological statement but a value statement. Even if we disagree with its ontological foundations or believe that it cannot be proven, nonetheless we can accept that it formulates a social fact, namely the fact that in our time freedom is not one value among many, but the supreme value, the value idea. A value idea is a value whose opposite cannot be chosen for a value. It is clear that in our times the opposite of freedom (unfreedom, slavery, etc.) cannot be normally chosen for a value. This obviously does not mean that actions are not guided by the principle of unfreedom in practice (which happens much too often); it means that the choice cannot be founded in or justified as a value. In ancient times whenever a nation was enslaved or oppressed or even wiped out, the oppressors called these actions by their proper names: oppression or enslavement of others could even be conceived of as virtuous actions. Nowadays, if a nation does exactly the same things, the claim is to have 'liberated' other nations, to have brought freedom to them, since oppression and enslavement are no longer considered to be virtues. Except for 12 years of Nazi rule, the value idea of freedom has never been questioned; however it has often been trampled underfoot in practice. All modern philosophies since Descartes's time have constituted freedom as the supreme value, although they have interpreted it in quite different, often even in contradictory ways. All human rights are interpretations of the value idea of freedom, but a particular kind of interpretation. They are interpretations which may serve as political principles since they can regulate political actions and are to be enforced by law. For example, the free choice of friends can be related to the value idea of freedom without contradiction, but it cannot regulate political action and it would be nonsensical to try to enforce it by law, which is why it does not belong in any catalogue of human rights.

Since human rights are only interpretations of the value idea of freedom in different contexts and relations, and from various standpoints, they must not contradict freedom. The moral implications they all contain are only derivative: they express the different qualities and aspects of freedom. Only freedom, the 'natural law', has an absolute moral value. This can be very easily comprehended. If there is a moral implication, there is an obligation as well. There are various obligations, for instance, the obligation to avoid something, the obligation not to interfere with something, and also the obligation to act according to values. Absolute moral obligation can be described by the Kantian formula 'you ought to act' in such and such a way. This very formula can be applied to freedom. The imperative that you ought to act according to freedom does not only command that you ought to respect the freedom of others and that you ought to avoid its violation but it also entails no lesser an obligation towards yourself. You ought to act as a free person: since you were born free and you are endowed with reason, you are responsible for your own freedom as well. In its inhibitory formulation it reads as follows: you must not enslave yourself since you ought to respect freedom in yourself. Among all particular human rights, it is freedom of conscience alone which has the same status. Thus 'freedom of conscience' is not only one interpretation of freedom among many, but is also intrinsic in its content. The Universal Declaration is quite correct when stating in its first article that 'human beings are endowed with reason and conscience'; it is justified in placing freedom of conscience in the paragraph about natural law.

All other human rights – both liberties and so-called welfare rights – follow a different pattern. The right to peaceful assembly or organization does not suggest that every human being ought to participate in peaceful assemblies and/or organizations, but that they can if they want to and that they should not interfere if others do. Needless to say if these rights entailed the same type of obligation as freedom does, they would contradict freedom – which they must not do. If the right to peaceful assembly meant that every human being should participate in assemblies, the human beings concerned would not be free; if the right to work meant that human beings were obliged to work (irrespective of whether or not they want to), they would not be free human beings either. In all countries in which rights are understood and enforced by law as obligations of the actors concerned towards themselves, and not just as obligations to respect or ensure the freedom of other actors, there is no freedom but tyranny.

The strongest proof of the statement that all rights are only interpretations of freedom and should be interconnected with freedom without contradiction, is the status of the right to life. This is the very right which occurs in all declarations of human rights and which usually stands in the first place. It entails the obligation to respect the life of others and it claims to positive laws which ensure the lives of the citizens of a state unless they violate those same laws. But as mentioned earlier, and as is obvious, the right to life is suspended in the case of war. This suspension is, however, normally supported by arguments on behalf of the value idea of freedom: you have to sacrifice your life in order to defend the freedom of your fellow citizens or to liberate other countries from tyranny, and the like. Whether the arguments express the real goals of war or serve only as rationalization is from this respect of secondary importance since I only want to argue on behalf of the priority of the value of freedom against all other rights. The right to life is always understood in terms of the supremacy of the value idea of freedom; it reads as follows: you can live if you want to (except in time of war). I wish to make the theoretical proposal that all rights can become controversial if they can be interpreted in different ways and if one interpretation – among many – could contradict the value idea of freedom in one or another respect. How can this happen if all rights are only different interpretations of the value idea of freedom?

I have proposed that not all interpretations of the value of idea freedom are (or can even reasonably be) attached to the list of human rights. However, it is a commonplace that the catalogue of human rights is not static but dynamic. Several interpretations of the value idea of freedom were not claimed as human rights in the eighteenth century but are claimed as such now, since the population of a particular country wants them to function in their capacity of political principles and/or wants them to be enforced by law. The authors of the declarations of human rights usually had a definite socio-political order in mind which they wanted to establish or certain particular actions which have to be taken. If new rights are consistently being claimed, the images of the socio-political order are constantly changing and people want actions to be taken which have not, or have only occasionally, been taken. The new rights claimed and/or accepted ones must not contradict the value idea of freedom to which they are equally related but they can contradict certain formulations of other rights which originally did not contradict freedom but may do so now in conjunction with new rights. In addition, various rights claimed in the same document can contradict each other as well. The Universal Declaration declares that 'No one shall be arbitrarily deprived of his property', where 'arbitrary' stands for unlawfully, which means basically that anyone can be legally deprived of his/her property; hence there is a hidden contradiction of the first sentence of the same article according to which everyone has the right to own property. The same declaration states that everyone has the right to work and to security in the event of unemployment, but again there is a contradiction involved: if everyone actually has his/her right to work, there can be no unemployment and vice versa. Confronted with this inconsistency, the liberal suggestion is to omit all socio-economic and cultural rights from the catalogue of human rights and to restrict the latter to political rights only, in order to eliminate contradictions.

I wish to challenge this suggestion on a number of grounds. Firstly, if the catalogue is restricted to liberal rights, the catalogue itself implies the image of a very definite order. The Universal Declaration is meant to be implemented by all nations. To restrict rights only to political ones would mean to universalize one particular political order, the liberal system, to the whole of humankind, which would contradict the value idea of freedom in one of its basic interpretations according to which every nation can choose its own type of government and social system. Secondly, the basic argument of liberalism, according to which political rights can be implemented without mobilizing economic resources whereas socio-economic and cultural rights cannot, simply does not hold true. There are certain rights in both clusters whose implementation does not depend on the wealth of a community and does not presuppose an additional expenditure by the state. The political right to leave (any) country and the social right to equal pay for equal work do not differ from each other in this respect. On the other hand, there are certain rights in both clusters which presuppose an additional expenditure on the part of the state or the community. Freedom of religion not only means that a citizen is not harassed because of his or her religious belief but also that the preconditions of religious worship are granted (for example, the maintenance of shrines, building churches, etc.). The right to a fair public trial, which necessarily involves the guarantee of professional legal counsel for anyone charged with any offence, involves just as much expenditure as health services do (even if not necessarily to the same proportion of the population). The difference is quantitative, not qualitative. If, however, we compare this political right to another social right, for example, to the right to equal access to tertiary education according to personal merit, even the quantitative differences are very questionable.

The third argument against socio-economic rights is that they are not universal: for instance, paid leave can only be a right for those who live on wages or salaries. However, the same holds equally true of certain political–liberal rights as well. The right to marriage and family has no bearing on those who are and want to remain unmarried, the right to asylum has a bearing only on those who are politically harassed. When speaking about the right of assembly or organization on the one hand, and about the right to work on the other, I described these rights with the formula: 'I can if I want to.' The above-mentioned rights, no matter whether liberal–political or socio-economic, have to be described by another formula: 'I have a right (to do this and this) if I am in need (of this and this because of my special situation) and if I want to (exercise this right).' For instance, I have a right to asylum if I am harassed politically (I am in need of asylum because of my special situation) and if I want to leave the country in which I am harassed. Another example is the following: I have the right to maternal support if I have a child (children) (I am in need of this support because of my special situation) and if I want such support. These rights from both clusters can also be described by a change of the formula such that the last part, my willingness to exercise my right, is omitted; for instance, I have the right to be considered innocent if charged with any offence until proven guilty. Another example of this transformed formula is: I have rights equal to other children even if I am born outside wedlock.

Thus it is sufficiently proven that the restriction of rights to political ones cannot be supported by logical argument. Needless to say the restriction of rights to socio-economic and cultural ones cannot be logically supported either. And I have already suggested that – since a catalogue of human rights implies an image of a particular socio-political structure – political rights without welfare rights express the image of a liberal, capitalist state, and welfare rights without liberties the image of paternalistic despotism. The Universal Declaration wanted to avoid both pitfalls but it had to pay a price for this: that of inconsistency. While enumerating all possible rights once claimed, it had no specific socio-political system in mind but a combination of several with a preference for a democratic, welfare state. The problem does not lie with the individual rights but in their sum total. The

Universal Declaration was unable to rank rights in a hierarchy since all such hierarchy would point towards one specific socio-political order.

The whole endeavour was theoretically doomed to failure, not because the idea of natural law is obsolete, and equally not because of the simple enumeration of socio-economic rights, but because of the lack of hierarchy among the rights. But it is precisely for this reason that I consider the contemptuous treatment of the Universal Declaration to be unfounded. It was and still is the best possible solution of the problem, since the rights contained in it do function as moral claims, as regulative moral ideas for human action and judgement. It is open to all possible political solutions which are in harmony with those moral claims. No government could be established on the basis of the sum total of these rights, but all governments could be criticized, to a greater or lesser extent, for a failure to implement one or another. The Universal Declaration expresses all needs for rights. It is not a catalogue of rights actually implemented here and now, but a catalogue of moral claims to various rights for which persons as human beings have to fight in order that they be implemented without contradiction. 'Without contradiction' means that no right should contradict the value idea of freedom, that is to say, 'natural law' and that no particular interpretations of freedom (actual rights) should contradict each other when implemented.

Natural law (according to which all humans are born free and are equally endowed with reason) is the source of all rights. This means among other things that every person and citizen has to have the right to claim new rights, and to interpret existing rights in different ways. As a result, if liberties are not ensured, there are no rights at all. When I said that socio-economic and cultural rights without political rights express the image of paternalistic despotism, this was something of an understatement, because economic, social and cultural provisos are not rights in themselves. They become rights only together with liberties. This statement seemingly supports the liberal argument, since it is undeniable that political rights are authentic rights even without socio-economic and cultural ones. However, I wish to argue that a catalogue of mere liberal rights basically contradicts the value idea of freedom as well and that this contradiction is responsible for all theoretical problems liberals have to face when it comes to socio-economic and cultural rights. The contradiction involves only one right, but this one is a fundamental liberal right: the right to property.

Although the contradiction between the right to property and the value idea of freedom (or natural law) is usually hidden, in certain cases it becomes explicit. Ritchie refers to the constitution of the state of Kansas from 1857 which, on the one hand, stated that 'All men are by nature equally free and independent,' and on the other hand, that 'the right of the owner of the slave to such slave and its increase is the same and as inviolable as the right of the owner to any property whatever.'[4] Ritchie adds with justified sarcasm that 'it had needed a civil war to settle the dispute' between the Bill of Rights and the seventh article of the same constitution. But let us refer to a less explicit case. The French Declaration of the Rights of Man states (XVII): 'The right of property being inviolable and sacred, no one ought to be deprived of it, except in cases of evident public necessity, legally ascertained, and on condition of a previous just indemnity.' We have seen that the Universal Declaration formulates the right to property in a similar way. However, it becomes clearer from the original version that the possible confiscation of property is formulated not as an action taken against individuals in criminal cases, but against social classes and strata, otherwise the reference to a 'just' indemnity would have made no sense at all. In what follows I shall examine firstly whether the right to property contradicts the value idea of freedom and whether the confiscation of property also contradicts it.

The right to property implies an exclusion by definition: if I have something, others are excluded from the use of the same thing. But it makes a considerable difference whether others are excluded from the use of the same thing without my consent or if some people (maybe in great numbers) are excluded from the use of similar things as well. For example, if I own a dress or a house or a car, I exclude others from the use of the same dress, house or car without my consent but I exclude no one from owning a dress, a house, a car of his or her own. However, if I own a factory which can only function with the labour of a hundred workers, I exclude these workers, by the very character of the wage-worker relationship, not only from using my factory as if it were their own without my consent, but also from owning a factory at all. If they did own one, they would not work in mine, and my factory would not be a factory but an agglomerate of dead machinery. Thus I exclude these workers not only from the use of the same thing, but from the use of a similar thing as well. If I interpret the right to property only as the exclusion of others from the use of the same thing, it does not contradict the value idea of freedom. If, however, I exclude many others (whole classes of people) from the use of similar things, the right to

----

[4] David George Ritchie, *Natural Rights, A Criticism of Some Political and Ethical Conceptions*, London: Sommerschein, 1895, p. 26.

property does contradict the value idea of freedom. The reason for this is easily seen. As mentioned, all rights can be formulated by the following formulae: 'I can if I want to'; 'I have a right (to do this and this) if I am in need (of this and because of my special situation) and if I want to (exercise this right)'; and 'I have a right (to do or receive this and this) if I am in need (of this and this because of my special position).' None of these formulae can be applied to the right of property if it is understood as the exclusion of others from the use of similar things. At any rate, the second two formulations have to be discarded since property has no relevance whatsoever to what I am in need of but to what I have. Thus only the first formula, 'I can if I want to' could be considered. If no one is excluded from the use of similar things, only from that of the same things, the formula: 'I can if I want' retains its validity. If, however, the right to property means the right to exclude others from the use of similar things, the formula: 'I can if I want to' has no validity any longer, since there is necessarily a considerable amount of people who cannot even if they wanted to. As a result, the right to property could only be related to the value idea of freedom without contradiction in a self-managed society, in a social structure in which no one would be excluded from the use of similar things.

Here we have to turn to the possibility of confiscation of property, to an option left open in almost all declarations of human rights. Undoubtedly, the confiscation of property by the state contradicts the value idea of freedom quite independently of the amount of indemnity. If the state can confiscate property, the formula 'I can if I want to' is no longer valid. Needless to say, this restriction of freedom is meant to correct the general restriction of freedom involved in the right to property as the exclusion of (many) others from the use of similar things and thus as the realization of distributive justice. If, however, we interpret the right to property as the right to exclude others from the use of the same, but not from similar things, there is no need to leave open the option for confiscation. General self-management can be substituted for this option, in harmony with the value idea of freedom.

Hence the right to property is the Achilles' heel of liberties. Only if it is interpreted according to an image of a self-managed society can this right be related to the value idea of freedom without contradiction. Moreover, only if it is interpreted in that way, can all other liberties possibly be realized together by all persons. The well-known objections against the formal character of liberties are based on the justified consideration that the exclusive character of property wih regard to similar things ensures an economic power for the wealthy for the optimal use of their rights, whereas those excluded cannot make proper use of the same rights. Self-management would equalize access to the realization of liberties without putting an end to the formality of rights which belong to freedom since it leaves rights open to different interpretations. Moreover, certain welfare rights which are now claimed from the state as various forms of state intervention could be implemented without the latter (such as security against illness or disability) if society were self-managed. If everyone is proprietor, unemployment benefits make no sense, at least not in their present form. They should only be granted to those who do not want to have (or share) property or to work, which have to be acknowledged as rights too. The more so since everyone's access to ownership is a right only when it can be described by the formula: 'I can if I want to' and never if it is described by the formula: 'I should,' since the latter would contradict the value idea of freedom.

To sum up my argument: if we have in mind a self-managed society, we could accept all human rights claimed up until now in such a way that no particular right would contradict the implementation of the other one and none of them would contradict the value idea of freedom, that is to say, natural law. With one exception: this particular right is enumerated in all modern catalogues of human rights, and I do not see any way in which its contradiction with the value idea of freedom could be eliminated. This is the right to education. Education is a right but it is at the same time compulsory, at least at the elementary level. The right to work or to peaceful assembly or to participate in organizations or to property (in both of its interpretations) are not rights at all, if work, participation in organizations or assemblies, or ownership are compulsory. The contradiction could easily be resolved if the right to education only meant the right to higher education. In this case, however, those who object to the formal character of liberties may reasonably argue that without compulsory elementary education even the minimum preconditions of the implementation of rights would be missing. The Universal Declaration tries to overcome this difficulty the wrong way. Mainly in order to emphasize that the right to education is a right proper, it states in the third point of Article 26 'Parents have a prior right to choose the kind of education that shall be given to their children.' This is undoubtedly a right, but it contradicts the value idea of freedom at least in one respect: it grants parents, not children, the free choice, even though it is children, not parents, who are educated. All the rights of the citizen and the majority of other rights are only granted to adults. This means that for instance no one under 18, 21 or 24 respectively can participate in an election or be elected (depending on the laws of the state) but this of course does not mean that parents decide whom their children ought to elect. Thus the problem is far from being solved by the Universal Declaration. In addition, I cannot see any possibility of eliminating this contradiction, not at least in the present and foreseeable future. I can, however, imagine a society in which education becomes as natural for everyone as play and where the right to a compulsory education – a basic contradiction – could be eliminated in this form from the catalogue of human rights, and this right should be narrowed down to higher education, without any reference to parents' rights to decide upon their children's education. Having thus resolved the last dilemma, all rights could be interpreted without contradicting each other or without either one of them contradicting the value idea of freedom.

I started from the assumption that human rights functioned in the classic declarations of the eighteenth century not only as moral claims but also as political principles for action to be taken, and that the catalogue of human rights (whether narrower or broader) was designed for a definite socio-political order. I have argued that the human rights enumerated in the Universal Declaration cannot function as political principles. No common action can be taken according to them, they are not designed for a definite socio-political order, (even if they imply a preference for a democratic welfare state) and some human rights enumerated in the Declaration contradict each other, hence these rights are rather moral claims. I have also argued that being mere moral claims is not a shortcoming of the rights of Universal Declaration, since we are living in a world in which human rights are usually not implemented. Last but not least, I stated that all the rights claimed (except for the right to compulsory elementary education) can be conceived of without any contradiction between each other and the value idea of freedom, that is to say, the natural law, to which all rights have to be related, since it is the axiom, the self-evident starting point of the whole enterprise, as long as we interpret the right to property as the right to exclude others from the use of the same things we own, but never from the use of similar things. A catalogue of human rights designed for a self-managed society would be a catalogue without contradictions. In this new catalogue, human rights could function again as political principles and not only as moral claims. Of course, at the present moment this is true only on a theoretical level, not on a practical one. But all the classic declarations could only apply certain catalogues of human rights in practice because these rights have already been designed theoretically. Without Locke's theory of human rights, there would not have been a Declaration of Independence; nor would there have been a Declaration of the Rights of Man without Montesquieu. Whether the political principles of a democratic self-managed society will ever be applied in practice at all is an open question. But they cannot even be in principle, if their elaboration is not given previous theoretical consideration.

7

On Being Anti-Nuclear in Soviet Societies

Ferenc Fehér and Agnes Heller [1]

This paper seeks to substantiate a prediction that runs counter to the cherished hopes, illusions or, sometimes, even delusions of the Western peace movement. Stated baldly our prediction runs as follows: of all the possible autonomous social movements, the anti-nuclear movement is the one least likely to become of any consequence and least likely to exert an impact on the future course of Soviet societies.[2] In a somewhat more cautious formulation, we can state that, should anti-nuclear movements emerge in Soviet societies on a wide scale, they will either immediately become bearers of other, broader and more complex, social issues, or will degenerate into state sponsored peace carnivals. It is this view which we shall seek to defend here.

Our main interest will not be to enter the debate concerning which of the existing 'peace' or 'anti-nuclear' groups in Soviet societies are state-sponsored and which are genuinely autonomous, although the ability to draw a distinction between the two is crucial to our argument here. To put it in a nutshell, official peace organizations are, in our firm view, part and parcel of the strategy and policy of the ruling strata in the Soviet Union, for reasons which are either obvious or which will become clear in our presentation. On the other hand, and principally in the USSR, there were and perhaps there will again be independent militants trying to launch a genuine campaign for bilateral nuclear disarmament. Their fate is both predictable and inevitable: most of them have already been arrested, and they will be convicted for

---

[1] Originally published in English in *Telos* (Saint Louis), No. 57, Fall 1983.
[2] For the purposes of this paper, 'Soviet societies' designates the Soviet Union and its East European empire and not the Soviet societies of Asia.

'slandering the socialist society'. Their activity has raised no wide interest in that society, nor is it likely to do so in the future, for reasons which constitute the subject-matter proper of this paper. In one country, the German Democratic Republic, there is a pacifist movement which is, overwhelmingly, though not exclusively, religious in nature, weak but not unsupported in certain strata of East German society, which pays lip service to the party ideology (as it simply must do in order to survive) but is to some extent autonomous, and which is pacifist in the strict sense and therefore not specifically anti-nuclear. On the lighter side, there is a Soviet regime, Rumania, where the state plays, in grandiosely launched official campaigns and with the unmistakable *Beigeschmack* of Vienna operettas, the role of an autonomous peace movement following closely a strictly orchestrated and centrally supervised scenario. Hungary is, of course, once again 'open' and extremely inventive: she keeps squaring the circle. The country invented the non-official but not entirely autonomous peace movement which protects itself extremely vigorously from even the presence of dissident elements in its ranks – testifying thereby to its degree of autonomy. All in all, this is not a very impressive inventory, and in what follows we shall try to explain the causes of the widespread disinterest found in Soviet societies for peace or anti-nuclear initiatives, something which contrasts markedly with the West European scene.

A further qualification seems necessary. We are relying here entirely on our personal experiences, and on the reported and recorded personal experiences of other observers, and not on any wide-scale scientifically based surveys or opinion polls, with all the uncertainties and inaccuracies that such methods entail. We can only give an assurance that we have not tampered retrospectively with our personal impressions, experiences and recollections.

Finally, it is necessary to distinguish between the following perspectives when discussing attitudes in Soviet societies to nuclear weapons and their eventual use: the view from the top – that from the base, official and non-official, Soviet (in the sense of Russian) and East European. The top, by which we mean the *nomenklatura*, the ruling apparatus, has worked out a homogeneous medium of public communication which we will try to penetrate further below. For now, let us note simply that the *nomenklatura* claims for itself the role of sole advocate and champion of peace. According to its public claims, the fate of peace is directly dependent on the strength of the Soviet Union, including its military might. When others build up their nuclear arsenal, it is labelled a threat to world peace. On the other hand, when the *nomenklatura* does the same, its sole motivation is the promotion of global peace. Therefore the officialdom, including professional peaceniks, however broad-minded and ready to admit past errors and excesses, will never acknowledge, not even in a hypothetical scenario, that Soviet nuclear armaments could be the source of a potential threat to humankind.

The social 'base' has several different views on this, as indeed they have on many other questions. On the question of nuclear armaments, however, this distance from the official position is clearly evident in their argumentation, though not as far as the end result is concerned. Nonetheless, the 'base', which, in Soviet societies, almost always reveals itself in confidential conversations, and in some cases through *samizdat* publications can be clearly distinguished from the 'top': it has its own separate interests, considerations and ways of thinking. The distinction between 'official' and 'non-official' is nearly, but not entirely, identical with the distinction between 'top' and 'base'. The 'top' might play upon the feelings of the 'base' which cannot be expressed in the official language and media, but only through 'confidential meetings of information'. Conversely, the 'base' occasionally speaks the language of the 'top' in the private space as well, though sometimes with such frankness that officialdom cannot openly acknowledge this language as its own. Therefore the distinction between 'official' and 'non-official' largely overlaps, but is not entirely coextensive with the distinction between 'top' and 'base'.

Somewhat more consideration deserves to be given to the distinction between Soviet (Russian) and East European, although here, once again, the conclusion we draw is much the same; that, in our view, the anti-nuclear movement does not have serious chances in either version of Soviet society, albeit for different reasons. One of the major features of the (highly reactionary) consensus in the post-Stalin paternalist state between 'top' and 'base' is Russian chauvinism. There is no space here to analyse this phenomenon though it has received a good deal of attention in several recent studies.[3] For our purposes, it will suffice to point to a recent paper by the 'dissident Marxists', Roy and Zhores Medvedev,[4] which assimilates almost entirely the perspectives

---

[3] Its best analysis can be found in Victor Zaslavsky, *The Neo-Stalinist State*, New York/ Brighton: M. E. Sharpe/Harvester, 1982.

[4] It is almost entertaining to detect the symptoms of their assimilation to Russian imperial chauvinism: at one point the Medvedev brothers speak of the 'dark days' of the Cuban missile crisis. (Roy Medvedev and Zhores Medvedev, 'The USSR and the Arms Race', *New Left Review* 113 (Nov.–Dec. 1981), p. 13). But for whom were they dark? Obviously, there is absolutely no reason for socialists to worry about American strategic positions, particularly not when the whole elaborate ballet takes place within the framework of a capacity for overkill. Nor is there, however, any need to feel 'humiliated' in the name of the

of the ruling Soviet-Russian apparatus, which they are otherwise out-spoken – if narrow minded – critics of, at least in so far as nuclear armament is concerned. Identification with the Russian apparatus, its interests and considerations, for obvious reasons, is entirely missing from the occupied East European scene. This makes the separate analysis of the two scenes methodologically necessary.

I THE *NOMENKLATURA* AND THE NUCLEAR THREAT

As mentioned, the official and vigorously advertised self-image of the ruling apparatus is its complete and exclusive identity with 'the cause of peace': in its own image, it alone represents peace-loving humankind against all sorts of warmongers. Is this to be understood as a simple deception of the politically naive, a mere exercise in propaganda? The answer is perforce much too dialectical: yes and no. Of course, it is deception and propaganda. Firstly, the leadership in the USSR has never renounced, and never can renounce, their claim for the victory of what they call the 'world revolutionary process' and what, in simpler terms, means the global triumph of the Soviet system of the 'dictatorship over needs'. (To what extent such an exclusive dominance would be a viable and long-term solution, is another question.) Such an option is obviously incompatible with the excessive claims for love and peace constantly made by the official peaceniks of the regime. At least theoretically, the self-professed goal of a 'world revolutionary process' has to comprise wars, as one of its options; and possibly, though not necessarily, also a limited nuclear war, or at least the limited use of nuclear weapons.[5] These days it is almost forgotten, notwithstanding

---

Soviet missiles. For, as Alan Roberts asked quite correctly, which are the 'socialist bombs'? (A. Roberts, 'Preparing to Fight a Nuclear War', *Arena* 57 (1981), pp. 45–93.) We can recall our feelings then, those of very heretic Khrushchevite reformist communists. Once again Khrushchev bungled it, we felt, and thus endangered anew the chances of structural reforms, hinted at so often but always postponed. But, of course, here it is being only East European and not Russian that makes all the difference.

[5] Very often, the genuine intentions of Soviet (Russian) leaders are spelt out by their East European sycophants. We strongly recommend the reading of the following quote stemming from Heinz Hoffman, Minister of Defence of the GDR, for Western peace activists: 'With all the suffering that would be caused to the peoples, especially those of the capitalist world, in this final and decisive conflict between progress and reaction, it would be nonetheless a just war on our part. We do not share the conception advocated in the peace

that it is a historical fact, that Stalin, in the period following World War Two, when he would have had to have been aware that in future all global wars would, sooner or later, turn into a nuclear clash, nevertheless always emphatically declared that only 'the given war' could be prevented; wars as such remain inevitable as long as capitalism exists. True, this thesis of his, together with several others, was revised by the 20th Congress of the Soviet Communist Party. But the 20th Congress is now dead and forgotten, and its main decisions, Khrushchev's very superficial and limited criticism of Stalin, have been largely revoked; and, specifically, who knows whether or not Stalin's views of the inevitability of wars have 'confidentially' been restored with binding validity. The sole certainty is that the Brezhnev–Andropov leadership approves (in the case of others), but does not practice or imitate, unilateral (nuclear or non-nuclear) disarmament. Finally, it is difficult to see where the Medvedevs take the following conviction from: 'no serious official statement has ever envisaged the USSR winning such a [nuclear] war. In fact, the Soviet population is told that global nuclear war is lunacy and that no one would survive it.'[6] Obviously, there is a great amount of confusion in statements regarding such a highly sensitive issue as a 'winnable' nuclear war, and Soviet marshalls and East European ministers of defence, just like American Presidents, talk irresponsibly and untruthfully about it. However, the fact remains that, from Marshall Malinovski, and his speech at the 22nd Party Congress, onwards, one could quote from all Soviet Ministers of Defence and Warsaw Pact Commanders-in-Chief sentences which state or suggest that the 'socialist community' will retaliate in kind for any nuclear strike, and this retaliation will result in the annihilation of capitalism. By implication this can only mean that a nuclear war is seen as winnable. But, more importantly, and this applies to both superpowers, no one sacrifices so much wealth and energy on preparations for a war which political leaders regard as unthinkable. But the permutation of this sentence into another with the meaning that the preparations for the nuclear war imply *ipso facto* that the powers concerned are in fact prepared to wage a thermonuclear war would be equally wrong, once again on both sides. In all probability, a certain instability in strategical

---

movement even by progressives, that a just war is no longer conceivable in the nuclear age, nor do we accept the thesis that a nuclear-missile war would not be the continuation of the politics of struggling classes, but a nuclear inferno, doomsday.' Heinz Hoffmann, 'Sozialistische Landesverteidigung', in *Aus Reden und Aufsätzen*, 1974 bis Juni 1978, Berlin: Einheitsverlag, 1979, p. 221.

6 Medvedev and Medvedev, 'The USSR and the Arms Race', p. 18. The seriousness of this statement is borne out by our quote from Minister Hoffmann, see n. 5 above.

thinking concerning the winnability of a nuclear war reigns supreme in all leading political circles and, if anything, this is an extremely dangerous factor. This instability is fuelled by the total moral irresponsibility of the Soviet and American ruling strata. Both think in terms of success alone, and neither regards as morally inconceivable (if they consider it to be physically possible) the perspective of our survival as humans in a world the greater part of which shall have been exterminated by a war unleashed as a result of their conjoint efforts. Without doubt then, the claim of the peace apostles of the *nomenklatura* is an exercise in shamelessly deceitful propaganda.

On the other hand, there are genuine elements in this claim as well. Although we have stated several times that, in our view, the Soviet dictatorship over needs is not a socialist system,[7] it is true that up until now the leading apparatus has found it impossible to break formally and publicly with the socialist vocabulary and state explicitly the real social objectives of the new society. However, as long as they remain within the framework of a socialist phraseology, they simply cannot dismiss peace as a central slogan of their policy, the ultimate objectives of socialists and the dream of eternal peace being mutually inseparable. Therefore, peaceful gestures are deceitful, but integral parts of their public performance. Much more importantly, Russia suffered terribly in two world wars, so that therefore the word 'peace' appeals there to everyone, and the denial of an ultimate peace objective is virtually impossible for any government. But there are even indications that in certain periods, and during the rule of certain leaders, the instability of strategical thinking mentioned above was present to much less a degree than in others. For instance, after Stalin's death, Malenkov seemed to believe in the unwinnability of a nuclear war, which would threaten the whole of our civilization (though it is hard to tell whether he argued this for tactical or other reasons). Khrushchev, born comedian as he was, seemed to have been genuinely shocked by Mao Tse-tung's humanitarian perspectives of global emancipation.[8] It was the 'moderate' and 'realist' Brezhnev who invested all his hopes in the military superiority of the USSR and who, therefore, can be suspect of having had delusions regarding the winnability of a nuclear war. But even in his case we find indications to the contrary. His insistence on the SALT treaties

---

[7] See our book, written with George Markus: *Dictatorship Over Needs*, Oxford: Basil Blackwell, 1983.

[8] Mao Tse-tung was perhaps the only statesman of the world who was harmoniously optimistic about the outcome of a nuclear holocaust in which the majority of humankind would perish, leaving the rest to live freely as he stated at the Moscow World Conference of the Communist Parties in 1960.

stem, of course, from a number of purely strategic, or rather tactical, considerations but they indicate, even in this mediocre and otherwise morally totally unscrupulous man, a measure of realism arising from fear.

At present, and as far as we can see it, guiding principles and considerations of the ruling Soviet apparatus regarding the winnability of a nuclear war are, in our view (apart from technological expertise for which they are totally dependent on their specialists), composed of and conditioned by the following, often contradictory theses. Firstly, they have constant fears about being outmanoeuvred by the Americans. The Medvedev brothers argue correctly, and this is a result of the technologically parasitic and dependent nature of the economy of the dictatorship over needs, that every new round, all technologically new families of nuclear weapons and their carriers have always been introduced by the American military complex. (They, of course, fail to add that the Soviets have not only immediately copied the new inventions but have regularly overproduced them in the vain hope that the new invention will be the 'last word', thus giving them ultimate superiority.) This being so, the Soviet leadership is constantly on the alert and ready for a new cycle in the armaments race. Secondly, and in blatant contradiction to the above, while the Soviets have a technological inferiority complex, sociologically and politically they have an increasing feeling of superiority over the West. They are more and more convinced, especially after Vietnam and the Watergate affair (which for them was the ultimate proof of the contemptible lack of authority in this unruly society), that the West has very weak knees and that a combination of menacing gestures and peace-loving phrases will force the Western countries into important political and economic concessions. Thirdly, the relative strength of the military–industrial complex is constantly growing in the Soviet Union. Castoriadis's thesis about a 'stratocracy', a military-ruled society, is arguable, even after Poland and martial law. However, the Medvedev thesis according to which there is no military–industrial complex in the USSR because everything is controlled by the Party, is not a proposition worthy of serious discussion, because it is not only sociologically absurd, but also logically incorrect. Ultimate Party control and arbitration does not eliminate the existence of the military–industrial complex. The question is how the cake will be cut and divided, and here all lobbies, the military more than others, have a say. But finally, to add one more feature to the set of contradictions, while the role of the military is growing constantly, so that a formal seizure of power cannot be excluded somewhere in the future (though it would certainly imply a formal rupture with the socialist facade, a major earthquake in Soviet history), the only telos which would legitimize the army's rule – victory in a global nuclear war – seems, in the final analysis, to be excluded. This is partly because in both systems the soldiers are more well versed and therefore more sceptical than the civilians about the chances of survival, and this consideration will finally prevail, or so we hope, over instability in strategic thinking. In part though, it is also because, as the Medvedevs note with respect to Western Europe, the Soviet Union, should it want to conquer the globe, certainly would not want to inherit a space full of nuclear debris.

We have described both alternative strategies of the ruling Soviet apparatus in matters of nuclear war. In sum, we have to state that whichever of the two will be realized, both exclude the existence of autonomous anti-nuclear movements, as far as the intentions of the 'top' are concerned, and these much more emphatically than the existence of any other movement aspiring for a measure of autonomy. Should the ruling apparatus decide to launch a nuclear war in a suicidal gamble, and should it start to prepare for it, it is obvious why they would not tolerate the existence of autonomous anti-nuclear movements. However, should they decide on behalf of the incomparably more realistic alternative, and in our opinion ultimately they will do so, and should they use nuclear parity, or their eventual minimal superiority, as a shield and means for global expansion, they cannot tolerate anti-nuclear agitators either. In fact, it is easier and more realistic to project a compromise between a politically toned-down and neutralized labour movement (an eventual successor of Solidarity) and the ruling apparatus, than one between the latter and any anti-nuclear movement that means business. There is no member of the ruling oligarchy, whether hawk or dove, hard-liner or 'liberal', who would not be absolutely convinced of the exclusive prerogative of the oligarchy to decide in all matters nuclear.

II THE BASE

It could be objected that the preceding discussion is equally applicable to the behaviour of the American power elite. In all probability it is. After all, if we could overhear confidential Capitol Hill or Pentagon conversations we would, more than likely, hear remarkably similar views, even if they are supported by different, technocratic, arguments.

Yet it is not so much the existence of democracy and public opinion in one society and their total absence in the other that we want to emphasize here – even though we disagree profoundly with the neo-Leninism of the Medvedev brothers which sees the differences as insignificant. What we would like to emphasize rather, is that the social base, even though its interests are far from identical with those of the 'top', is, for a number of reasons which we will analyse below, over-whelmingly uninterested in supporting any serious anti-nuclear move-ment. The militants of attempts at the latter may suffer persecution and serve long prison terms without even acquiring the halo of martyrdom that is conferred upon some of their colleagues in persecution, for instance militants of religious or national freedoms.

The first and overriding factor is that while the average Western citizen's life is determined by insecurity (particularly heightened during the last decade in the face of an ever-deepening capitalist depression), the life of the subject of Soviet societies is determined by a total lack of freedom. In our view, the dominant and rapidly accelerating general insecurity provides an answer to the question: why is it that the anti-nuclear movement flared up precisely now, after nearly a four-decade-long coexistence with the Bomb.[9] In fact, increase in insecurity is the

---

[9] The following objections could be made even to our raising such a question. Was it not reason enough for starting the anti-nuclear movement now, one would ask, that Schlesinger, then Defence Secretary, spoke already in 1973 about the possibility of 'surgi-cal' nuclear strikes which did not imply Armageddon? Was it not reason enough that, much later, President Reagan mentioned the abstract possibility of limited nuclear wars, even if this option was later most resolutely rejected (including the futile denial of the authenticity of the President's statement) by his staff and the State Department? Is it not reason enough that new weapons keep emerging which are either 'pure', so that they 'only' kill humans, but do not destroy cities and industry, or which are limited, therefore allegedly only annihilate a part of the world, not the whole? Is it not reason enough that the part of the tension which had been eliminated at the end of the Cold War, was reimported into Europe by the medium-range missile issue accompanied by the vigorous language of anti-communist cru-saders plus a near total destruction by the recent administration of all communication between the superpowers? These facts are undeniable and they, in their ensemble, do not only contain the moral indictment of American foreign policy; they also demonstrate its ineptitude, which finally succeeded in undermining the deterrent character of its own deterrent in a part of public opinion. They are also partial, but only partial, not primary, factors in the upsurge of anti-nuclear movements. First of all, we are positive that any sur-vey of the political climate of the political climate of the fifties, when there was no peace movement, except the official pro-Soviet world organization, would show a much more undisguised display of American nuclear superiority and much more untarnished threats to use them, both by the press and the politicians. Moreover, even if public opinion was perhaps not familiar with the details, basically everyone knew that MacArthur categorically demanded the use of nuclear (and laser) weapons against Chinese troops. In the event, the option was turned down by the White House. But the Korean crisis could have equally served as an encouragement to a future use of, or a future abstinence from, nuclear weapons. Much more importantly, and this is what we regard as the crucial factor, if one looks at the actual parallels of foreign policy it will be immediately clear that while in

only all-embracing answer we can find to the 'anti-nuclear phenomenon'. While it seems to be beyond reasonable doubt that the Reagan
administration is the worst post-war government of the United States,
we do not think that any objective analysis could point out any fact
corroborating the actually heightened danger of a nuclear war caused
by this administration. There are, of course, many aspects of the activities of this superpower which sustain such appearances, such as the
mentioned, near-total rupture of communication with the other superpower. We do not deny either the fact of an enormously increased
military budget under Reagan, nor its socially scandalous character
when seen alongside the attempt to progressively demolish the welfare
system. What we deny most emphatically is that an increase in the
military budget is an automatic indication of an increased threat of
nuclear war.

If we accept this, we shall see anti-nuclear movements in the West as
symbolic movements full of positive democratic demands, but also full
of rhetoric and intolerance in romantic gestures which give vent to the
feeling of insecurity engendered by the collapse of the affluent society,
the disappearance of job security, fears for a genuinely threatened
environment and a livelihood threatened by an excessive and uncritical
industrialization. It would also account for the fact that the movement
is tainted with important elements of anti-American nationalism,
especially in West Germany and in the United Kingdom. This new anti-
Americanism, a just punishment for the haughtiness of a dominant
position now lost, in all probability for good, a feeling which, despite its
often leftist vocabulary, is not necessarily leftist in character (in fact, in
Germany it can be, and often is, ultra-rightist, or bears long-held and
hidden grudges for 'wartime humiliations') is central to the movement.
The psychological, instead of sociological, way of argument about the
imminent dangers of the present situation used by the anti-nuclear

---

the United States the belligerent rhetoric has become fortified, indecision has only grown,
and this great power suffered humiliations, like the one inflicted by Iran, which would have
been inconceivable 15 years earlier, without seriously considering military retaliation. (Or
if it did consider such action, it must have been quite effectively discouraged by its military
experts and this is also a telling fact.) At the same time, Soviet aggressivity keeps increasing
year after year, and the USSR has been involved in its Vietnam, the war in Afghanistan, for
a third year. (Needless to say, the latter serves only for Andropov as an excuse for the
Central American policy of the USA. He mentioned in a recent interview, in a lucidly
Machiavellian comparison, that the USSR defends its national interests in Afghanistan to
the same extent as the USA does in Central America.) The fact of the Afghan war, as well as
the blatant disregard which surrounds this fairly obvious and public constellation,
convinces us again that it is not the upsurge in US war preparations, but the general
Western upsurge of the feeling of insecurity (with a number of collateral factors) that triggered the present dynamic of the anti-nuclear movements.

movement, the main bearer of this anti-American feeling, is most telling about the dominant atmosphere of insecurity as the very basis of the movement. Should the question arise as to whether Western Europe is exposed directly to any danger from the United States, no one would answer in the affirmative. A statement like this would not normally make sense. As far as the Soviet threat is concerned, one can rather witness a near-hysterical toning down and underestimation of the very substantial danger of the Finlandization of Europe, to a point where certain activists, like Rudolf Bahro, are actually advocating such an option.[10] Logically speaking then, one scenario remains: the psychological argument which runs as follows. We, by which we mean the Western alliance, are too strong, too threatening. This could either conclude in a loss of self-control our our part, or provoke a loss of self-control on the part of others. In both cases, we, the West Europeans, are likely to be sacrificed. Very clearly, this is a straightforward case of disturbance stemming from insecurity, one, in which the Bomb really loses its deterrent character, for, after all, who would be deterred from anything if at the other end people see themselves in a complex mental state of being too weak because they are too strong?[11]

Nothing like that can be found in the oppressive atmosphere of the neo-Stalinist state. We basically agree with V. Zaslavsky in his structural description of the post-Stalin paternalism which is just as unfree as Stalin's state was but which, under Khrushchev, closed the devastating periods and cycles of 'revolutions from above' and, in exchange for confiscated freedom, provides a certain type of security. This is a security of unfree life, of a life without political objectives and activities, a life without genuine culture, a life without the burden of having an opinion of one's own, but undeniably a life not exposed, except on the top, to the risks of competition, of losing one's prestige because of incompetence or sheer bad luck in a dynamic and egoistic society, a life which does not demand the unpleasant business of governing one's own fate. Therefore everything people like and dislike in this world, has hardly anything to do with insecurity, and can only be expressed in and through another overriding category: lack of freedom.[12]

---

[10] See his interview with *Le Nouvel Observateur* (26 June 1982, pp. 36–7).

[11] At this point, we simply wish to state with emphasis that all this is indeed a criticism of the movements but not a condescending and ironical statement of their futility. Their democratic potentials are enormous and have a crucial importance for non-doctrinaire Western radicalism.

[12] As one can learn from the interesting article of J. Kis, 'Quelques idées pour l'opposition hongroise', *Esprit*, 1983, a specific type of insecurity and collateral anxiety is emerging now in the relatively well-off countries of Eastern Europe (Hungary, Czechoslovakia, GDR). They look at Polish and Rumanian shopwindows and ask: when will this happen to

Of course, all this does not at all mean that fear plays no role in the life of Soviet society. On the contrary, under Stalin, fear became a way of life for the Soviet state subject and has remained so ever since. But this fear is a clear-cut, easily comprehensible, easily internalizable feeling, not even similar to the polyphonic and objectless anxiety which stems from the insecurity caused by Western capitalism. Needless to say, the lack of insecurity (the obverse of which is the self-renouncement of our freedom) is not an asset. One can see its devastating results on both poles of Soviet life: in Solzhenytsin's quest for a strong authority and his contempt for 'weak democracy', and the ever-increasing consciousness of the ruling apparatus, sometimes even surfacing in the still sporadic and immediately suppressed publications which treat freedom as a chimera and the strong state and paternal guidance as the only social realities.

What are, in our experience, people afraid of in Soviet (Russian, not East European) societies, or, what are they not afraid of? Above all, the average 'citizen' there does not live in fear of nuclear war. In fact, the nuclear threat hardly ever enters his or her daily thoughts and ruminations. When the Medvedev brothers write that 'a preemptive strike by the United States is an ... imaginable and frightening scenario to the Soviet leadership'[13] they may well be right. However, they are once again identifying with their favourite subject, the ruling apparatus. If we are speaking of the average citizens, their general feelings are widely different. Not even the famous ecological issue, the peaceful use of nuclear energy, was ever widely thematized in the unofficial public opinion of the Soviet (Russian or non-Russian) societies for reasons which are almost self-evident. Societies governed by the 'dictatorship over needs' are 'asinine' societies. They push industrialization to pathological extremes, but never satisfy consumerist needs. Therefore people, being well aware that there is no way back, now yearn for satisfaction, even saturation, by industrial consumer goods, and they could not care less about pollution, ecological consequences and the potential dangers of the peaceful use of nuclear energy. It belongs to the full truth that, in this respect, there is a discrepancy between popular feeling and the attitudes of dissident intellectuals. A significant part of the opposition, especially in the USSR, is deeply concerned about problems of environmentalism and the 'cancerous' growth of industry. The Medvedev brothers (of whom Zhores in particular, during his

---

us? But this is such a concrete type of insecurity, with such a tangible object that it cannot perhaps even be compared to the Western type.

[13] Medvedev and Medvedev, 'The USSR and the Arms Race', p. 17.

years of emigration, did some extremely valuable work in exposing nuclear power station catastrophes in the Soviet Union, catastrophes which have, needless to say, never been mentioned in the press) warned Soviet public opinion about certain irreversible consequences of Khrushchev's agricultural escapades right back in the early sixties. Industrialization has been one of the main hates of Solzhenytsin, from whom the adjective of 'cancerous' growth stems. However, at least at this stage, these are overwhelmingly the feelings of intellectuals and, by and large, they are at odds with people who want more consumer goods, irrespective of the natural costs at which they are produced.

In addition, Soviet authorities (both in the USSR and in Eastern Europe) go out of their way to keep social imagination shielded from fears of a nuclear holocaust. When the Medvedev brothers mention that 'there is no planning in the USSR for mass survival in a nuclear conflict: shelters are non-existent in the new Moscow housing districts, while civil defence training in the provinces is confined to perfunctory bus trips in to the forests,'[14] the statement, according to our personal experience, is correct. Yet it betrays an excessive confidence in the humanity of a government which (or the predecessors of which but with whom they accept historical continuity) sent millions to extermination camps, if all this is interpreted as a sign of peaceful intentions. This total and (if Soviet leaders believe a single word of their own propaganda) criminal neglect of the protection of the populace is part of a wider plan. Soviet authorities are, through secret police reports, certainly not unaquainted with the disinterest of the populace in nuclear threat, and they want to keep them in this state of disinterest. Therefore everything that even distantly reminds them of the dangers of a nuclear holocaust is removed from public display. Not only are there no shelters or plans and exercises of a civil defence training programme. Movies available in abundance in Western cinema and television programmes about nuclear doomsday are generally banned from Soviet media.[15] In military training courses for civilians (at universities, sometimes for high school students), the lectures tone down the eventual consequences of a nuclear attack sometimes to a comic-book level. It is, thus, a precondition of unhindered strategical planning and the unperturbed and exclusive prerogatives of the ruling apparatus over all strategic matters to keep the social imagination in a

[14] Medvedev and Medvedev, 'The USSR and the Arms Race', p. 18.
[15] We heard, but could not verify, that Peter Watkins' *The War Games* was shown on Soviet television. If this is true, it is a remarkable, and obviously tactically motivated, exception to a generally very strict rule.

state of dangerous passivity. Thus people will not, or to a much lesser degree, interfere with the superior wisdom of the apparatus.

Nor are people in Soviet (Russian) society afraid of the 'Western enemy'. This statement calls for immediate qualifications. The general argument on behalf of 'peaceful Soviet intentions' is the fact of the enormous losses in World War Two. Apart from the minor flaw in the argument that it was first of all the populace, incomparably more than the apparatus even in relative terms, that suffered the losses (the party leadership in Leningrad survived the blockade, while hundreds of thousands died of famine), and if this is not simply a pro-Russian racist argument, two objections can be levelled against it. While people will certainly not forget the World War (this is why the slogan of peace should always remain part of the officially stated policy objectives), the actual world of experience of the overwhelming majority of the population of the USSR, those below 45 years of age, is not shaped any longer by World War Two recollections but by other events, the importance of which in so far as they impinge on the chances of anti-nuclear movements, we shall immediately address. Further, the extent of losses in a previous war works more than one way in any national community; it can either stymie, or reinforce militarism.[16] In the same spirit one could say, without slandering a much-suffering nation, that certain, unfortunately very wide, strata within it, behave as any other national communities do: they are most reluctant to wage a war which would entail excessive casualties, and they are ready to support any military action which ensures an easy and costless victory.[17] As the Soviet populace is, we repeat, not afraid of the 'Western enemy', this simple but fundamental bifurcation works in this case against, not for anti-nuclear movements.

But why are they not afraid of the West? The answer to the question can be divided into two parts. As to general Soviet (Russian) attitudes towards Western Europe, the Medvedev brothers sum up the situation so succinctly that we have nothing to add to it

> If a television commentator from Norway, Sweden, Greece, France, Italy, Holland or Spain arrived in Moscow, what evidence would they

---

[16] For instance, in France after World War One the crippling losses of the war had, despite the victory, a paralysing effect both on the leadership and populace, in the critical days of the German invasion, while in Germany of the same period they fuelled an aggressive, even suicidal militarism.

[17] Whatever our methodolological reservations, this is borne out powerfully by V. Zaslasky's clandestinely performed sociological investigation about popular reactions to the Soviet invasion of Czechoslovakia, see *The Neo-Stalinist State*, op. cit.

find amongst the Soviet public of the fear of aggression from *Europe*? Almost none ... It could be argued that West Germany is a special case, and, indeed, until 1958–1962 there was still an anxiety amongst ordinary people and sections of Soviet officialdom over possible revanchist tendencies on the German Right. The memories of Nazi aggression were still too fresh to allay all suspicions about Bonn's ultimate intentions, whatever common sense might suggest. But the perception of a 'German threat' has slowly receded with time, especially since the emergence of *Ostpolitik*; and although not completely extinct, these fears no longer play an important role in forming the general Soviet view of Western Europe.[18]

As to fear of the United States, not even these authors, who, as we have argued, identify with the feelings of their enemy, the ruling apparatus, can produce evidence of any feeling other than that of a hurt national pride. For instance, it is conceivable that the espionage flights of the U-2 planes, of which the Soviet public only learned retrospectively (after the first was shot down) that they had been going on for years, did perhaps provoke a retrospective feeling of offended nationalism which spilled over even beyond officialdom. Equal, or similar, feelings can be stipulated in connection with the Cuban missile crisis (the Medvedevs themselves are evidence of it!), although of course it is hard to tell how widespread such feelings were. However, there are at least two solid reasons which point to an absence of fear about the 'American enemy'. The first is a very widely held contempt in the USSR for American qualities of valour which is strangely mingled with an envy for their wealth and an appreciation of their liberal constitution (this curious mixture is sometimes present in the same person who makes voluntary statements on behalf of a strong authority). Yet such a mixture is not at all unusual in unfree societies. In our experience, Soviet (Russian) people never really believed official propaganda about the standards of living in American capitalism, not even when the propaganda touched upon serious realities (such as the situation of the blacks), but they almost always believed when it depicted the 'moral disintegration', high criminality, wide drug addiction, lack of respect for authorities and 'sexual licentiousness'. There is no recognition for American military performance in World War Two in generations whose fathers, because of Stalin's criminal mistakes and whims, often had to storm German trenches and fortresses without artillery, and certainly without air cover, to perish superfluously by the hundreds of

[18] Ibid., pp. 8–9.

thousands. The Korean War with its absence of a decisive victory hardly did much to bolster respect or fear; and the Vietnam defeat, despite the enormous technological superiority of the Americans, undermined its vestiges. It is a matter of self-esteem for the average Soviet citizen, and it is also socially rewarding, not to be afraid of an army of gum-chewing addicts who rebel unpunished against their superior officers. Secondly, the Medvedevs underestimate the general intelligence of the Soviet public if they believe that their 'ordinary' Russian citizen was unaware of the fact that the West (American in particular), both as far as the number of bombs and the long-range carriers are concerned, enjoyed unchallenged nuclear superiority between 1945 and 1950. After all, the USSR had, at the end of the war, an army of 20 million, so that huge masses of people simply had to be aware of certain military realities. Soviet citizens, according to our experience, knew about this superiority perfectly well and therefore, they also had to come to the conclusion that if the United States, for a number of reasons which cannot be analysed here and which perhaps do not even figure in popular Soviet fantasy, did not attempt to destroy the USSR then, they certainly would not dare to do so in an age of nuclear parity, if not in that of Soviet superiority.

Further, there is amongst the populace no fear of the possibility of an impetuous and unilateral Soviet action provoking a nuclear war. This confidence (which we share as well) must not be considered as a vote of confidence in ideological tenets: it is a politically neutral but widespread feeling. There is a well-established image of Stalin behind it and the firm belief that, at least in this respect, all Soviet leaders have remained orthodox Stalinists. Stalin's image was the exact opposite of Trotsky, of the latter's leanings of a 'Red Bonaparte'; Stalin, on the other hand, can only be seen as a 'cautious Ghengis Khan'. He certainly intended world domination but not only did he master the resigned wisdom that this would not be achieved in his lifetime, and not only did he feel himself powerfully confirmed in his caution by the crippling defeats of the first year of the war but, most importantly, this real founder of the dictatorship over needs, contemplated, sometimes over-anxiously, the capacities of the 'Soviet world-system' to absorb, economically and socially, what it had conquered with military might. Naturally, the intricate details of this strategy never percolated down to the minds of the 'ordinary' subject of Soviet society. Nonetheless, people understood one cardinal and permanent touchstone of Soviet statesmanship: do not reach out for more than you can consume, but once having grabbed it, keep it for good. Brezhnev's rule *de facto* ended when he violated this principle by embarking on the unwinnable war in Afghanistan, and we are only now witnessing the beginning of a long route along which the chickens shall come to roost. It goes without saying that this attitude can be explained as shrewd imperialism as well as the realistic observance of the 'patriotic interests' of the USSR, but in both cases, it does not generate fear of nuclear adventurism either in the enemies or the supporters of the regime. In this sense, the Soviet 'citizen', however unpolitical s/he might generally be, is politically more conscious and perceptive on this score than the over-politicized Western anti-nuclear activist. S/he considers the Bomb to be what it in fact is: a deterrent, up until now the only guarantee against the new world wars.

Finally, militarism, a marked and ever-increasing feature of Soviet society is not likely to fuel anti-nuclear passions for a number of reasons. First, and here we have to quote again the Medvedevs because of their accuracy, the 'citizen' of Soviet societies, either in the USSR or elsewhere, does not hold the military responsible for his incomparably lower standards of living than those of West European or American counterparts: 'Soviet defence spending, contrary to a widespred belief, is not generally perceived as a major cause of their economic difficulties by the Russian people. The ordinary Soviet citizen blames the omnipresent bureaucracy for shortages, inefficiency and poor quality products, not the army.'[19] Nor is this simply an instance of 'false consciousness'. These days we already have some analyses (Zaslavsky, Castoriadis) of the hermetically separated world of the military complex, of the so-called 'closed factories' which pay higher wages and salaries, ensure incomparably better social amenities creating thereby a distinct wage-earning stratum which is much better of than the rest of the Soviet wage- and salary-earners. In addition, G. W. Breslauer, in a new book on Khrushchev and Brezhnev[20] demonstrates that Soviet leaders, from Malenkov to Brezhnev, relied invariably on the 'marginal products' of the military industry whenever they wanted to satisfy the demands of the population with really modern and good quality products, and not on 'peace industry'. But, equally importantly, Zaslavsky also convincingly analyses the army as a major channel of upward mobility for wide social strata in the USSR, in particular for the village conscripts who do not have an internal passport of their own. In the army they learn industrial skills, they have some experience of the urban life otherwise unattainable to them, and when discharged, some of them can even obtain the cherished internal passport.

[19] Medvedev and Medvedev, 'The USSR and the Arms Race', p. 20.
[20] *Khrushchev and Brezhnev as Leaders: Building Authority in Soviet Politics*, London, Boston, Sydney: George Allen and Unwin, 1982.

What are the Soviet people afraid of? What are the really frightening experiences of those below 45 years of age? The most frightening experiences, and, at the same time, the menacing future options of the average Soviet citizen are conventional wars and armed conflicts in the outer reaches of the Soviet empire – principally in Asia, but also in Europe – in which Soviet soldiers have been, or could be, involved, and the recurrence of which threatens eventually to spread over the Soviet homeland as well. These conflicts could take place between 'socialist' and capitalist states, as well as between those of 'real socialism'. The conflicts we have in mind are the Korean War in which a fortunate coincidence of events ensured that Soviet contingents were not deployed (a 'fortunate coincidence' which, however, was purchased at the price of hundreds of thousands of Chinese 'volunteers' killed or wounded); the Vietnam War, where, again Soviet 'volunteers' could have been used (and, in fact, the American administration anticipated it when calculating the chances of a frontal attack on Hanoi); the 1956 police actions against Poland and Hungary, and their repetition in 1968 against Czechoslovakia, all of which finally turned out to be small-scale operations from a military point of view, although, there is absolutely no telling when a new edition of such 'liberating operations' will cost tens of thousands of Soviet lives; the Ussuri war in 1971 between the USSR and Maoist China, which in fact demanded at least thousands of Soviet and tens of thousands of Chinese lives, and in which major battles raged with ultramodern weapons, just short of a limited nuclear conflict; the constant Chinese–Vietnamese tensions with the Soviet partner in the background, a flare-up of which in 1979 triggered Soviet fleet manoeuvres and troop concentrations in defence of a country whose cause and regional ambitions mean absolutely nothing for the average Soviet citizen; and finally the Afghan war which, after three years, has cost, according to more or less reliable sources, more than 10,000 Soviet lives. The Chinese danger, the 'yellow peril' is the overriding nightmare for Soviet citizens, who now have the same feeling as European countries once had of facing the apparently endless Russian human mass, this steam-roller of the Russian Empire. People in the USSR generally believe that it is only technological, that is, nuclear superiority that can guarantee their safety and act as a deterrent against immense conventional wars with their Asian neighbour. However, this feeling works against, not for anti-nuclear movements in the USSR. No doubt, should China in 20 to 30 years build up its own nuclear arsenal to the present Soviet level, a feeling similar to that found in present-day West European countries could grip wide strata of the Soviet population. Until this entirely different constellation emerges, however, the Russian people are unlikely to abandon their principal fear of conventional war. They are, therefore, also unlikely to be grasped by anti-nuclear sentiments.

III EASTERN EUROPE: TOP AND BASE

In analysing East European Soviet countries, there is hardly a great need to devote much space to an analysis of the 'top'. There can be, and indeed there are several important differences between each of the countries of the region and their respective ruling apparatus. However, in respect of the strategic problems of nuclear armament and preparation for a nuclear war, they are mere emanations of the Soviet Russian apparatus, and there is one absolute precondition of their existence: they must not take foreign policy initiatives of their own.[21] In this sense, each of the particular ruling apparatuses can be understood through what they have in common: serving Soviet strategic interests which are also presented in each nation as being in the interests of peace.

More can, and should, be said of the attitude at the 'base' which is equally unfavourable for nuclear movements as that of the 'base' in the USSR, but for not entirely identical reasons. East European Soviet society too is one of unfreedom and fear, not of insecurity and anxiety, and we have already seen that it is the latter that favours and promotes the West's largely symbolic anti-nuclear movements. However, in order to understand the political climate, we have to ask our earlier question again: what are people afraid of and what are they not afraid of in this region? East European countries, as occupied states, possess no great fear of 'American aggression'. Should Soviet predominance in this region somehow miraculously cease, each nation would in all probability choose a course entirely different from its present one. Possible courses can be characterized by capitalist as well as genuinely socialist solutions. For all this, however, one could safely say that no inhabitant in any of these countries who is not incorporated in the power apparatus, regards the United States as an enemy.

However, there is a more sophisticated formulation of the same problem. One could contend that these countries have a 'West German

---

[21] As is well known, Soviet hostility towards Ceauşescu's regime, one of the most oppressive in the region, is conditioned precisely by the Rumanian's flirting, mainly for internal political reasons, with sham-national independence and a foreign policy of his own.

feeling', namely the argument so widespread in the West German anti-nuclear movement that the American target is the Soviet Union and that West Germany will be used as a battlefield. Such a feeling has, indeed, emerged in certain 'neutralists' of the region. For instance, Imre Nagy, the martyr of East European democratic socialism who, in his famous *Memoranda 1955*, in which he formulated his programme which he tried to put to test in the short-lived Hungarian Revolution of 1956, explicitly spoke of the necessity of becoming neutral, lest Hungary become a battlefield for the superpowers. But in post-1956 generations this feeling of a danger is clearly fading. The reason is simple. As a result of the deep disillusionment felt in Eastern Europe about the absence of Western support in Hungary in 1956, which was to be further corroborated by the cynical tacit approval of Soviet actions in Czechoslovakia in 1968,[22] it is difficult to see precisely who in the East would believe that the West was capable of the extremely audacious action needed to bring the world to the brink of holocaust. Put another way, if the West has never intervened in Eastern Europe in the past when it was in a position of superiority, then why should it do so now? In short then, the West confronts a deeply rooted problem of credibility in Eastern Europe which will further militate against the formation of independent peace movements on a large scale. There is no fear of a nuclear clash between the superpowers because of an excessive American zeal to 'liberate' Eastern Europe in the region concerned.

Nor is there any fear of a Soviet nuclear strike or threat. The idea of a possible Soviet nuclear attack on any East European target immediately ceases to sound as absurd as it might first appear if we imagine an all-out and dogged Polish resistance to a Soviet Army inter-vention. In fact, had Stalin had nuclear parity, it would not be possible

---

[22] In fact, we know from the book by Z. Mlynàř, *Night Frost in Prague*, London: C. Hurst and Co., 1980, that the American approval was more than tacit. Brezhnev briskly informed the captured Czechoslovak leadership about his secret negotiations with President Johnson in the following words: 'I asked President Johnson if the American Government still fully recognizes the results of the Yalta and Potsdam conferences. And on August 18 I received the reply: as far as Czechoslovakia and Rumania are concerned, it recognizes them without reservation; in the case of Yugoslavia, it would have to be discussed. So what do you think will be done on your behalf? Nothing. There will be no war' (p. 241). This remarkable piece of statesmanship, once again a strongly recom-mended reading for West European anti-nuclear militants so concerned about the capacities for American belligerence, does not deserve particular attention for the recip-rocal cynicism inherent in it, which has been stipulated by us from the beginning; only for the imbecility of American foreign policy. In effect, it was an open recommendation to act against Rumania (Yugoslavia could not then be a target but Rumania could), as well as against Czechoslovakia.

to exclude that he might have tried his hand on Yugoslav cities for his realism had its limits when he met weaker opposition. But *au fond*, East Europeans tend to appreciate the Soviet Army on their territory as a *gendarmerie* of the Soviet Empire. Its duties consist of maintaining 'order', the dispersion of eventual mutinies, the putting down of revolutions but not the transformation into nuclear wastelands of regions which are usefully incorporated into the mechanics of the Soviet world-system.

Pacifism, however, plays an incomparably greater role at the base of East European societies than in the Soviet Russian society, especially the religious version of pacifism. In a document issued by the allegedly 'independent peace movement of Hungary' which we have studied with the utmost scepticism, we can read, nonetheless, the following interesting statement: 'While the student movement has been dealing exclusively with disarmament, the religious groups, called *base communities* have been concerned with militarism in general. Having first appeared in the sixties, the base communities are spreading in Hungary. There are now about 300 such communities, each numbering about 30–40 persons. They are against military conscription and are seeking a civilian alternative to military service. They are truly pacifist, and are popular especially among Catholic laity.'[23] This is an important development and it displays the only equivalent in East European societies of anti-nuclear movements of Western Europe.

Such movements are possible when and where the militarization of everyday life becomes excessive and unbearable. The country *par excellence* for such a trend is obviously the German Democratic Republic, in which old-fashioned Prussian traditions are merged with Soviet authoritarianism. Let us quote briefly from *A Resolution of the Provincial Church Convention of Saxony in Halle on the Problem of Peace*:

We understand, affirm and advocate the security interests of our state. However, we have to spell out our concern regarding the fact that the military penetrates our whole social life in an ever-increasing degree: from military parades to the kindergarten, from closed forests to certain criteria of admittance into (tertiary) education, from children's toys to the training exercises of civilian defence. All this does not serve the real security and the future of our life. In result of it, anxiety will be generated on the one hand, people will be acclimatized to an eventual war on the

---

[23] *The New Hungarian Peace Movement*, ed. F. Köszegi and E. P. Thompson, London: European Nuclear Disarmament, 1982, p. 12.

other hand; perhaps discipline will be attained by it, but we are not going to be made capable of shaping peace creatively.[24]

Why are pacifist movements more successful in East European than in the Russian Soviet societies? One of the reasons is that in the former the army never provides such a distinguished avenue for upward mobility as it does in the USSR. Obviously where people complain about the militarization of life, the obverse of the picture must be a relatively increased role of the military which, therefore, has to serve as at least one of the channels of upward mobility as well. Some of the Warsaw Pact countries (in particular, Poland) have, indeed, armies and navies which are, as far as size is concerned, superior to some of the leading armies and navies of Western Europe. But these armed services are never entirely trusted by the Soviet leadership and therefore they are organically incorporated, through Warsaw Pact channels, in the Soviet Army. If, then, the Medvedev thesis of the non-existence of an independent military–industrial complex applies somewhere, it is to East European, not the Russian, Soviet societies. However, this means, irrespective of the measure of militarization, a reduced importance and social role for the army in these countries, which, unlike Soviet Russia, presents, socially, other possible avenues for upward mobility. A further reason is that religious freedom, including that of the sects which are to our knowledge even more hostile to the armed services than the Catholic laity, is far greater in Eastern Europe than in the USSR. All these factors together promote at least the possibility of a widespread pacifist movement.

But what will be, and what could be, the physiognomy of such a pacifist movement? Perforce, it has to be overwhelmingly religious and non-political. Its religious character is a more or less inevitable feature: this is the sole consideration which the 'socialist state', in its more liberal periods, is prepared to accept for the refusal of military service. If the ruling apparatus did otherwise, they would open the floodgates for a movement of general disobedience. As a result, even people with very mild, or no religious beliefs at all have to pretend to have a 'conscientious objection' of a religious nature. The non-political character of the movement can be gleaned from the East German document we have quoted above. Obviously it would be totally unrewarding to make in-depth incognito analyses to decide whether

---

[24] 'Vorschlag: Reduzieren der SS 20 und der Panzer', 'Beschluß zur Friedensproblematik der provinzialsächsischen Kirchegefasst in Halle', in *Friedensbewegung in der DDR*, Texte – 1978–1982, ed. Wolfgang Büscher, Peter Wensierski and Klaus Wolschner with Reinhard Henkys, Hattingen: Edition Transit, 1982, p. 207.

those wording the document indeed think the way the document suggests. The important fact is that, as pacifists, they have to accept the authority of the state in all policy matters except the one on which they are assembled and organized: the refusal of participation in (even potential) violence. Therefore, for reasons of principle this movement is not capable of influencing state strategies.

IV WESTERN MOVEMENTS – EASTERN MOVEMENTS: IS A DIALOGUE POSSIBLE?

If, as we have argued, there are no serious chances for an independent anti-nuclear movement either in the USSR or in the East European Soviet societies, can a reasonable dialogue be maintained between the Eastern opposition and Western movements, the latter being from the late seventies onwards overwhelmingly centred on peace and ecology issues? The very formulation of our question will, we think, immediately provoke hostile comments from many West European militants. Why a dialogue only with the opposition, several of them will ask? Why should we isolate ourselves from the official peace organizations? Our answers to these questions should be clear from our view that the official peace organizatons form an integral part of official Party policy and strategy. As long as these organizations refuse even to admit that Soviet nuclear armaments could, even hypothetically, become a source of danger to humankind, they remain purely functional to official ends and in no way independent.

The single most important question for us remains, however, whether movements genuinely intend to meet movements or whether they are content to make purely symbolic gestures. Thus, if Western militants are serious about cooperating with movements in the East, they do not require much political astuteness to recognize that genuinely autonomous movements are few and far between. And further, they must recognize that the record of cooperation with these movements to date is hardly one which Western leftists can be proud of. The two major peace movements of Western Europe, the British and the German, sometimes after a mild symbolic gesture of protest, sometimes even without such a symbolic gesture, turned over the page on Poland, December 1981, in the history book. And the anti-nuclear militants who uncritically participate in peace carnivals, refusing, by and large, to address the question concerning who their Soviet counter-

parts and codemonstrators have been recruited by, and, further, refusing to ask any questions about the well-being of Sakharov, this
super-Oppenheimer, the only genuine scientific hero of the anti-
nuclear issue in the USSR, and also, who turn a blind eye to the fate of
the autonomous Soviet peace movement which was under arrest or
house-arrest during the visits of Western peace activists, will make
absolutely no contribution to the cause they themselves deem to be
cardinal for the future of present-day civilization. Precisely for this
reason we cannot emphasize strongly enough the significance of
gestures within the anti-nuclear movement which seriously question
the value of the official Soviet facade of 'peaceful intentions of the
socialist community', which demand that acts, not only flattering words
should emerge from the Soviet leadership, deeds which testify to at
least a minimum of tolerance towards autonomous social movements
without which there is not the slightest hope of the peaceful solution of
world conflicts. In particular, E. P. Thompson, one of the theoretical
and practical founders of the West European peace movement,
demands vigorously in his recent statements and speeches that no
credit should be given to the Soviet pose of the 'sole guardian and
trustee of the noble cause of peace'. Whatever the actual wording of
these statements, they are beyond the credulous, or self-deluding, uni-
lateralism of the original British movement in that they demand
reciprocal action on the part of both superpowers as the sole basis for
credibility. Even if, for the time being, these important new developments remain on a gestural level (although they are represented in
several national peace movements ever more vigorously by groups of
varying strength), they shatter the illusions concerning Soviet societies
so widespread in the anti-nuclear movements, as well as counteract
Soviet and pro-Soviet manipulations and promote an at least more
lucid self-awareness of the movement itself.

The underlying dilemma can be formulated in terms of a 'communication disturbance'. Even where we are speaking of militants with
genuine intentions of combining political freedom and survival, we
must recognize that, in East and West, we are speaking of people who
have experienced their political socialization in radically different
social climates. One group lives in a world of insecurity, speaks the
language of insecurity (which for a decade now, has been replacing the
language of alienation) and therefore perceives several underlying
threats, in addition genuine ones, to the very existence of our civilization. But the movement is, at the same time, full of irrationalist intolerance and closed to rational arguments when its main values are
concerned, and this is true to a greater extent than in other movements.

The other group has been politically socialized in a society of un-freedom and speaks the language of unfreedom, and whether it does this with an approving or disapproving accent, does not really matter. The time perception of this group is short-term, they are not interested in the strategic issues of the world they are living in, nor are they par-ticularly concerned with hidden threats; the problems bothering them are much too visible. Therefore, on the one hand, they are much more realistic regarding several problems connected with the peace issue. For instance, as mentioned, the overwhelming majority of the populace of Soviet societies is, in our personal experience, adamant that the Bomb does work as a deterrent, otherwise we would already be up to our neck either in a new world war or equally devastating regional wars, for instance between China and the Soviet Union. On the other hand, they are just as blind and impenetrable concerning certain dangers, mostly the ones which are in the focus of the Western anti-nuclear militant, as their Western counterpart is concerning certain others. There is no way to convince the populace of an under-industrialized area of any Soviet society which lacks elementary industrial goods and other social amenities, often even electricity, that a nuclear plant could have dangerous side effects. The fact that they have no say whatsoever in the efficacy of safety regulations is really just an appendix to a dangerous indifference.[25]

In the final analysis, the 'communication disturbance' and its causes boil down to the following formula. A certain type of social activist in the West lives in anxiety about the potential suicide of a civilization. The Doomsday atmosphere (a term which is part of today's fashion-able lexicon), has to be understood in a literal sense, for up until now, there has never been a whole civilization (only single communities) that can contemplate committing suicide. The notion therefore carries a half religious, half mystical aura (irrespective of the reality or irreality of the alarm signals and predictions). Its sense of time is the following: perhaps we are beyond the point of no return; its mythology a set of dramatic opposites: life versus death, health versus the 'cancerous tumor' in the body of civilization, organic versus artificial. The ultimate content of this anxiety is the emphatic feeling of a New Fall, the doubt, in many already the conviction, that 'progress' is poison. Very clearly, this is the most important and most influential romantic movement of the postwar world.

---

[25] One must not interpret our objectivity as wise remarks of the *au dessus de la mêlée*. We are painfully aware of the extremely slow process in which we, after leaving a Soviet society, came to realize that certain issues advocated vigorously by our Western friends are not simply expressions of a collective neurosis.

To the extent that there are movements in Soviet societies at all, and not just isolated moral fighters, they express a diametrically opposite life-feeling. For them, there is not enough progress. Progress has not kept its word, true enough, but in a different sense: it has never brought affluence which was the underlying promise held out to those who accepted 'the temporary restrictions', and it certainly has not brought freedom. The sense of time of this type of activist works with is once again the exact opposite of the Western anti-capitalist romantic: not Doomsday, the approaching and menacing end of a civilization, rather infinitude, the endless duration of a world which, perhaps, may be habitable but which is certainly not the promised land of progress. As a result, the mythology is different as well. 'Darkness at noon' is still a relevant symbol here but it means now the darkness of the tunnel that never ends. If there seems to be a light at the end of the tunnel, it is only a will-o'-the-wisp, a promise that never comes true. This is a world in which the myth of eternal repetition prevails, this myth of disillusionment, where everything always starts anew only in order to end in the same, humiliating and frustrating way. Then the story commences again.

Is there, then, a possibility of dialogue between two forces so differently socialized? We believe that there is such a possibility provided that both speak the language of freedom and democracy. It is futile for the Western militant to seek for people in a world totally alien from his or hers who have his or her life experiences. It is not futile, nevertheless, but rewarding to look for allies in a struggle to control fundamental social processes now entirely in the hands of small and ruthless power elites. If survival and democracy (and for socialists this means radical democracy) become combined issues, both in East and West, a genuine dialogue may begin.

8

The Great Republic

Agnes Heller[1]

A utopia can be utopian to a greater or lesser degree. The model of the Great Republic is a utopia in the least possible degree. If the 'utopian mentality', as Mannheim put it, is strong, the utopian character of the utopia is relativized. Thus, in the view of those who share the utopian mentality, a utopia is not utopian at all, but a socio-political model ready for implementation. Only those who do not share such a mentality would denounce the model as 'utopian'. However, the model of the Great Republic does not live exclusively in the utopian mentality. Political movements, for instance, have already attempted its implementation in a particular region of the world, and whilst they may have failed, this was due to the intervention of external forces. Of course, the external provenance of its dissolution does not offer proof of the viability of the model, for one can still argue in a sceptical, but not entirely unfounded spirit that, had the attempt to establish the Great Republic not been crushed by force (and here we refer to Hungary, Czechoslovakia, Poland and, much earlier, Austria), the project would have eventually dissolved as a result of endogenous factors. However, such considerations are irrelevant, for I have not stated that the model of the Great Republic is not utopian. I have only insisted that it is utopian in the least possible degree.

The model of the Great Republic was conceived in Europe, east of the Elbe. I deliberately refrain from using the term 'Eastern Europe', for the tradition of the Great Republic is shared by certain Central European societies and only some East European ones. Further, there is no one single model of the Great Republic but several. However, all

---

[1] Originally published in English in *Praxis International* (Oxford) 5:1, April 1985, also published in Spanish as 'La Gran Republica' in *Revista de Occidente* (Madrid), N.45, February 1985.

have certain basic features in common, indeed sufficient to warrant our calling them models of the Great Republic. In addition, all of them have been formulated by thinkers who grew up east of the Elbe, or were carried and motivated by political movements belonging to the same region. Cultural traditions are, of course, never hermetically sealed, least of all radical traditions. They influence one another, and sometimes even shape themselves in accordance with the image of the other; they share basic concerns, and even aim at certain similar solutions. Despite this, and perhaps because of it, they remain distinct. The model of the Great Republic though, has never made an appearance in the modern history of Britain; the American model has always been deeply rooted in its own tradition (the only democratic *tradition* one can mention); French postwar social movements, especially those of May 1968, have borne very little resemblance to the Great Republic.

Certain features of the Great Republic were sketched first by Kant. It is odd to think of Kant as a philosopher belonging to a tradition from east of the Elbe, but in many respects this is what he was. The way in which Kant formulates the proper relationship between morals and politics,[2] his criticism of 'unsociable sociability', his emphasis on *sensus communis*, the place he attributes to judgement in politics, his suggestions, albeit vague, for a combination of representation and participation, all this and so much else, already intimates the theme of the Great Republic.

The most radical theorist of the Great Republic was, without doubt, Rosa Luxemburg. She undertook the task of moulding her orthodox Marxism into a model of the Great Republic. Her emphasis on the spontaneity of movements, on self-education via participation, her commitment to the idea of councils and, simultaneously, to the idea of representation, the way she formulated the proper relationship between politics and morals (very much like Kant) – all these and so much else were but variants on the theme of the Great Republic.

The same tradition spawned another great radical thinker in Hannah Arendt. She interpreted the American Revolution through the prism of that tradition. Her insistence on the 'insertion' of a 'social sphere' between the political and the private, the cause of so much mis-

---

[2] Dick Howard, in a recent study, 'From Marx to Kant: the Return of the Political', *Thesis Eleven*, No. 8 (1984) (Melbourne), makes some very interesting remarks about the Kantian understanding of the relationship of politics to morals. He writes as follows: 'Politics differs from morality because of the form of its judgments. The key to a theory of politics is the reflective judgment that proceeds from the particular to the universal' (p. 86). And Hannah Arendt's increasing preoccupation with the theory of judgement is well known.

understanding on the Western Left (which has always believed that she was a 'conservative') was a recurrent theme within the tradition of the Great Republic.[3] It is small wonder then that Arendt was enthusiastic about the institutions which mushroomed during the 'ten free days' of the Hungarian revolution in 1956, and that she discovered a sisterly spirit in Rosa Luxemburg, whose intentions she had understood so well.

Many studies have been written about the differences between Hungary 1956, Czechoslovakia 1968 and Poland 1980–1. Without disregarding these differences, which in certain respects are crucial, all three attempts should, in my view, be regarded as variations on the theme of the Great Republic. Of course, the latter is not *the* tradition, but a radically democratic (and socialist) tradition belonging to that region east of the Elbe, a region which is also rich in conservative traditions, most of them nationalist (some racist), several authoritarian or fundamentalist (of every possible provenance). What is 'in between', namely the liberal tradition, is extremely weak, excepting Czecho-slovakia. In certain instances, both conservatism and radical demo-cracy draw their strength from the same sources. Possessive individualism is despised in both quarters, so is goal-rationalism oriented to private interest. The ideal of community is highly acclaimed in both theories, and both also demonstrate an enthusiasm for ideas, a certain kind of populism and the primacy of the practical over the pragmatic. A stubborn version of romantic anticapitalism (both leftist and rightist) prevails in the respective theories, a rejection of piecemeal approaches to social change and an inclination towards institutional-ization and a certain predilection for continuous discourse. The latter has often been a target for self-criticism ('we talk forever, instead of acting').

The historical background behind all these behavioural patterns, patterns of action, world-views and beliefs is easily located. I will not, however, dwell on genesis, but rather on outlining my own version of the Great Republic, no particular feature of which, however idio-syncratic the design, has been invented by me. Each and every one of them has been invented by social movements, and all theoretical inter-pretations have been equally drawn from one or another philosophical attempt at their generalization.

---

[3] It was Andrzej Walicki who drew my attention to the fact that the line of demarcation between 'private' and 'public' passes along different realms in the East European and Western democratic traditions. He insists that the distinction of the 'social sphere' in Arendt has undoubtedly an East European streak. I would add to this that the inter-pretation of the 'social sphere' in Arendt is highly idiosyncratic.

Alec Nove, in his recent book, *The Economics of Feasible Social-ism*, writes the following about a future socialist society: 'Political assumption: a multiparty democracy, with periodic elections to a parliament ... The notion that several parties are needed only when there are separate social classes is clearly false.'[4] The notion is clearly false in my view as well. Yet its falsity is far from self-evident in the eyes of many democratic socialists. Castoriadis among others, to mention only this outstanding philosopher of democratic socialism, would strongly disagree with such a political assumption. In his view, an 'auto-nomous society' and representation are mutually and absolutely exclu-sive. He is unable to understand Rosa Luxemburg's fury at the dissolution of the Constitutional Assembly in any terms other than tactical ones. However, far from being a tactical consideration, for Luxemburg this was a crucial tenet, for she could not conceive of any socialist society without a multi-party system, representation and general elections to a parliament, nor could she conceive of a socialist society without constitutional guarantees for human rights. Neither was it for tactical reasons that the Hungarian Workers' Councils immediately committed themselves to a multi-party system and parlia-mentary elections. The resolution of *one* workers' council demanding that there should be no parties at all was overruled by an overwhelming and very vocal majority.

In order to understand this problem, we have to go to its roots, and examine the status of the person in the Great Republic. Status is differ-entiated, reflecting three levels of interaction: it is, first, the status of the person qua person, secondly, it is the status of the person as a parti-cipating member in a social body, and thirdly, it is the status of the person as a participating member in a political body. In principle, all three forms of status are independent of one another. The person in his or her status qua person makes choices or decisions independently of the choices and decisions s/he makes as a participating member of a political or social body; or at least, s/he can make such decisions. Furthermore, a person as a participating member of a social body makes decisions independently of the choices and decisions s/he makes as a participating member of a political body, and vice versa. The person qua person has rights as a person, and again, these are independent of his or her rights as a participating member of a social or political body. The rights of the single person carry with them only one obligation: to respect the same rights in all other persons. However,

---

[4] A. Nove, *The Economics of Feasible Socialism* (London, Boston, Sydney), George Allen & Unwin, 1983, p. 197.

they do not impose any obligation to make use of such rights. Personal rights can do no more than permit a person to exercise them should s/he wish. One cannot be forced to exercise personal rights. The rights attaching to a participating member of a social body can be simultaneously obligatory and optional. Whether it is the former or the latter which applies depends entirely on the self-established norms and rules of the social body. The utilization of rights attached to a participating membership in a political body, on the other hand, is obligatory: political rights must be made use of. However, the rights of the person qua person are primary rights: the person must remain in a position where s/he can choose whether or not s/he wants to be a participating member of a social or political body.

The subject of the multi-party system of general elections to a parliament is the subject (person) qua subject (person) endowed with primary rights. It is assumed that the need structure of each person is unique, and, further, that each person is vested with a great variety of goals and options. Parties stand for typical goals and typical options. Persons voting for one or another party vote for them in order to have them represent their goals or options as typical ones. Of course, opinion cannot be represented but it can be voiced in the body politics of which the person is a participating member, as well as in the public domain which is not identical with any single body politic – for example, the media, occasional assemblies and the like, where everyone can give his or her opinion and address the whole public directly. The person qua person does not simply cast his or her vote: the person makes his or her voice heard in the public domain where the goals and objectives which the parties stand for are shaped as typical goals and objectives. It is an article of faith with some on the Western Left that any system of representation dooms persons to passivity. However, whatever can be stated of electoral passivity, if the typical goals and options the parties stand for are themselves shaped in public discourse, the citizens are far from being passive. What they delegate to representative bodies is only the right to legislate and execute in accordance with the typical options and objectives of the citizenry whose representatives they are. An elected representative body is not, however, coextensive with 'magistrates'. The elected parliament is a real sovereign, it wields power, and it is precisely for this reason that checks and balances are needed against the hypertrophy of power within this body.

Let me now approach the model from a different angle. As mentioned, the third status of the person in the Great Republic is his or her participating membership in a political body. Briefly, the model combines direct democracy with representative democracy. Solidarity called itself a 'union'; in Hungary in 1956 bodies of direct democracy termed themselves 'councils' and 'revolutionary committees'. Terms, however, matter very little. What does matter is the idea itself and this can be described as follows: persons are members of political bodies which raise political problems of public concern and primary importance. These problems are solved by debate in which everyone gives his or her opinion. A resolution is then passed which embodies the opinion of the membership on the issue under discussion. The common opinion has to be represented by one (elected) member of that body in a body politic, the membership of which consists of the elected members of various primary and democratic political bodies. (For example in Hungary in 1956 these were local workers' councils, the Budapest Workers' Council and a National Workers' Council.) Democracy is indeed direct in all primary bodies and everyone's opinion is voiced and acknowledged. Both primary and representative political bodies are invested with sovereignty. They wield a real political power. Thus the sovereign political body is divided into, first, the parliament and, second, the workers' councils. Strictly speaking, the polity is characterized by a structure of dual power, the underlying assumption of which is that a system like this is the best device for preventing power from becoming an agency of domination. In addition, the 'dual power' structure is not a temporary device. The view that all power should be taken over by the agencies of direct democracy is radically rejected, and for good reasons.

Let us have a brief look again at the operation of direct democracy. Every member of the political body participates here in decision-making. However, it cannot be assumed that in all cases under discussion the resolution will reflect the will of all. Sometimes, obviously, the majority view will be embodied in the final resolution. Even moral pressure of a kind cannot be completely excluded in a procedure like this, nor can the eventual emergence of a false consensus. While electing representatives, people are far less exposed to moral pressure than in the bodies of direct democracy. Moreover, in the bodies of direct democracy, only the main political issues are discussed; every affair simply cannot be discussed. Persons want to live, work, make love and do other things besides participating in a body politic. If all affairs are discussed in the bodies of direct democracy, in the end none will be discussed, for people will be exhausted and will lose interest. And if this were to be the case, then, again, a few would decide for everyone, the few whose interest in politics overrules all their interests in life. A system of direct democracy can, in principle, degenerate into a system of domination as easily as the representative system. This insight provides the inspiration for the idea of dual power and dual sovereignty, the combination of direct and representative democracy. It is not the division of power which is the novel idea here but the division of sovereignty. And, further, it is not the idea of popular sovereignty that is novel here but the coalescence of nominal and real sovereignty. The citizenry is no longer a mere nominal sovereign which delegates its powers to the real sovereign, for it delegates certain powers and not others. The decision as to which issues belong to the jurisdiction of the delegated power remain entirely with the citizenry. It is to be discussed and rediscussed in the public domain and eventually decided by referendum (plebiscite). In addition, decisions like this are not made once and for all, but in each case separately and continuously. The model operates in such a way that every political issue can be discussed in the institutions of direct democracy if participating members of such political bodies believe that they should be. This is so irrespective of whether the same issues are also discussed in the parliament. The latter cannot pass laws without the consent of the bodies of direct democracy. If a conflict between the two sovereign bodies emerges, the issue should be rediscussed in the general public sphere (or domain) and in the political bodies of direct democracy simultaneously, in order to achieve a consensus via discourse. A state constituted by a dual sovereignty of this kind could be defined as Aristotle defined the city-state: 'the sum total of its citizens'. And this holds true even if the distinction between the 'real' and 'nominal' sovereign remains valid in respect of *one* of the two powers, namely the representative body. In other words, the state is not abolished here but defetishized.

Up to this point I have briefly discussed the status of the person qua person (the individual citizen endowed with rights as such) and the status of the person as a participating member in a political body. Let us now examine the third status which attaches to a person when s/he is a participating member in a social body.

The model of the Great Republic separates the political sphere proper from the social sphere. The latter is the sphere of property-holding and welfare.

The main issue which arises here is the generalization of property-holding. The 'right to property' is defined here in such a way that each and every member of society has the right to be the owner of the wealth s/he has created and to the disposition of that created wealth. Further, s/he has the right to dispose of the objectives, programmes and strategies of all institutions which s/he is a member. Thus the social basis of the Great Republic comprises the generalization of self-management. Institutions, from those of production to those of health and education, should be self-managed. The model of generalized self-management does not imply that every economic or social institution is self-managed; the citizenry can decide otherwise in certain cases and for certain reasons. At the same time, the model of generalized self-management is a general model. No fixed pattern is set as the rule of operation for any institution. The model implies only that the rules of operation for any social institution should be established by the members of those institutions instead of being superimposed on them by any agency of social domination. This is tantamount to the subjection of instrumental and functionalist action to practical reason, and not to the project of eliminating instrumental action or a functionalist division of labour.

Self-management can be actualized in different modes and forms. A factory can be owned by a collectivity. All decisions concerning the operation of the factory can be decided by all participating members of that collectivity. Or, alternatively, the collectivity can elect a permanent decision-making body with rotating membership. Or again, the collectivity can instruct experts to prepare drafts for decisions while upholding the right to check, approve or disapprove such drafts. The members of a collectivity (factory) can be the shareholders of the factory and decide upon all major issues only at shareholders' meetings: this solution is much more viable in large enterprises. State ownership should be exceptional. One must take the main slogan of the Hungarian Workers' Council in 1956 seriously: 'We shall relinquish neither land nor factory,' – neither to the capitalist proprietor nor to the state. In institutions other than productive ones, self-management is tantamount to the abolition of social hierarchy.

The person's status as a participant member of the social body is similar to his status as a person; s/he has the right to co-decide and to participate. S/he has the right not to do so and to give instead only a tacit consent. If people lost interest in participating in the decision-making process of a body politic, degeneration is the result. A danger like this is not acute in a social body. Economic and social questions in our workplace or in our social environment, questions whose consequences concern us in the most direct way, normally capture our interest anyway, and if we do not care to participate in one or another concrete case, a real (tacit) consent can be presupposed.

The model of generalized self-management does not exclude two extremes. At one extremity we find communities in which not only property but the whole of life is shared (the kibbutz would be an example), while at the opposite extremity there is private ownership. If the individual's private management means self-employment, there is no social problem at all. But how about employing the labour of others? This possibility can be both included and excluded within the model. Given that I have opted for a plurality of ways of life, I would rather include this possibility under certain social limitations. If everyone has the opportunity to be the owner of social wealth (in a dispositional sense), it must be assumed that if someone accepts as an option being employed, this option satisfies his or her needs.

Theorists of one or another version of the Great Republic repeatedly address the problem of the economic viability of such a model. In drawing lessons from the devastating consequences of the social experiment of 'the dictatorship over needs', they insist on the maintenance of market regulations, probably combined with a kind of central planning. It is indeed of great importance to prefigure and project the economic (and social) *modus operandi* of a society which legitimately can be called socialist; nevertheless, I wish to keep the discussion on a more abstract level. Commodity production and market regulation are certainly presupposed by the model; however, the type of market existing within it would obviously differ from the capitalist and post-capitalist market in many respects. Collective ownership of the means of production, collective management, on the one hand, and the political structure of the Great Republic, on the other hand, together forge new ways of life, and distribution is, after all, always embedded in a particular way of life. The future market may be co-regulated by the state as a dual power, that is, the whole citizenry, in its capacity as political agent and participant, can set limits to market relationships, limits which simply cannot be foreseen now. Even if we reject the idea of wholesale and centralized planning, we can still insist that the structure of dual power should redistribute social wealth from taxes and levies paid by the collectively owned productive units. How much would be redistributed and in what way, is again a matter that has to be decided in public debates (in the public domain, in the agencies of direct democracy and in the parliament), for it is a socio-economic matter which needs to be subjected to political decision. However, the model is to work in such a way that state paternalism should be decreased and, eventually, completely eliminated. How?

Here we can only hint at certain features which point in this direction. Members of a collective decision-making body can invest a part of their profits in vital services (schools, hospitals, homes for the aged, even subsidies for cultural institutions). The difference betwen present practices and the future practices of the Great Republic is the latter's predominantly social rather than economic nature. The decisions are made collectively, the institutions serve the collectivity. Furthermore, the co-owner of a productive unit might obtain his or her share of the accumulated profits of the unit after retirement, precisely as a co-owner or shareholder. Very little room is left here for paternalistic need imputation. If all members of a collectivity decide collectively in matters of social expenditure, if they achieve consensus via rational value discourse, then all side-effects and consequences are freely accepted by everyone concerned, and their needs are thus no longer imputed.

All these (and several other) factors change the *modus operandi* of the market. Firstly, the labour market is relegated to the niches of society. Secondly, most of the services, among them long-term services, are not marketed at all. Redistribution here cannot be conceived according to a pattern the terms of which are, firstly, atomistic individuals racing for success, secondly, the state as the sole redistributive agency and thirdly, the act of redistribution understood as the use of part of the assets of the successful individual competitors to satisfy the primary needs of the unsuccessful individual competitors via need imputation (providing elementary services and welfare payments). The pattern must change even if competition, this time among self-managed productive units, remains in force, as does the need for redistribution itself. To sum up, the decrease in, and the eventual abolition of paternalism and paternalistic need imputation is a matter of principle, whereas the forms and modes of achieving this are matters of trial and error.

There are loopholes in every model, and the present one is no exception. All models are duly modified in their implementation, if they are ever implemented. The idea of the Great Republic is, as I have emphasized at the beginning, utopian. It is one utopia among many which may serve as regulative and constitutive ideas for the actualization of societies under the evidence of the golden rule of justice. The utopian character of this utopia is however relativized precisely because there have been social movements which have, time and again, raised it as a realistic (achievable) goal.

Let me, finally, turn to some general theoretical implications of the model of the Great Republic. The Great Republic is conceived as a self-governed society. But this does not capture the specificity of the model. All radically democratic socialist models make a plea for self-government. Thus I only address the unique features distinguishing this particular utopia from other utopias.

The utopia under discussion does not imply the disappearance of power relations. It evokes the long-standing idea of the division of powers with certain decisive modifications. The division of power is the division of sovereignty, making it possible for everyone to wield some political power in person. Economic and social power is collective, thus everyone wields economic and social power in person as well. All persons have equal rights and possibilities to be the participants of two powers (the political bodies of direct democracy, and the self-managing bodies of society). Further, they have equal rights and equal possibilities as persons to elect their representatives. A division of power of this kind secures the proper checks and balances needed for the reproduction of symmetric reciprocity (relations which exclude domination).

The model maintains the division between civil society and the state in a way adequate to the division of powers. Further, it maintains the division between the 'social' and 'political' domain. However, the two divisions do not overlap.

The social sphere is the sphere of self-management. Persons as members of self-managing institutions do not address political, but rather socio-economic matters. They set the rules for their operations. What they decide in common is the operation of such particular institutions. Self-managing bodies are concerned with purposive rational decisions on the one hand, and with engendering value standards to guide purposive rational decisions on the other hand. The way of life of the collectivity is also set by the collectivity within whose framework the individual way of life of members is determined to a varying degree depending on the character of the collectivity and on the rules established by the members.

Bodies of 'direct democracy' do not belong to the social sphere, but to the political sphere proper. However, they do belong both to civil society and the state. In their sovereign capacity they are the state (although not the whole state). In their capacity as debating and acting agents they belong to civil society. If the state is to be 'the sum total of its citizens', at least one power has to be conceived which embodies the dialectical unity of state and civil society.

The representative (elected) bodies belong to the 'political' sphere – they are the state in contradistinction to society.

The model of the Great Republic is thus the combination of society and community. It is society proper, for at least three reasons. Firstly, although the person has three statuses, the primary status of the person is one qua individual person endowed with inalienable rights. Secondly, individuals qua persons do elect their representatives and, needless to say, the system of representation is a hallmark of society. Thirdly, commodity production and thus the market, remain in force.

Individual persons (as well as collectives) express their wants (although not all their wants) by buying certain satisfiers and not buying others. However, the model embraces the community proper as well, and again for three reasons. Firstly, the public domain is the domain of the community of argumentation. It is a pure community of argumentation, for persons are members of this community via their participation in its discourses, and in no other way. Secondly, the social sphere, as the sphere of self-management, consists of communities. Thirdly, political bodies of direct democracy are, again, communities. Both are not only communities of argumentation, but also communities of social and political action respectively. Communities of self-management can be very loose as well as tightly-knit within one and the same realization of the model. Communities of direct democracy can also be loose and tightly-knit. However, it is safe to assume that in one and the same realization of the model they are either more or less loose, or more or less tightly-knit.

The model, as we have seen, implies the subordination of instrumental action stemming from the functional division of labour to practical reason. It follows from this that practical (value) considerations can overrule instrumental or functional exigencies. One can object to this with the well-founded scepticism that market relations impose constraints upon the (productive) social bodies, forcing them to give priority to functionalist and instrumental considerations. This might, and again might not be the case. Taking too much for granted restricts the social imagination to a degree to which it should not be restricted. It is by no means absurd to presume that collectivities can experiment with the implementation of alternative technologies to secure the primacy of practical reason and ensure efficiency simultaneously. Nor is it at all absurd to presume that collectivities might choose to achieve less profit in order to make life meaningful. If one pattern remains the same (even if with crucial modifications), namely the market, but all other patterns are replaced, change in social exigencies and human attitudes cannot in principle be excluded. However far we may stretch our imagination though, one factor remains constant; the utopia of the Great Republic does not reject instrumental and functionalist considerations.

Yet, one objection cannot be neglected: the utopia of the Great Republic is demanding, both culturally and ethnically, although it is less demanding than alternative utopias of self-governed societies which reject representation on the one hand, efficiency on the other hand, and which advocate the total autonomy of both individual and society.

Although the utopia allocates primary rights to persons qua persons and it does not make participation (in social and political bodies) obligatory, the model can only work if the great majority of the populace is actively willing to participate. It is presupposed as a matter of course that if people were given the option of deciding their own fate, the overwhelming majority would be ready to do so emphatically and continuously. Continuity here, is a crucial factor. In turbulent times when a general change depends on participation, people are normally ready to participate. However, in this case, participation is almost always a 'short-term' phenomenon. It has already been mentioned that in social bodies where the interests of members are direct and permanent, exhaustion does not set in to the same extent as it does in political bodies. However, if exhaustion were to set in on the political level, the model could not possibly work either. Thus the model demands the perpetuation of motivation for participation. This motivation cannot be pragmatic where interest is rapidly exhausted; it must be practical. Practical motivation is invested in the practical: it is an ethical motivation. Briefly, the model works if one simultaneously presupposes the emergence of a strong public virtue, a citizen's virtue. Only on such a condition can willingness for active participation be both enthusiastic and continuous.

However, the model does not presuppose only the willingness of the majority of citizens to actively participate, but also their ability to participate.

It is easy to dismiss this problem on the grounds that every person is equally born with good sense, that nothing is more equally distributed than common sense – all this, and other such statements are only partially relevant to the problem under discussion. In part they are relevant for they permit the drawing of the conclusion that amidst familiar circumstances everyone can equally make use of his or her good sense. The problem still remains whether everyone can become familiar with the issues on which one has to have an opinion or pass judgement as a participating member of the community. And, more importantly, the problem still remains whether someone is able to formulate his or her opinion according to the intrinsic rules of practical discourse.

If not all citizens are familiar with the problems and issues on which they give an opinion or pass judgement, if not all of them are well-versed in the rules of practical discourse, discourse is going to degenerate in no time into a kind of 'power-speak'. And this is far more so in the political than in the social sphere. It is precisely for this reason that the model of the Great Republic is demanding.

First and foremost, all knowledge, every problem, concern, or question of political relevance must be made public. Kant's stricture applies completely to the Great Republic: keeping knowledge, information and options of political relevance confidential constitutes an infringement of the fundamental norm of a republic like this. Those keeping such information confidential have to face social sanctions. Secondly, every citizen has to be educated in practical discourse. Training in both theoretical and practical discourse must be the focal concern of all educational institutions, the primary ones included. Thirdly, access to education (and self-education) must be permanent on both a formal and an *ad hoc* basis. The social conditions for such permanent facility for education (and self-education) must be ensured. This does not mean that everyone has to go to school or university or even attend classes during the whole of one's lifetime; it means only that everyone has the right to and the possibiity of entering into any kind of educational process whenever s/he wants to.

The ethnically and culturally demanding aspects of the Great Republic are different in kind. Civic virtue is *expected* from each and every citizen. The conditions for education and self-education are provided for every citizen. To make use of them is a civil right, but not an obligation.

The Great Republic is not conceived as the utopia of 'the just society', but the patterns established by the model are recommendations for a just procedure. The main institutions of the Great Republic are prefigured so that they serve this purpose, and serve it well. The model includes, rather than excludes, socio-political conflicts and contestations. All norms and rules, all laws of the Republic can be contested as 'unjust'. But the conflicts and contestations are to be carried out via discourse or by negotiation. No conflict or contestation can be solved by force. This is so because the model is forged so as to secure the reproduction of relations of symmetric reciprocity and to block the re-emergence of social domination. Checks and balances against the socially enhanced relations of super- and subordination are built into the model.

But the model remains silent about relations of super- and subordination other than strictly social and political ones. In my view, this is correct. In a pluralistic cultural universe no socio-political utopia can undertake the task of designing an image of the good life, and should not even make an attempt to that effect. Social models need to say something about the citizen's way of life, but nothing, or very little about the way of life of good persons. The self-restriction of the model of the Great Republic, if seen from this standpoint, turns out to be more of a credit than a debit.

9

Class, Modernity, Democracy

Ferenc Fehér and Agnes Heller[1]

I METHODOLOGICAL PREMISES

1.1

Two terms of the tripartite title of this essay need a word of explanation. By 'modernity', we mean the period (and the region) in which capitalism, industrialization and democracy appear simultaneously, reacting to, reinforcing, complementing and checking each other. We use the word 'democracy' in a value-free way, in other words, not counterposed to liberalism as we are otherwise wont to do. It involves simply the following conceptual constituents: publicly (constitutionally) recognized pluralism, formally free citizenry, the trend towards an increasing political equality.

1.1.1

We state simply, without historical analyses of any kind, the fact of the more or less simultaneous emergence, later symbiosis, of democracy, capitalist organization of socio-economic life and industrialization. We do not call this symbiosis either 'historically necessary' or 'historically contingent'. Both descriptions would mean setting diverse factors into the homogenizing framework of a philosophy of history which we deliberately intend to avoid. We take them as facts or 'raw material' of our interpretation, and not as embodiments of so-called universal laws.

[1] Originally published in English in *Theory and Society* (Amsterdam) 12 (1983), in French as 'Classe, démocratie, modernité' in *Les Temps Modernes* (Paris) 40th Year, November 1983, in Italian as 'Classe, modernità, democrazia', *Critica Sociologica* (Roma), January–March 1983.

Our analysis will follow in the footsteps of at least one version of a tradition which can be legitimately called 'historical materialism', namely the contrasting of modernity with earlier (or precapitalist) periods. From the above it follows as well that we explicitly reject the customary historical materialist conception according to which one of these factors (the capitalist market organization of the allegedly eternal separate economic sphere) would determine the other two – 'in the last instance'. Such a 'determination in the last instance' contains, firstly, tacitly or overtly, an empty, overgeneralized statement regarding the whole history. Secondly, it replaces a rational understanding of a situation in which industrial capitalist interests, very often in conflict with express majority will, prevail in political decisions, by an alleged 'determination' which is a substitute for 'necessity'; a historical mythology.

1.1.2

In our view, modernity is a dynamic (in other words, unstable) co-existence of these different trends, in proportions varying from one society to the other, rarely in harmony, rather in more or less constant collision. Any radical position which embarks on explaining the vast period called modernity, has to account for all three factors and their interrelations. A monocausal explanation of any kind is either a self-delusion or an ideology.

1.2

Already our title points to the fact that we do not renounce the use of the category of class, a gesture which is so trendy nowadays. On the other hand, we certainly use it with substantial modification as compared to the thinker, Marx, whose name the category is mostly bound up with. Therefore it is appropriate here, at the start, to give a definition of our own.

1.2.1

Social classes are human social ensembles which essentially and consciously contribute to social change via purposeful action, in keeping with their own interests and/or needs.

1.2.2

Further, the dichotomous character of class relationship is crucial for us. The term in this specification stems obviously from the distinguished Polish sociologist, Ossowski. In the wake of Ossowski, we mean by dichotomous social relations mutually constitutive pairs of interconnected social entities, none of which can exist (or for that matter, come about) without the other. They are antagonistic relationships presupposing, in the very relation and in the social 'space' around them, inequality, hierarchy and subordination.

1.2.3

In contradistinction to Marx, and in harmony with Max Weber, we are going to speak of political and socio-economic classes as separate entities. Both clusters are dichotomous relationships (without this characteristic feature, namely this bipolar antagonistic structure, we do not acknowledge the existence of a class relationship at all), but the constitutive dichotomy lies elsewhere in each case. With regard to the political class, the economic roots of each partner can be different (we shall return to this later), this economic situation might or might not have a bearing on their political status (no true generalized statement can be made regarding this), but their political interrelationship affects both of them and it is precisely the latter that constitutes them as an antagonistic pair, a dichotomous entity. And obversely, in case of the only pure socio-economic classes, the modern bourgeoisie and the proletariat, the political aspects of their existence is not constitutive of their being an economically antagonist pair. In every consistently liberal–democratic country, politically and formally both of them are equally free. What constitutes their existence as (socio-economic) classes is the relation of economic dependence or exploitation, an economically dichotomous relationship.

1.2.4

In the spirit of our definition, we exclude from the cluster of class relationships those social ensembles which are dependent but the members of which behave, individually and collectively, as mere objects. Obviously, what we have in mind is the dichotomous ensemble of slave and slaveholder. (This immediately shows that while for us all class relationships must perforce be dichotomous, we do not recognize all dichotomous relationships as class relations.) This statement needs further corroboration, the more so as slavery can emerge even in modernity (consider the southern states of the United States which were regarded by Marx as capitalistic even if not industrialized).[2] Further, by this statement we clearly distinguish relations of personal dependence, which are not class-like in character, from relations of subordination and hierarchy without personal dependence which mostly are. (Needless to say, relations of subordination and hierarchy can be those of personal dependence as well but under the heading 'class' we are only speaking of the kind which is not.) For us, the concept of class, this arch-evil of leftist discourse, has a decidedly positive connotation as well: where there is class, there is liberty, at least a certain measure of it. It is paradoxical that we have to remind others, after decades of wilful opposition to reification, of the emancipatory aspect of reification as expressed in class existence. It is human relations which appear in class existence as relations of things, whereas the non-class relations of personal dependence are in fact relation of things (mere objects). This is so for a very simple reason. Persons living in a rigid world of seemingly unalterable personal dependence regard themselves (if they achieve the level of self-reflexion at all) as things, in that they accept their existence as parts of a process which has no alternative. But a process without alternative is nature. Anyone who does not distinguish himself/herself from nature, is not only unfree but is also unaware of the existence of freedom, in this sense a thing. The maximum that a network of personal dependence can give birth to is, at peaks of unendurability, the quest for becoming different which is the well-known basic pattern of all slave mutinies. However, sublime moments like those do not generate dichotomous class cohesion.

1.3

The incurable ill of Marx's generalized statement regarding history as class history in a famous passage of *The Communist Manifesto*[3] is that he confuses, or rather he merges, three disparate elements. One is con-

---

[2] Karl Marx, *Capital*, edited by F. Engels, Vol. 1. New York: International Publishers, 1970, p. 759.
[3] Karl Marx and Friedrich Engels, *The Communist Manifesto*, Berlin: Werke, 1964, Vol. 4, p. 462.

stituted by dichotomous social relations the antagonistic partners of which are sometimes political, sometimes socio-economic classes undistinguished from one another. The second is constituted by dichotomous social relations which, because of the mere object-like behaviour of the persons whose aggregate adds up to one of the constituents of the dichotomous pair cannot be termed class in the same manner as another antagonistic ensemble in which all members of both clusters behave like subjects. The third element of the Marxian use of the term consists of genuinely conflictual, but not dichotomous social relations (the classic case being that of guildmaster and journeyman).

1.4

Of course, all changes of definitions or interpretations of a category mean shift in values; ours is no exception. There is one major point which we retain in common with Marx in our definition of class: the emphasis on the conflictual character of history. This emphasis has a positive yield: the commitment to radical action. This is why our conception of class is functional, not structural.

1.4.1

The main shift in value resulting in our definition originates from our distinction of social position (behaviour) from social action. All our sympathy lies with those who are oppressed and who, therefore, are often reduced to the level of objects, but we expect relevant change only from those who purposefully act upon history. Moreover, we even regard as dangerous the failure to distinguish those shaping and those only suffering history. The latter usually project their frustration in eruptions of hatred creating power vacuums but not emancipation.

1.5

We maintain just the contrary to what G. Cohen stated regarding classes, namely that classes are, if anything, structural.[4] We regard them as non-structural, which has the following meaning. Firstly,

---

[4] G. A. Cohen, *Karl Marx's Theory of History: A Defence*, Oxford: Clarendon Press, 1978.

classes can, and nearly always should, be conceived of in terms of E. P. Thompson's description of the English working class: as 'classes in the making'.[5] But if classes are permanently 'in the making', they are never the fixed, circumscribed, static elements any meaningful structural analysis should operate with. It is rather the dynamic trend, not the blueprint, of the social edifice we can decipher from classes and their conflicts. Secondly, and in keeping with our definition, there is no such historical period, either in modernity or prior to it, when the totality called society could be reasonably exhausted, or accounted for, by the entities called 'class'. Of course, a theoretical undertaking like this can be performed. The work of Poulantzas is the material proof of the possibility of constructing a social totality by elements uniformly called classes,[6] but we deny the meaningful character of an undertaking like this. In it, all fundamental differences between social ensembles simply evaporate. Finally, the explanatory value of the concept of class is crucial but not universal (all-embracing) as required by any consistent structuralist conception. This statement has a double meaning. First, there is no universal class. None of the particularistic class entities contains the dynamis, the actualization of which would lead to the abolition of all classes (or conflictual ensembles). We consider the well-known Marxian–Lukácsian predilection for such a class a myth. Secondly, there is no such social ensemble which could serve as the universal basis of the interpretation of all social phenomena. Both the exclusive approach to the fundamental problems of a society prior to modernity from a class position, and the similarly exclusive approach to many cultural problems pre-eminently social in character in any society, show the futility and sterility of the universalistic structuralist method.

II POLITICAL CLASS

2.1

What are the characteristic features of political class as distinct from the socio-economic one? Firstly, the dichotomy constitutive of that

---

[5] E. Thompson, *The Making of the English Working Class*, Harmondsworth: Penguin, 1980, pp. 8–10.

[6] Nicos Poulantzas, *State, Power, Socialism*, transl. by Patrick Camiller, London: New Left Books, 1978 and *Classes in Contemporary Capitalism*, transl. by D. Fernbach, London: New Left Books, 1975.

class relation implies hierarchy and subordination but, as has been mentioned earlier, not necessarily a type which is economic in nature. In the so-called pre-capitalist era it was not at all excluded that the politically dominant partner in a dichotomous relationship was the economically inferior. If the Roman patrician did not happen to be a big slaveholder, he was, as a rule, less rich than certain urban elements of the *plebs*, and similar financial power proportions can be observed between the top of the medieval city *Bürgertum* and several layers of the landed gentry. There is no general explanation of this contradiction except perhaps one: the economic prevalence and the political dependence of the city as against the countryside in a pre-industrial period. Further, and irrespective of the relative financial strength of the constituents, the sources of income are usually different here which makes coupling political prerogatives with economic subjection difficult, if not impossible. Thirdly, the political character of the political class had a very direct and unambiguous meaning: the dominating partner of the relation exercised its power directly, without delegating it, and with the clear intention (not always with the net result) of depriving the other of all facilities and avenues of political life. This statement is adequate to the self-characterization of the period in question. It is in these terms that Aristotle described the political aspiration of the *demos*, and the Roman historians portrayed the duel of patricians and plebeians.

2.2

If later the theorists of the modern age declared the whole period of political classes an era of unfreedom, it was more than modernization, or the high and mighty attitude of the Enlightenment to 'prehistory'. This was a true statement despite the fact that we uphold our former assertion: where there is class, there is (a certain measure of) freedom. The exact meaning of unfreedom in the era of political classes is the following:

2.2.1

That the politically dominant partner exercises its power directly, instead of delegating it, had one major consequence, restricting the general freedom. The direct exercise of power is not equivalent to the public sphere's being the exclusive property of one political class. Such a state of affairs is characteristic of oriental despotism alone, and, in terms of our definition, it even contains a self-contradiction: oriental despotism excludes political class. Just the contrary, in a world where there were political classes, the politically inferior partner had almost always been publicly dissatisfied with its inferior position. This public dissatisfaction even created a new public sphere. But, and herein lies the unfree character of the era of the political class, the direct exercise of power is certainly equivalent to the other statement that the politically dominant partner was the only recognized and exclusive source of all rights. This is precisely what is meant by Weber when he mentioned the 'illegitimate power' of the medieval cities. Of course, overgeneralized statements are dangerous here as well, and for instance, in Renaissance city-states the source of legitimation and the whole (male) populace, directly (but in fact not equally) exercising political power was almost coextensive. But *civis Romanus* was not identical with the *citoyen* or citizen. The new body politic as created in the United States or in the French Revolution presented a breakthrough precisely by the shift of authority and legitimation to Everyman.

2.2.2

The last political classes were the workers and the women. The political class of the workers presents an extraordinary case due to the early egoistic aspiration of the bourgeoisie to couple, perhaps for the first time in history, absolute economic predominance with declaring itself the sole source of legitimation. In result of this tendency, the proletariat was for a period simultaneously a political and a socioeconomic class. This was observable not only in the very restricted electoral proportion of the workers, a general feature of early bourgeois Europe, but also in the harsh legislation against the right to self-organization of the working class by a legislative power, the electoral basis of which was more or less coextensive with the class of the bourgeoisie (plus the ennobled bourgeois and the bourgeoisified nobles). This situation had had a unique yield: the short-lived but nearly unanimous gaining of ground by Marxism (and other radical doctrines such as anarchism, anarcho-syndicalism and the like) in all countries in which the workers formed a political class simultaneously with their gradual transition into a socio-economic one. (Which provides an explanation for why the workers remained so unideological in an otherwise stormy class history in the United States: they started immediately at the stage of the socio-economic class.) Women

represented a political class to the extent that they had become
conscious of their 'gender cohesion' (identity consciousness being
central to our conception of class formation) and had remained a class
everywhere up until their formal equality in every respect was not
recognized. (Which is obviously not identical with the end of the
'women's question'.) The abolition of the political class existence of the
workers did not only mean that they had been transformed into a
socio-economic class (together with their partner in dichotomy, the
bourgeoisie), but also that they had completed the system of parliamentary democracy by the class struggle for political (not for 'human')
emancipation.

2.3

What put an end to the history of political classes?

2.3.1

The first factor is well-known to all students of Weber: he, correctly,
bound up the emergence of socio-economic and the demise of political, classes with the universalization of market relations.[7] At this
point, Marx's impact on Weber becomes clearly visible. The socio-
economic class, a crucial entity, the aggregate of individuals whose
behaviour is primarily motivated by economic factors (as distinct from,
and counterposed to, others) is the unique and inimitable product of a
moment in world history: of capitalism. In order to avoid misunder-
standings, the question on the agenda is not whether people earlier
were 'less or more egoistic' but rather whether they had consciously
separated the economic from the non-economic in their system of
activities, in order to subject all latter to the former – and these are not
identical questions. It will suffice to point to Soviet industrialization,
undeniably an event of modernity which is economic in character, and
in which the motivation to act was, both for dominating and dominated,
extra-economic. Therefore it is appropriate to term the latter a society
of which the existence of socio-economic classes is no longer characteristic.

---

[7] Max Weber, *Economy and Society, An Outline of Interpretative Sociology*, ed. by
Guenther Roth and Claus Wittich, New York: Bedminster Press, 1968, Vol. I, pp. 302–
305, Vol. II, pp. 927–932.

2.3.2

The second factor was the universalization of democracy as a project. Emphasis is added to the last word: the actual process in which the full system of formal rights has become completed, was very slow even in the small number of countries where it has in fact been completed. But it is a crucial difference whether or not the project of democracy is universalistic in nature. As the rule of the *demos* excluded, even as a project, the slave, the barbarian and the woman, Athens' celebrated democracy could not produce socio-economic classes. For in our firm view, it is not only the development of capitalist economic organization plus industrialization that creates democracy (as its own 'super-structure'): the interrelationship works the other way round as well. The existence of socio-economic classes is just as much a precondition, as it is a result of industrial development, the capitalization of the world, and democracy as a universalistic project. Only the formally free individuals (whose aggregate is the socio-economic class) are capable of self-consciously positing their system of needs as infinite and insatiable and of establishing a conscious hierarchy of life activities under the hegemony of the economic ones. Both activities, in their entirety the life system of faustian man, are absolute preconditions of profit-oriented manufacturing industry, both can be conceived of, at least as a completed system, only as a result of the universalizing project of democracy. All monocausal conceptions of historical materialism which simply deduce formal democracy from a mysteri-ously self-moving and automatically increasing system of capitalist and industrialist activities, miss this basic point.

III SOCIO-ECONOMIC CLASSES

3.1

3.1.1

Socio-economic classes are dichotomous ensembles in which one constituent cannot by definition exist without the other, the reci-procally interdependent existence of which is based on an economic system of domination (of one over the other, and several others not belonging to the dichotomous ensemble). It is a system which does not necessarily imply political discrimination of the dominant partner or any other group of the population, even if it might imply discrimination of this type. The existence of the dichotomous ensemble must be central to the subsistence and self-reproduction of the given society.

3.1.2

We believe our definition of class (which is, as becomes visible at this point, shaped after the model of socio-economic classes) to be more precise than the customary ones which operate with ownership title, income brackets and the place occupied in the social division of labour, even if we do not regard these secondary characteristic features to be entirely irrelevant. The first problem with the customary definitions is a double one. On the one hand, any of their constituents mentioned above might play a certain role in the emergence of the dichotomous relationship which has been defined functionally as the agent of social change: alone, in combination with several factors, mentioned or not here. On the other hand, it is the constituents of the customary definitions that are comprehensible through social conflict and not the other way round. (This is why our definition dealt with function alone and disregarded genesis). The second problem with the customary definitions is that they totally neglect that constitutive interdependence which Ossowski aptly termed 'dichotomous'.[8] In this way, socially important strata (for instance, the peasantry), which in a world no longer containing political classes, simply cannot have a dichotomous counterpart, will be included in the functionally dramatically different class relationship. (A similar problem is presented by the sterile debates about the 'middle classes'.) Further, if the dichotomy is not interpreted as expressive of economic domination and contributing, consciously or unconsciously, to social change which is central to our definition, then truly dichotomous ensembles, but such as cannot possibly be called classes (for instance, debtor and creditor), will be included in the network of class relationship by virtue of their being economic and dichotomous in character. The ownership title is undeniably an integral part of class relation but without the key concept of dichotomy based on economic domination, all attempts at its interpretation will be wasted in the artificial mental exercises as to whether the title is 'real' or simply a legal window-dressing. As to income

---

[8] Stanislaw Ossowski, *Class Structure in the Social Consciousness*, transl. by Sheila Patterson, Chapter V, New York: Free Press of Glencoe, 1963.

brackets, it was Ossowski again who pointed out in his criticism of Marx how unclear the use of this category is with regard to class distinction. For instance, when positing land, labour and capital equally as proprietors, Marx analyses the sources of income; when contrasting labour to capital, he speaks of a relationship of exploitation in which income (its source and its amount) plays only a secondary role. Except at peak and at nadir, income brackets do not tell us much about a position occupied in a system of economic domination, and in themselves, they do not reveal anything about class affiliation. The place occupied in the social division of labour (if it is, as usual, narrowly understood as a place in social production) provides better yields for a theory of stratification than for a theory of classes. While the former is certainly crucial, it is, equally certainly, dependent on a class theory. It is always the dichotomous system of economic domination, its particular character, elasticity or rigidity, its inner dynamics and the like which determine the given system of stratification. And as to theories of social mobility, we fully agree with Schumpeter's ingenious remark: for anyone who gets on the bus at a given moment (which may or may not be important), the socially relevant fact is that the buses are constantly crowded, in other words, that the social roles are established and fixed.

3.1.3

However, our insistence on the definition of classes as fundamental and dichotomous ensembles expressive of economic domination is a terminological distinction which only achieves relevance if it spells out something essential of society. In our view the definition communicates the following basic knowledge:

3.1.3.1. In its pure form, as a dynamic and tendentially growing dichotomous entity, this ensemble is expressive of an industrial society. (The obverse of the statement is not necessarily true: not all industrial societies are based on a dichotomous ensemble which can legitimately be called class.) This is so because it is only industry that ensures a dynamic and expanding form of economic domination.

3.1.3.2. Even if this dichotomous ensemble can be coupled with political discriminations (e.g. S. Africa), this is not only 'not necessarily so'; even advocates of economic domination and hierarchy regard such discrimination as an anomaly. The 'normal form' of the functioning of the dichotomous ensemble which we term class is the liberal–democratic version.

3.1.3.3. The liberal–democratic character of domination does not eliminate the crucial social fact that in the society a particular economic domination, namely the capitalist, prevails with its necessary political results, with political and non-political social hierarchy and subordination. This fundamental fact is also inherent in the definition.

Therefore it is the dichotomous character of the socio-economic class and it alone which unifies in its being all three elements of modernity (industrialization, democracy and capitalism), which upholds and reproduces them as an ensemble, and which, to a certain extent irrespective of its extension and quantitative proportion, guarantees the self-reproduction of modern (industrial, liberal and capitalist) society. This makes the definition substantial and legitimizes the use of the category of class with certain important methodological reservations. But being a many-factor definition, it yields several alternatives of social action on both poles.

3.2

What characterizes the dichotomous ensemble of bourgeois and proletarian? (Needless to say, within the ensemble, our attention will be focused on the second.)

3.2.1

Both are open classes. To some extent, openness characterizes political classes as well, as against the caste, the slave's existence, tribal life, patriarchal order and the like. But in the case of socio-economic classes, openness has very definite additional nuances.

3.2.1.1. Class affiliation in modernity is not an 'inborn' situation. Undoubtedly, being born a worker's son or daughter means having less chance to become a bourgeois, or an intellectual, than being born a bourgeois's son; being born a bourgeois's son means more chances to remain in the economically (and tacitly politically) privileged class. But it is indeed a chance as far as the individual is concerned, and here

Schumpeter's simile[9] can, and should, be reversed. The buses always remain crowded in a particular society, but for the individual it is probably the particular bus he or she gets on that counts (its being more or less crowded, its direction and the like), not the fact that the buses are crowded in general. And the abstract chance to get on a better bus is in principle constantly present, and, equally in principle, for everyone.

3.2.1.2. The dichotomous ensemble of social classes both receives and emanates life styles external to them from, and into, the 'outer space' of society. It is generally the first dynamic that is stressed: the imitation of the nobility by *le bourgeois gentilhomme*, the 'bourgeoisification' of the working class. Nevertheless, the second dynamic is at work as well. To mention only one but crucial example, unionization has introduced forms of social behaviour in the upper strata of the so-called 'middle classes' which would have been unimaginable in the nineteenth century. When the leading, well-paid and highly positioned public servants strike against a conservative government which does not respect their material interests, they behave in keeping with emanated working-class habits and values. This is another indicator of the openness of classes.

3.2.1.3. There is free social space around both partners of the dichotomous socio-economic classes. In the socially 'closed' world (in tribes, castes, estates), transcending the boundaries of the world one was born into could only mean two things (except suicide, social limbo). It either meant a self-transfer to a closed world of another type (for instance when a nobleman or noblewoman joined the Church) or it was identical with the submersion into the cosmos of non-articulation, of thingified existence (when, for instance, a poor free man, being indebted, became a slave). This was a situation drastically different to that in modernity in which the voluntary farewell to both of the ways of life in the dichotomous ensemble (in other words, living as a freelance intellectual, a self-sustaining peasant, an artisan or simply as a private person on 'one's own wits') is a perfectly legitimate, socially recognized situation.

3.2.2

Therefore it is a utopian dream (explicitly manifest in practically all socialist doctrines of the nineteenth century except that of Rosa

---

[9] Quoted in Ralf Dahrendorf, *Class and Class Conflict in Industrial Society*, transl., revised and expanded by the author, Stanford, California: Stanford University Press, 1959, p. 220.

Luxemburg) to expect that modern society as a whole can be reduced to the bipolarity of two classes alone. It is utopian not in the sense of an Ought which is socially productive, but in the sense of an impossibility and an unfeasibility which is socially counter-productive. It is also a fairly negative utopia. The dream remains perforce a dream because many tasks of social reproduction can only be executed outside the dichotomous ensemble of the two socio-economic classes. It is negative as well because it would eliminate the free social space around the two classes rendering thereby two open classes into two closed ones.

3.2.3

Both entities are, to use Thompson's category again, 'classes in the making'. Even though both partners of the dichotomous relation are what Gouldner and others call, to some extent in every period of their development, 'flawed' classes,[10] there is a serious historical difference. In its early era of emergence, the English working class (which Marx used as the ideal type for generalization and which Thompson studied empirically), was the paragon of a 'flawed' class, a conglomerate of the most heterogeneous elements, as far as social provenance, life styles, permanence of occupation and social aspirations were concerned. In a later period in which capitalism and industrialism started to diverge (for instance, in Britain, there was a capitalized but non-industrialized nobility and an economically dominant bourgeois–industrial class), the dominant bourgeoisie became 'flawed'. This means, first of all, that it emanated its own life style to others (e.g. the 'bourgeoisification' of certain strata of the working class) and received life styles from others (e.g. the imitation of the landed gentry and the hereditary nobility by the bourgeoisie of several countries). But it equally means that the bourgeoisie integrated, either through the channels of split ownership or those of split social control, certain strata (managers, technocrats and the like) into which were originally and functionally not bourgeois. Meanwhile, the 'flawed' character of the working class does not cease to exist. That class which is called 'new working-class', or the phenomenon of the proletariazation of certain groups of intellectuals, demonstrates the ongoing 'flawed' nature of the working class, even if to a much reduced degree as compared with the bourgeoisie.

---

[10] The term appears frequently in A. W. Gouldner, *The Future of Intellectuals and the Rise of the New Class*, London: Macmillan, 1979.

3.2.4

What are the characteristic features of the 'proletariat', or the aggregate of workers, as a socio-economic class?

3.2.4.1. The actual social position of the members of this aggregate is identical irrespective of their being employees of joint-stock companies, private capitalist enterprises or state-owned industries. Here Marx's assertion remains valid: being a wage-earner is a social relation which will not be changed either by increased income or by the shift in the individual or collective person of the owner-proprietor. It will only change if everyone becomes a proprietor both in the sense of enjoying and disposing of social wealth.[11]

3.2.4.2. As a result, there is an 'us–them' relationship on the shop-floor. This dichotomy, without the presence of socialist or radical ideologies of any kind, creates a social division between those belonging and those not belonging to the working class. It also determines what can legitimately be called 'working class culture' (now increasingly the subject-matter of investigations by radical British historians). The 'us–them' contrast is the first and fundamental manifestation of the identity consciousness of the working class.

3.2.4.3. We categorically reject the Marxian–Lukácsian distinction between the empirical and the imputed consciousness of the working class. The elitist–Leninist consequences of this distinction have been discussed to a sufficient degree, so we need not enter into them again. We only add that with this rejection, the distinction between a 'class in itself' and a 'class for itself' is discarded as well. But, of course, the fact that a thesis has socially dangerous consequences is no argument against its truth. Therefore we would like to point out that if there is any relevance in the now voguish theories of the 'rule of the intelligentsia over the working class'[12] their truth is much more poignant before than it is after a political revolution, coup or take-over of power. Imputed

---

[11] Karl Marx, *Lohn, Preis, Profit* (in particular Chapter IV *Werke*), Vol. 16, Berlin: Dietz Verlag, 1963.
[12] Alvin Ward Gouldner, *The Future of Intellectuals and the Rise of the New Class*, a frame of reference, theses, conjectures, arguments, and an historical perspective on the role of intellectuals, and intelligentsia in international class contest of the modern era, London: Macmillan, 1979. Ivan Szelényi-György Konrád, *The Intellectuals on the Road to Class Power*, transl. by Andrew Arato and Richard E. Allen, Brighton: Harvester Press, 1974.

consciousness is nothing but an intellectual project reflecting intellectual aspirations rather than actual working-class options, a project
which is imposed on parties representing working-class strategies. In
our firm view, there is only one working-class consciousness: the
empirically given, however complex the assignment may ocasionally be
to give a fair assessment of it. And this holds true, however much it may
be the duty of socialists under certain circumstances to take a detached
and critical attitude to precisely this empirical consciousness, of
course, without believing that they are entitled to substitute their own,
'more correct one', for it. Class consciousness has two forms: identity
consciousness and aspiration consciousness. Without the first, no
socio-economic class can exist, which is one of the most powerful
arguments against the theory of intellectuals as a class. But the
assertion cannot be simply reversed: not all people who are conscious
of belonging to the same 'cluster' constitute a socio-economic class. All
Catholics are aware of the fact that they belong to such a 'cluster', yet
they do not constitute a socio-economic class. Identity consciousness is
not a simple reflex of the social condition of an ensemble, as well it is a
powerful impetus to seperation (from the 'alien' ones) and to identification (with the similar ones), again irrespective of the existence of
radical ideas in the socio-economic class. Logically speaking, aspiration consciousness can be:

1 zero – which is hardly ever a collective constellation rather a case
   of individual apathy,
2 identification with the given, actual situation of the class which is a
   positive, even though problematical, feeling and not equivalent to
   zero consciousness,
3 mobility aspiration of individual members of the class in order to
   abandon its framework, life styles and conditions without an
   active interest in the unchanged fate of the others, and
4 a collective determination (a majority attitude but hardly ever a
   sum total of individual decisions) to change the collective situation. This latter is the state (and the precondition) of radical
   action.

Aspiration consciousness (instead of imputed consciousness) is not a
simple swap of terminology; first, because its presence or absence does
not create two alternative modes of class existence; second, because,
tortuous as may be to state its exact content, proportions and trends, no
one is entitled to substitute a 'more correct' consciousness for the
actually existing one.

3.2.4.4. Working-class existence in general is characterized by un-satisfying work conditions. The more emphatic the argument for the value of job satisfaction, the more depressing and frustrating the feeling of dissatisfaction with work conditions. Given that in practically all industrially developed societies of modernity, 'protestant ethics', in the Weberian sense of the word, became prevalent irrespective of the religious profession of the populace, this feeling of dissatisfaction runs counter to the most important of inner motivations. What Marx stated about the alienated character of work under capitalist conditions, and on which a whole edifice of *Kulturkritik* has been built, has remained true but proved to be one-sided. Industrial dynamics ought to be changed, patterns of technological development should be modified as well, in order to eliminate the alienation of work and the resulting frustration.

3.2.4.5. Non-identification with the workplace is generally charac-teristic of the socio-economic class of the workers in result of the above and other circumstances. But given that the capitalistically industrial-ized world is wholly 'artificial' in the sense that domicile and workplace are, for the first time in history, entirely separated from one another, the alienation from the workplace transforms the working-class into the homeless *par excellence* of modernity. This creates a life-feeling which has social and political consequences which are destructive for capitalism, to be analysed later. Unionization might have eased, but it has not fundamentally changed, the authoritarian character of factory management.

3.2.4.6. The working-class is evicted from the relationship of owner-ship, if the control of social wealth means decision-making.

3.2.4.7. It was Ossowski again who pointed out a fundamental character trait of working-class existence in contrast with the bour-geoisie. He remarked that this bipolar relation is not identical simply with the conflict of property versus non-property. Often working-class people claim to be the proprietors of their labour power (they contend that their collective description as man*power* is more than a figure of speech) as against the proprietors of the conditions of work (produc-tion). On this widespread feeling are built a mystified social economy and a revolutionary natural law. In Marx, it is the labour power alone that will remain of the edifice of the old world to serve as raw material for the construction of the new, in Proudhon, all property which is not identical with the worker's ownership of his or her own labour power is 'theft', the former alone is 'natural' property.[13] It is a 'natural claim' (precisely in the sense of natural law) that all relationships *not* built on the only natural property, on labour power, should be declared 'inauthentic' and 'illegitimate'. This attitude had been repeatedly exposed to scholarly criticism but it has remained ineradicable from the actual life-feeling of the workers, once again irrespective of the level of political radicalism observable in the socio-economic class of the workers.

3.3

What kind of political strategies can be built on this existence of the aggregate of workers as a socio-economic class?

3.3.1

The point of departure of the analysis is that the emergence of democracy, the abolition of political classes, separates industrial from political conflict. Our view clearly deviates from Dahrendorf's position, which ascribes this separation to the rise of capitalism.[14] But it is enough to point to countries like Argentina or several Asian dictatorships without unionized workforces but certainly with a capitalist organization of economic life, in which industrial conflicts have remained pre-eminently political in character precisely because of the absence of democratic institutions, to see that Dahrendorf has inadmissibly homogenized two factors. It is the very fact that the United States started at a point where the political class of workers did not exist in it at all, which accounts for the Bolshevik option remaining constantly marginal in its history.

3.3.2

The statement of separation of industrial and political conflicts should not be mistaken for two further statements. Firstly, it does not imply that industrial conflicts are devoid of political aspects, even less,

---

[13] Pierre Joseph Proudhon, *What Is Property?* An Enquiry into the Principle of Right and of Government, transl. by B.R. Tucker, New York: H. Fertig, 1960.
[14] Ralf Dahrendorf, *Class and Class Conflict in Industrial Society*, translated, revised and expanded by the author, Stanford, California: Stanford University Press, 1959.

secondly, that in a parliamentary democracy social conflicts, originally at least partly economic in nature, cannot develop into a situation which is to all practical purposes revolutionary. It will suffice to think of May 1968 in France to see that just the contrary holds true.

3.3.3

Our statement has a double meaning. Firstly, the famous 'hydra of revolution', this phantom of the nineteenth century, is not lurking in each strike, at least in non-totalitarian systems, and secondly, in a democracy (in other words – in a state of affairs where political classes no longer exist) there is no Jacobin–Bolshevik solution to the problems of the socio-economic class of workers, however pressing these problems might be, however tempting this solution might look.

3.3.3.1. A political revolution (and in a popular view, Jacobin–Bolshevik action is identical with political revolution *sui generis*) can only emancipate the political classes and transform them into socio-economic ones, a task already completed in a democracy.

3.3.3.2. A political (Jacobin–Bolshevik) revolution which has the publicly professed goal of elevating the socio-economic class of workers into the position of a ruling class, even if for an allegedly limited duration of a historical transition, either sets an impossible task for itself or else it simply makes false promises. Elevating the working class qua working class into the position of the ruling class means the symbiosis of incompatibles. On the one hand, it implies the generalization of the particular form of aspiration consciousness which aims at the identification with the actually given working-class existence (a situation in which every, or almost every, worker would allegedly remain worker), on the other hand, the generalization of the particular form of aspiration consciousness which aims at the transcendence of the working-class existence (a situation in which every, or almost every, worker would allegedly intend not to remain worker any longer). This is clearly impossible, and the yield is more than a logical contradiction. The social result is the oppressive rule of an omnipotent apparatus over myriads of state wage-earners, of course in the name of those same wage-earners. Unfortunately, Marx's own prophesy, formed with such pathos, that the workers can only lose their chains, is not true. New, even more powerful ones can be forged for them, this time ironically in the name of their own emancipation.

3.3.4

In the arena of genuine political struggles, there are then the following alternative political options built on the characteristic features of the existence of the socio-economic class of workers.

3.3.4.1. Not only logically, but also actually, the first option is precisely the one the relevance of which we have rejected above: the Jacobin–Bolshevik programme. (It is first in the list in the sense of its international role and relative strength.) After 60 years of political experience with the outcome of the project, one can now be legitimately suspicious whether it was not an outright self-delusion from the start, and not just simply the missing of a historical bus, that Lenin waited so vehemently and so much in vain for a German (French, etc.) revolution, similar in type to October. Jacobinism certainly was a Western blueprint of social regulation. Moreover, Western industrial societies, even after having reached the level of the abolition of political classes, can, and for a long time to come will, generate a Jacobin–Bolshevik opposition, eventually even a powerful one. However, they cannot tolerate a Bolshevik revolution, at least as long as the majority of social actors have retained their internal freedom of action. Viewed from this standpoint, it is no wonder that the countries in which the Bolshevik–Jacobin project had genuine success in the name of the working-class were precisely the ones which were industrially under-developed, and the project took root even in them in regions which were mostly rural in character and, most importantly, unfamiliar with democracy. The working-class, after having gone through the phase of emancipation into a socio-economic class, commits several egoistic mistakes (such as supporting ultra-nationalistic movements which corrupt the workers with the benefits of chauvinistic escapades) but never the masochistic one of willingly abandoning the results of its social emancipation and willingly transforming itself into a dependent mass of state wage-earners. A change of this kind can only be the outcome of a coup or an overwhelming external force. Historical differences between the countries might play a significant role regarding the relative weight of a Jacobin–Bolshevik opposition (in France, understandably, it has been quite strong for half a century, in the United States, equally understandably, it is nearly non-existent), but the limits to its advance are clearly set.

3.3.4.2. The second option is that of a 'stationary' policy in terms of a customary social-democratic strategy. Its overwhelming feature is a dominant stagnant aspiration consciousness, one which emphatically identifies with the worker as employee but which is either uninterested in, or watches with suspicious eyes, all projects of a radical change of the general situation of the socio-economic class. Propaganda slogans about their 'treason' are not only somewhat dubious on the part of those who introduce (or promote) a system in which routine strikes are kept in check by powerful armies. An accusation like this misses the main point. The social democrats do not betray, they rather jealously guard, certain limited interests of the socio-economic class of the workers. They are also justified in rejecting the Jacobin–Bolshevik project which will not cure the disease, but only cripple the patient for a lifetime. But their strategy has two inbuilt weaknesses and deficiencies. On the one hand, there are several constitutive features of the very existence of the socio-economic class to which their programmes do not respond at all (dissatisfaction with, and alienation from, work and the workplace, the non-proprietary position of the worker). On the other hand, they are, in result of the very structure of their movement, incapable of even raising problems concerning the industrializing logic which is so crucially important for the socio-economic class of workers. The social democratic strategy in its customary sense is the passive interpretation of the interests of the *Arbeitsnehmer* (employee).

3.3.4.3. In principle, and in the last years increasingly in fact as well, there is a novel option. In terms of ideology and political strategy, it does not transcend the level of the employee (in other words, it makes no suggestion how to abolish the conditions under which the workers further constitute a socio-economic class). However, it is an active and resolute agency of the *Arbeitsnehmer*. Its characteristic features are the following. First, it is a non-Jacobin, non-Bolshevik project, partly because of its indifference to all ideologies, partly because of its anti-authoritarian leanings. Secondly, it is totally unaffected by all programmes of self-management as the latter do not offer new material incentives but, predictably, put additional burdens on the shoulders of working-class militants. Third, it translates all social grievances and demands into the pecuniary language of real incomes. This latter makes its advocates insensitive to economic rationality, only sensitive to a policy of uninterrupted salary and wage augmentations. As this tendency is represented without any limitations imposed by a system of workers' ownership but with the vigour and zeal of an unrestrained collective egoism, an aura of Bolshevism is unjustly created around it by its enemies. However, and even without being Bolshevik, this policy could overthrow capitalism (or rather cripple it beyond chance of survival) without creating a new world of emancipation. In the vacuum, either neo-Bolshevism or neo-Fascism can take over. A generalized lie of the aspiration consciousness inheres in its tendency to translate all social questions into the language of salary increases, a trend which socialists alone are entitled to criticize. It promises that all members individually, and thereby the whole class collectively, can transcend the social condition of the socio-economic class with the aid of such actions as in fact simply reproduce this class, or destroy the preconditions of its existence, preparing the ground for a social situation much more disadvantageous than that of liberal capitalism.

3.3.4.4. Another even more widespread working-class policy is directed not so much against the structure of the socio-economic class as against the structure as a technological syndrome. Its main enemy is Prometheus, the titan of creativity, its utopia is *Schlaraffenland*, this world of dreams where there is no alienated work, or work at all for that matter; its historical heroes are the Luddites who destroyed the first manufacturing machinery. This movement is anticapitalist as well, but for its participants capitalism is primarily identical with the spirit of productionism. Their target area may range from ecological reforms to a total deindustrialization. (Most recently, it is Cornelius Castoriadis who gives most resolute voice to these demands.)[15] The main slogans are spontaneous actions, absolute equality, autonomy (which stands for absolute political freedom). We have repeatedly pointed out that the last two postulates are in irreconcilable conflict with one another. Because of the deep embeddedness of industrial needs in the man of modernity, this movement does not stand any serious chance of ever becoming a majority option, but it can be an important ally of various sorts of radical working-class policies.

3.3.4.5. Finally there is another radical option, the one advocated by us, which couples non-Jacobin, non-Bolshevik political radicalism with a generalized movement of self-management understood as workers' ownership. It has four distinctive features. Firstly, it aims not at statist confiscation, but at the universalization of property by a general self-management movement which ensures title of ownership

---

[15] Cornelius Castoriadis, Daniel Cohn-Bendit, *De l'écologie à l'autonomie*, Paris: Éditions du Seuil, 1981.

for the workers or employees of factories or enterprises. This statement needs further qualification. It is important for us that self-management, in principle implementable in a system of nationalization, should take place in the framework of a general workers' ownership which does not exclude the nationalization of certain strategically important factories or groups of enterprises. (By 'important' we mean, on the one hand, prosperous enterprises which ensure the monetary backing of the state's fiscal policy; on the other hand, and in drastic contrast with the former, enterprises which work, for one reason or the other, with deficits but the subsistence of which is necessary from a national point of view.) It would be an unfair argument, even though a favourite tenet of all types of biased conservatism, that a wide system of nationalization would necessarily lead to totalitarianism. But property and title of ownership are not mere words. Should the state be more than a simple agency of redistribution, but rather the actual owner of all means and preconditions of production, such a monopoly position would necessarily create (if not outright presupposes in advance) a stratum, no matter whether it is called a ruling intelligentsia, bureaucracy, statocracy, which would organize society on the principles of hierarchy and subordination. This may well be the only solution in modern times (which we very strongly doubt) but if it is so, then socialism becomes an impossible option. On the other hand, we do not deny that a system of generalized workers' ownership creates a number of problems which entail initial, perhaps recurring confusion and limited functioning of administrative and fiscal machinery. These are problems arising in connection with the cooperation between factories and enterprises, on the one hand, municipalities, on the other. Equally, there will be inevitable problems between single units of production and the central institutions of investment and the central fiscal machinery, not all of them easily resolvable through taxation policies. However, these costs of a universal system of ownership, the only positive transcendence of capitalist private property, seem to be inevitable.

Secondly, this policy involves maintaining an industrial dynamic within ecologically reasonable limits and in a way that industrial growth should grant possibilities of changing the technological patterns so that the problem of work dissatisfaction may be gradually solved. Thirdly, the new aspiration consciousness plays a central role in initiating and implementing this policy. The theory of the 'new working class', so voguish a decade ago, having now totally disappeared from the political and the sociological scene, was not the expression of a new social identity but rather that of a new social aspiration. It was a radical attempt, still pregnant with future potential, to resolve the paradox that the Jacobin–Bolshevik scenario could not. It was an attempt to theoretically establish the existence of a social ensemble which is the workforce of industrial production, which has at the same time a politically leading role without being a 'ruling class' and which transcends the alienated cosmos of job-dissatisfaction and hostility towards the workplace. Finally, all this can be realized if the socio-economic class of workers remains 'collectively conscious' (which, in more simple language, is equivalent to the statement that most of its members are aware) of the fact that they represent an open class, and that they can only achieve victory if they live up to this open character and the expectations stemming therefrom. This has a double meaning. The open class of the workers has to emanate its own way of life to other social groups in a way palatable to them, and, at the same time it has to accept the persisting plurality of life styles in the new order.

3.3.4.6. This turn would mean a radical act (rather, a radical process) but not a political revolution. The difference between the two is perhaps more than theoretical hairsplitting. Whereas it is un-deniable that a radical change, as we conceive of it, needs modifica-tions of the political structure, sometimes decisive ones, it is a fatal mistake to identify the decisive act of change with seizing (crushing and ultimate reshaping) state power. This is so even if the original will to change is not the Bolshevik one aiming at the elimination of poli-tical democracy. Moreover, it is only the Jacobin–Bolshevik scenario that can indeed achieve its own political goals by seizing and fashion-ing state power after a totalitarian pattern – one of the other ones mentioned by us. Anti-industrialist radicalism simply has nothing to do with state power. Social democracy needs power in the traditional sense of electoral victory but it mostly does not implement even the changes necessary according to a wide public opinion. What we called the option of the active representation of the employee would need state power to implement sweeping nationalizations, but certainly not the crushing and totalitarian reshaping of this same power. And finally our own selected option is the exact opposite of that Bolshevik scenario. Let us here quite emphatically restate that after the act of political emancipation, in other words, the disappearance of political classes, all political (Jacobin–Bolshevik) revolutions cannot be but anti-emancipatory.

IV STATE AND CLASS

4.1

The relation of class to state (and vice versa) is the subject of a long and violent debate. The two extremes of the debate are roughly the following:

4.1.1

'The state (and together with it, all institutions of the political sphere) are independent of all aspects of economic power.' The most representative partisans of this view, for us untenable, are such a distinguished scholar of social thought as Hannah Arendt, a genuine radical when it comes to the problem of polity *sui generis*.

4.1.2

'The state is simply an "agency" of the economically powerful class. All its decisions are aimed at implementing political decisions which serve capital.'

4.1.3

We do not accept either of these positions. In our view, the inter-relationship between state and class has to be regarded as 'in the making' as well. In an earlier period, when classes were political in character, when therefore political power was not delegated, but directly practised by one of the political classes, the state was indeed a direct representation (as a result, not an 'agency') of the dominating political class. We adopt a 'middle of the road' position in the debate between Engels and Perry Anderson. Engels contended that the state of the absolute monarchy could be regarded as already bourgeois in character in so far as it constituted the balance between nobility and bourgeoisie, and not as the direct representation of the former.[16] Perry

---

[16] Friedrich Engels, *The Origin of the Family, Private Property and the State*, Marx-Engels Selected Works, London: Lawrence and Wishart, 1968, p. 588.

Anderson maintains that the state of the absolute monarchy was an expression of the will of the nobility pure and simple (but at least a complete and uncontaminated expression of their, and no one else's, interests).[17] (This is, of course, a debate between ideal-types while the polemicists are not visibly conscious of it. The secret model interpreted by them in two different ways, is French absolutism. If we look at the early periods of Russian monarchy, we cannot but fully agree with Anderson, but if we look at what is called, with a somewhat questionable terminology, English absolutism in its early phase, we cannot but fully agree with Engels.) We believe that neither Engels nor Anderson takes into consideration the 'in the making' character of the absolutist state which was indeed originally the representation of the whole of the nobility. At that time, there were no political functions beyond the extension of this nobility, and no part of it was entirely excluded from practising some political functions. As long as this situation existed, the Anderson thesis was valid, and this was the ideal situation for the restoration of which the dissatisfied and rebellious nobility of the Bourbons strove. On the other hand, the very fact of the separation between court and countryside nobility, the insertion of an (ennobled) bureaucracy between monarch and hereditary nobility showed ('in the making') how the state embarked on a change which had to lead to a bourgeoisification of the body politic. But even here, the character of representation of the political class, so much different to the socio-economic one, comes flagrantly to the surface. It was primarily the new, already politically conscious, bourgeoisie and not the 'economically exploited' peasantry (exploited mostly by a rural bourgeoisie) against whom the state defended the politically dominant class. And this is true despite the fact that several peasant rebellions and an endless number of violent incidents in what is usually called the *guerres de farine* were put down by state power, as state powers are generally wont to put down famine mutinies. Once again, the conflict was expressed primarily through political confrontation, not through economic exploitation.

4.1.4

As long as the classes are political, in other words, as long as the will of the dominant class is the only publicly recognized will in society (in the

---

[17] Perry Anderson, *Lineages of the Absolutist State*, London/Atlantic Highlands: New Left Books/Humanities Press, 1975.

sense of being the only source of legitimation and rights in general), the state is a self-conscious expression of this minority will. Political classes disappear gradually, liberalism establishes its institutions equally gradually. The history of pre-Victorian England testifies to the revolutionary tensions in a body politic, which is gradually under way towards the construction of the completed edifice of liberalism whenever the process of such construction is too slow whether internally or externally. However, to the extent that liberalism develops its institutions (never spontaneously, almost always under the impact of a 'push from below'), the state ceases to be the domination of a political class. This state of affairs is not identical with the following statement: no socio-economic class has a crucial influencing role on the state of affairs of the body politic. For example, as already mentioned, as soon as the early bourgeoisie was in a position to exercise its economic power over social and political life through bureaucracies, castes of officers and the like to which it usually delegated a part of its power,[18] it immediately legislated against the existence of trade unions, those organizations born out of a mere identity, and not radical aspiration consciousness of the socio-economic class of workers. When banning trade unions, the modern state directly represented the minority will of bourgeoisie. But this was an exception rather than the rule.

4.1.5

Here we find the *locus classicus* of the divergence between the logic of democracy and the logic of capitalism. In itself, the second logic could be easily conceived of in concubinage with a direct and public representation of a minority will, with the majority remaining socially mute. For the last time here, we refer to the capitalist employment of the semi-slave, at least racially dependent, workforce in South Africa or, earlier, outright slavery in the capitalist plantation economy of the southern states of the United States. But since it so happened (through no necessity, but equally through no contingency, simply in fact) that capitalist organization of economic life was born together with, even promoted by, democracy in gestation, capitalist economic power has to take into account democratic principles when it comes to its political representation. And there is, with all imperfections that modern democracy might have, one fundamental rule which has to be respected in

---

[18] See Marx, *Der achtzehnte Brumaire des Louis Bonaparte*, Werke, Vol. 8, Berlin: Dietz Verlag, 1964, pp. 149–158.

any liberal or democratic system. *Consensus omnium* may be only a value ideal of modern democracies; but the majority principle cannot be circumvented. All self-conscious political representation of a minority will, as against the majority, is regarded as a tyranny, and as such as something negative, in modernity.

4.2

In order to better understand the tortuous ways through which a minority will (the will of the bourgeois class) prevails, while democracy, with its majority principle, remains still, and is certainly more than a mockery, we have to raise a simple question: how does the state function? In an ultimate abstraction and simplification, one can sum up the functions of the modern state in the following way. Firstly, one of them consists of the ensuring of the existence of the nation state against external threats. A further function consists of ensuring its economic growth, which is, in contrast to earlier rural communities, to huge empires with a stationary economy and the like, the precondition, even if not the guarantee, of individual well-being. This latter is the source of legitimation of the establishment as well. The last main function consists of ensuring 'law and order'. This last point has been deliberately formulated in a vague way. The status and the content of 'law and order' can, and does, range from the most tolerantly democratic to the most intolerantly conservative, but 'law and order' of some sort must exist. No society can lastingly live in either a 'permanent revolution' or in permanent upheaval and chaos.

4.2.1

From this it follows above all, that in the majority of liberal parliamentary states there is nothing in the constitution (very much in contrast to a popular belief widely held on the Left) that would prescribe capitalist organization of society. Very interestingly, it was Habermas, who, in an interview, pointed out this character trait of a state (the West German) designed in a truly conservative spirit. There is an equally popular answer to this on the Left: that constitution is only a piece of paper, what is important is the will of the bourgeoisie. We do not deny that in the empirical majority of the cases it is the interest of the bourgeoisie that prevails, but we definitely do not share the view that a constitution is 'just a piece of paper'. An accepted document with the backing of legitimation is a substantial social power. If there is no such social power in most modern parliamentary states which would prescribe the capitalist logic of economic and social organization as the only legitimate one, this constellation opens a wide avenue of radical action without a Bolshevik scenario towards the replacement of the capitalist logic by a socialist one. It is equally unacceptable to us to answer the problem in the following way: in the decisive hour the state and its authorities would 'anyhow' act with force against even a majority will for socialist change. This is a so-called true statement regarding the future, in regard to which there are no true statements. Chile, 1973, confirms this view; France, 1981, falsifies it.

4.2.2

But as long as the economy (and the society as a whole) is capitalistically organized, the state can only accomplish its tasks if it follows the interests, not necessarily the will, of the bourgeoisie. Before entering into the detailed discussion of this distinction, let us give an example to illustrate the crux of the matter. No matter what the life span of the monetarist policy will prove, no matter how well or badly it will serve bourgeois interests, large-scale tax-cuts on behalf of the rich have been the will of many (perhaps most) rich people, as already expressed in the Goldwater programme of the mid-sixties. However, on the one hand, in the middle of the economic boom, on the other hand, in the throes of an increasing political crisis caused and fuelled by the Vietnam war, such a policy was not in the interest of the bourgeoisie as a whole. Therefore it was only with Reagan that the actual implementation of monetarist policies in the United States set in, at the nadir of the economic crisis when it was at least reasonable to believe that such a policy would serve well the interests, not only the will, of the bourgeoisie. As a result, all three functions, and not because of any conspiracy, but simply in order not to turn into social dysfunctions, are implemented on behalf of capitalist groups. It is difficult, if not impossible, to introduce a whole political and economic strategy which serves the interests of the bourgeoisie alone. There are unmistakable class priorities in each programme in a class-dominated world but there must be built-in compromises as well. External threats are turned into wars or reconciled in pacts according to the (well or badly understood) interests of the bourgeoisie. Economic growth can also take place only in keeping with capitalist principles: sometimes by protectionism, sometimes by its exact opposite, namely the participation in supranational economic organizations. As well, the internal order is preserved in harmony with bourgeois interests. This could, and by socialists naturally should, be criticized, but all conspiracy theories simply miss the elementary social fact, that a state based on a capitalist socio-economic establishment would become dysfunctional, if it were to act otherwise.

4.3

Is the distinction between the representation of the interests and the will of the bourgeois by the state relevant in any sociological sense?

4.3.1

The relative independence of the state from all direct manifestations of the will of the bourgeoisie can mean a corrective principle both in a conservative and a democratic sense. In either case, such a direction implies an inevitable social tension. Bismarck's second *Reich* is a case study of the conservative correction of the will of the bourgeois. There can be no doubt that his brand of parliamentarism (with an exaggerated system of prerogatives and a cult of the monarch which later proved fateful to the second *Reich*) was not in harmony with the will of a considerable part of the bourgeoisie: hence the liberal opposition against Bismarck and his successors. There can be equally hardly any doubt that the system was bourgeois in character in the sense that it served the interests of the bourgeois. Both rightist radical (for instance, Nietzsche) and leftist radical (for instance social democratic) opponents admitted this. The equally classic case study of the democratic correction of the will of the bourgeoisie, on behalf of its interests, is the New Deal. A wide documentation is hardly necessary here, it will suffice to point to a large part of upper middle-class public opinion which treated Roosevelt as almost a 'commie' because of his flagrant violation of the will of upper bourgeois circles through his social policy while he was simply, but wisely, defending the interests of the bourgeois establishment. Whoever now reads Galbraith, a self-professed advocate of capitalism in so far as liberal capitalism 'softens its edges', will clearly see the self-awareness regarding the pro-capitalist character of the reforms implemented by the New Deal. But a more simplex and more elementary case mentioned by K. Polanyi will show that corrections of this kind are rather the rule than the exception. In *The Great Transformation* Polanyi stresses that the British state had to introduce protective legislative measures on behalf of the industrial workforce in the early nineteenth century or else the British Army and Navy very soon could not have found able-bodied young men for their services.[19] Restraining bourgeois greed in exploiting the workforce was certainly against the will of the then bourgeoisie, upholding the service level of the British Army and Navy, guarantor of imperial greatness and expansion was, with equal certainty, in the interest of the same bourgeoisie. Very simply, the state based on a capitalist organization of economy and society cannot always, not even very often, be the direct expression of the sum total, the aggregate of the individual bourgeois wills. But it can never eliminate, not even in its apparently most radical measures, capital as a social relation.

4.3.2

We have to return once more to the question: when will the state resort to force to put down social reforms? In other words, when will the state act as a proper agency of the bourgeoisie?

4.3.2.1.   Firstly, when a radical programme appears on the field, militantly and menancingly, but without being capable of winning majority support within the socio-economic class of the workers itself, and/or in the 'open space' around the working class. The crushing defeat of the *Spartakusbund* is the classic example of the first eventuality, the defeat of Austrian social democracy and the *Schutzbund*, at the hand of Dollfuss's Catholic Fascism and the Austrian Army illustrates the second possibility.

4.3.2.2.   Secondly, it happens when the flight of capital abroad (and with it the economic disintegration of the country) assumes such dimensions as to threaten the normal economic functioning of the country in question. In cases like this, the state which has, according to the customary composition of its bureaucracy, anyhow pro-capitalist leanings, acts in the name of 'order', and usually gains support of certain lower middle class strata which would otherwise support social reforms. The flight of capital or at least the threat of its flight is a habitual weapon of the bourgeoisie. The total disintegration and economic destabilization applied against leftist governments has been often used

---

[19] Karl Polanyi, *The Great Transformation*, Boston: Beacon Press, 1957, pp. 165–166.

but the classic case is certainly presented by Chile. There can be a two-fold answer to this on the part of socialist radicals: the alternative of Jacobin–Bolshevik terror which we unconditionally reject, in contrast to which we certainly prefer the come-back of even a liberal-conservative government (if it is not terroristic itself), and a system of protective measures on behalf of the national capital based on a wide popular support which is not necessarily, but at least can be, efficient against such tactic.

4.3.2.3. Thirdly, reactionary state intervention occurs when the leftist strategy is active but negative and creating at least the appearance (which rightist demagoguery can put to use proficiently) that it will result in a general disintegration, or when it overtly advertises its aim of extermininating the traditional middle classes. Italy in 1920–22 is the classic example of the first (and it is the historians' duty to determine how much was appearance, how much reality of the negativism which could be so skilfully exploited by Mussolini), Spain, 1936, of the second danger. It has to be added that in these cases it was not the state *sensu stricto* which acted against socialist movements. In Italy, the traditional conservative–liberal state had to be taken over by rightist revolutionaries (and, despite a far-reaching tactic collaboration on the part of the royal bureaucracy, the *Marcia su Roma* was indeed a take-over). In Spain, the state, at least nominally, was in the hands of the socialist radicals, as a result, the rebellious army, traditionally a political authority in Spain, generated a new state power out of itself. As is amply documented by nineteenth- and twentieth-century Latin America, and twentieth-century Asian history, it is particularly dangerous if the army has a political role even in a formally parliamentary system. Such a role repeatedly overthrew mildly liberal regimes in South America, crippled a formally full-fledged parliamentarism in prewar Japan, plunged countries in Asia into civil war to emerge with consolidated and extremely bloody dictatorships.

4.3.3

We are not selling any universal panacea in the form of the strategic alternative we are opting for but it certainly has advantages which might prevent the state from intervening into the implementation of socialist reforms as a direct agency of the bourgeoisie. The first is keeping nationalization to a minimum of absolute necessity which at least to some extent can dissipate the fear of totalitarianism and enhance the expectation of an increased economic rationality. The second is that our option regards the state as the neutral locus of redistribution (to be realistic and fair: neutral to the measure of the possible), not an agency of another social force. In other words, the goal of the social change is not an 'agency swap' but a transformation of the supreme political authority. Finally, our option admits the use of force only to the degree of paralysing, not exterminating social factors which endanger the whole system of democracy and which would like to reverse majority decisions by violent means, and even this on a temporary, not on a permanent basis. Retroactive history is not much more than an intellectual game, but as the example is provocative, we would like to state the following. We admit the right, moreover the moral and political duty, of a combined communist, social democratic and liberal majority government in 1933 Germany to enact the long-term imprisonment of the Nazi ringleaders clearly preparing for an anti-constitutional *Machtergreifung*, to enact the disbandment of the Nazi party and the short-term internment of the SA troops, but we would not admit even in retrospect the moral or political legitimacy of a mass extermination of the members of the Nazi movement, a politics the like of which was widely practised by Lenin's regime of mass terror after 1917.

4.3.4

It is important, here as well, to keep in mind that what we have called modernity is the conflict-ridden coexistence of capitalism, industrial development and democracy with their separate and even divergent logics. Therefore the conflicts which face radical movements after implementing a crucial social change cannot be reduced to the proverbial one: the resistance of the expropriated *ci-devants*. One could even say that, granted a correct handling of socialist strategy, this resistance is the least important of all possible conflicts facing a leftist government. Other conflicts, equally resulting from the three logics, can be roughly the following:

4.3.4.1. Social conflicts, directly economic in character stemming from the logic of industrialization. For example, the Russian Revolution created for itself the greatest and most dramatic of all conflicts (if one can give credit to Stalin's famous self-admission to Churchill)[20] by

---

[20] Winston S. Churchill, *The Hinge of Fate, The Second World War*, Boston: Bantam Books, Houghton Mifflin Co., 1977, pp. 434–435.

forcing tens of millions to abandon the rural way of life that they and their ancestors had lived for centuries.

4.3.4.2. National conflicts, either in the form of tensions between ethnic minority groups with the majority nation, or in the form of the fight for a truly federative system. The whole history of the Soviet Union after 1917, that of Rumania after 1947–8 is full of conflicts of the first type, while Yugoslavia is a classic case study of the second. Needless to say, it is only the poorest version of a party 'histomat' which treats the existence of nation, multi-national state and its internal tensions as simply deducible from a 'capitalist base'.

4.3.4.3. Religious conflicts which are mostly related to the fact that the parties of the Left implementing a change are customarily and traditionally, even if not exclusively, atheistic. A populace religious in its majority may simply be afraid of the atheistic zeal (not without good reason, as the immediate aftermath of the Spanish Revolution and the whole post-October history of Russia demonstrated). But the radical take-over may be implemented in a country in which the social organization itself is theocratic (consider the Chinese occupation of Tibet). If this happens in the spirit of Lenin and Stalin, the population faces a tragic ensemble of measures combining with originally emancipatory intent, a form of execution which concludes in genocide.

4.3.4.4. There are very often conflicts, partial in nature, which are related to ecological or feminist considerations and while they mobilize wide masses against governments with leftist programmes, they have nothing to do with advocating capitalist interests. Up until the last decade, leftist movements were fairly indifferent, if not outright hostile, to feminist demands, and up until this very day, socialism is almost without exception indifferent to ecology, apart form certain propaganda exercises.

4.3.4.5. And finally, perhaps overwhelmingly, there are the conflicts related to an earlier existence of capitalism with its adequate life styles which are, however, not identical with any bourgeois resistance to socialism. People certainly have to re-educate themselves in order to accept collectivistic values and life styles instead of the individualistic ones.

4.3.4.6. In all these conflicts, the different logics of modernity come to the fore and socialists commit a tragic mistake if they reduce this variegated syndrome simply to a 'survival of the vestiges of capitalism'. If they do so, the mistakes, truly fatal in their political results, are two-fold. Firstly, they allocate as the centre for eliminating these conflicts an overcentralized state, the least appropriate of all authorities for the task of transition. Secondly, they overestimate the role that the earlier socio-economic class of workers can play in such a social transformation. The genuinely radical social change can only be the yield of the contribution of an overwhelming majority.

V PERSPECTIVES

The different logics of modernity offer different global perspectives, with varying chances of longevity and/or realization.

5.1

Our prediction is that pure capitalistic logic (with or without an adequate parliamentary system) will have the smallest chance of survival and global predominance, for several reasons.

5.1.1

It became clear already at the beginning of the century that Marx's fore-cast of an entirely capitalized world (which was, paradoxically, the firm conviction of Marx's arch-enemies, the pro-capitalist conservative statesmen as well) had turned out to be totally false. Only the minority of the regions held in capitalist colonization had assimilated the capitalist logic of socio-economic organization. They had either survived on the ruins of their traditional systems or combined its vestiges with an underdeveloped capitalism.

5.1.2

The more democratic capitalism is, the less chance of longevity it has. In a democracy, the needs, created by the capitalist logic of endless quantitative increase, can be freely and publicly articulated, but they cannot be satisfied to the same extent, at least not without increasing difficulty. This failure creates ever-increasing tensions within the system.

5.1.3

For the first time, after decades of phrases about 'world economy', a genuinely global economy came about, which means (a) disjointed but mutually interdependent *loci* of industry and raw materials, (b) multinational economic organizations, (c) palpable limits to free circulation, accumulation and investment of capital as predicted by Rosa Luxemburg. In order to avoid permanent crisis, a global economy would need a new framework of institutions which cannot be elaborated on a decolonized basis of capitalist nation states.

5.1.4

Liberal capitalism has a very serious competitor in the form of the so-called 'dictatorships over needs', the systems which call themselves socialism but which are the complete negations of everything socialism has ever stood for. The countries in this system live permanent crisis as well (for reasons different in nature) but they have a remedy against the unlimited expansion of needs: the very system of dictatorship. They cannot eliminate capitalism globally, or if they could, they themselves would soon collapse as they have no rationality basis of their own. But they can very effectively, in a political and military sense, set limits to the expansion which is vital for the survival of capitalism. They are also capable of exploiting the inner tensions of capitalism to some extent.

5.1.5

In spite of the present monetarist wave, we estimate the chances of longevity of industrial, liberal and capitalism to be far greater in a welfare state, for two reasons. Firstly, Galbraith in all probability is right when he regards the so-called 'techno-structure' as the more dominant factor within the capitalist management, rather than the entrepreneurial class *sensu stricto*, and while the first needs a paternalistic state, heavy taxation, development of education, skilled work, welfare benefits, it is only the latter that can thrive on tax-cuts and tight fiscal policy. Secondly, it was likewise Galbraith who, as mentioned, correctly pointed out that the reason for capitalism's survival was that it had 'softened its edges'. If, in a system of monetarism, this process of 'softening' is going to be reversed, the results will be unpredictable. And at least one consequence seems to be certain: the repoliticization of the citizenry touched off by sensitive economic issues, a generally increased level of radicalism.

5.1.6

Therefore, in all probability, the system based on the existence of the dichotomous socio-economic class is doomed. The only open, and the only relevant, question is whether what follows it will be a world more or less humane.

5.2

The chances of a general victory, at least of a widespread breakthrough are rather on the side of one of the anti-democratic solutions which overrule capitalistic logic and the several versions of which, according to their particular organization, can have several different relations to the logic of industrialization.

5.2.1

One of them is a type of modern totalitarianism with a leftist ideology which is a political society (in the sense of the supremacy of the state over 'civil society') and which, in contradistinction to rightist totalitarian systems, is the sole proprietor of the precondition and the means of production. Without entering into a detailed characterization of this society (which we have done elsewhere), here only the following should be stressed from the standpoint of our problematic *sensu stricto*.

5.2.1.1. It is a society which, by implication, excludes the logic (and all remnants) of democracy, radically and without trace.

5.2.1.2. It is a society which, with certain ups and downs (such as the intermezzo of the 'proletarian cultural revolution'), not only preserves the logic of industrialization but drives it to socio-pathological extremities, often causing enormous losses of human lives, and ecological catastrophes.

5.2.1.3. As far as class existence is concerned, dictatorship over needs means a devastating combination of the openly professed political prerogatives and domination of earlier political classes with the economic *plein pouvoir* of the one dominant socio-economic class. As such, it means a complete withdrawal of all results of an earlier emancipation.

5.3

There is a solution, at least logically, which means the prevalence of the industrial logic over the other two, which is implemented in a ruthlessly undemocratic way but with a liberal ideology and which has a contradictory relation to the logic of capitalism. The socio-economic structure we have in mind is called, in the wake of Szelényi, the 'state mode of production'. The specification that it exists as a logic rather than an actual option, has two explanations.

5.3.1

A 'state mode of production' as an anti-democratic solution of the present global crisis is only feasible if the technocratic–bureaucratic branch of the 'flawed' class of the bourgeoisie exercises absolute control over the economic existence of the proprietor and the political existence of the wage-earner. A situation like this yields, however, only one version of two social states of affairs, both self-contradictory, therefore transitory.

5.3.1.1. In the first, the realization of the absolute control of techno-bureaucracy over the entrepreneur unwittingly eliminates market competition, abolishes the initial capitalist logic of society without acquiring any kind of pseudo-socialist legitimation. (Or if it does, it will simply be a new edition of a dictatorship over needs, somewhat irregular and eccentric as far as its genesis is concerned.)

5.3.1.2. In the second, if emphasis is laid on the total political control of the wage-earner, it has to re-emancipate the bourgeois, in which case it will be a subgroup of the rightist totalitarian systems but with an inadequate, because initially technocratic–liberal, ideology.

In both cases, the state mode of production seems to be a contradictory formula, the probable fate of which is demise and a relapse into the dichotomous society of socio-economic classes from whose crisis it was born. While it reduces democracy to nil in the name of a 'progressive liberal' technocratic ideology and morbidly overdevelops industrializing tendencies, it can offer no relevant, even if non-emancipatory solution to the problem of transcendence of class existence.

5.4

A final alternative version is presented by the unexpected formula, emerging in the last decade, the traditional fundamentalist tyrannies. They are thriving on the ruins of a colonial or half-colonial system. Through either traditional life styles or religious doctrines which are at the same time organizing social principles or through both, they have preserved archetypes of ancient social frameworks and patterns hardly compatible with either industrialization or with capitalism. This does not at all mean that they are incapable of sometimes even very prosperous economic activities. Our characterization simply indicates an organically inherent incapability of developing an industrial or capitalist logic of their own, while it does not exclude a parasitic symbiosis with the economic world system of capitalism.

5.4.1

As far as democracy and class existence is concerned in this system, the situation is even more threatening. Fundamentalism is not only totally incompatible with democracy. It even abolishes the category of citizen in that it does not tolerate any distinction between the (religiously defined) good man and the good citizen: the latter must be identical with the former. This has, however, the menacing implication that the whole problem of class existence will be reduced, or dissolved, into the problem of castes or the exclusive contrast of fidel and infidel.

5.5

Our option, classless society via the radicalization of democracy, has very limited chances indeed.

5.5.1

Among its potentials are the so-called radical needs, at least the particular cluster of them which points towards a radicalized democracy. We have discussed them elsewhere.

5.5.2

Further, it has negative bases:

5.5.2.1. The gradual exhaustion of the economic and sociological reserves of the capitalist logic;

5.5.2.2. The nightmare evoked in many millions by the repeated holocausts of the totalitarian solution, a negative feeling which has very positive repercussions;

5.5.2.3. The visible emergence of ecological limitations to an endless industrializing expansion;

5.5.2.4. The danger of nuclear wars created by practically all other solutions.

5.5.3

Its main categories are:

5.5.3.1. Generalized self-management in the form of workers' ownership;

5.5.3.2. Decentralization of state power; its reduction to the role of an agency of redistribution;

5.5.3.3. Politically active citizenry continually realizing what Habermas called 'undistorted communication';

5.5.3.4. Democratic (non-hierarchical) relations within the factory and a conscious shaping of technological development with constant consideration of work conditions adequate to humane individual development (if need be, and on the basis of a democratic consensus, at the expense of the accelerated industrial expansion);

5.5.3.5. No class relationship but the further existence of interest conflicts between *ad hoc* groups or the state agency of redistribution and certain groups of industrial, etc. branches.

There is indeed a very small chance for all these categories to be combined in a lasting and global social constellation. But if this is the only chance of a human survival worthy of the name, as we believe it to be, who can discard its chances offhandedly, limited though they might be?

10

An Imaginary Preface to the 1984 Edition of Hannah Arendt's *The Origins of Totalitarianism*

Agnes Heller [1]

The twentieth century will go down in annals and books of history as the age of totalitarianism, and Hannah Arendt will certainly remain the classic source of any forthcoming interpretation of the origins of totalitarianism. True enough, any chronicle by a contemporary, an eye-witness, lacks in certain historical perspectives, even if the witness's story is told in the past tense; for this past is still the 'past of the present', and not the historical past of the bygone. This holds true for Hannah Arendt's book as well. Yet it was precisely a certain lack in perspective that made her book powerful. As a deeply involved observer, she gave her testimony in a case which is still far from closed. Her theoretical commitment to understanding totalitarianism, her practical commitment to a stand against totalitarianism and her emotional re-enactment of the path leading to the Golgotha, merge fully in a unique compound.

Arendt's approach totalitarianism is strictly historicist. She resists the temptation of easy explanations. This is why she insists that totalitarianism, far from being indicative of our having relapsed into some kind of premodern (incidentally Asiatic) barbarism, is rather the offspring of our modern, Western culture, a new form of modernity. She sums up her position in the preface to the first edition in the following manner: 'The subterranean stream of Western history has finally come to the surface, and usurped the dignity of our tradition.' The explanations of totalitarianism are, therefore, to be sought in the dynamics of development, not in underdevelopment, in the Occident, and not in the Orient, in certain tendencies specific to our own eternal

---

[1] Unpublished manuscript.

human nature. This seminal discovery (which of course has never prevented legions of scholars from endlessly pondering the Asiatic mode of production as the possible source of Soviet totalitarianism) has, to my mind, only one flaw. Arendt remained an evolutionist in so far as she attributed a certain kind of necessity to the factual sequence of historical events. Since totalitarianism was, in her view, the novel offspring of Western modernity, it could only emerge after all previous events of modernity had already unfolded. However, the fact that history unfolds in a certain way does not prove that it could not have been otherwise. In my view, the totalitarian option had been present since the dawn of modernity, at least on the European continent, and it was due to certain 'accidental' (but, at least, undoubtedly not 'necessary') factors (to our everlasting historical fortune), that the nineteenth century took a turn towards parliamentary liberalism, rather than an early form of totalitarianism. However, since alternative histories cannot be written, either for better or for worse, Arendt's reconstruction of the origins of totalitarianism remains valid.

If we read *The Origins of Totalitarianism* together with its companion volumes, *The Human Condition* and *On Revolution*, the message of the first work becomes even more explicit. In Arendt's view, there are two ideal-types of modernity: the democratic and the totalitarian. Neither of them is simply a political system. Rather, they constitute two different cultures, diametrically opposed to one another. Each culture has a singular moral, psychological, sensual texture of its own; each operates with an imaginary contrary to that of the other. Each enhances attitudes and practices counterposed to the other. Fortunately or unfortunately, however, real histories rarely produce ideal-typical, pure cultural types. Although I am convinced that Arendt's typology is, in the last instance, revelatory, the understanding of the development of totalitarianism after Stalin calls for certain refinements and further specification. In her 1966 preface to *The Origins of Totalitarianism*, Arendt refers to the 'rich recovery of the arts during the last decade' as 'the clearest sign that the Soviet Union can no longer be called totalitarian in the strict sense of the term'.[2] Arendt, as so many among us, drew far too hasty conclusions from certain phenomena associated with the Khrushchevian intermezzo. Almost two decades have again elapsed since this preface was committed to paper, and totalitarianism has remained vigorous, indeed, it has even gained more ground. If Arendt lived today, she would surely

---

[2] Hannah Arendt, *The Origins of Totalitarianism*, 2nd ed. London/New York: Allen & Unwin/Harcourt Brace/Jovanovich, 1966, p. 12.

write a new preface to her book, as she did every time historical junc-
tures called for further explanation. The greatest tribute I can pay to
her memory is to try to perform this task in the year 1984. In doing so, I
shall address three problems; firstly, Soviet totalitarianism; secondly,
the emergence and dissemination of totalitarianism and totalitarian
political practices in the so-called 'Third World', and, thirdly, the
decline of totalitarian movements in Western Europe without the disappearance of certain factors enumerated by Arendt as contributions
to the 'origins' of totalitarianism.

I

No redefinition of the notion 'totalitarianism' makes Arendt's ideal-
type obsolete. The way a social system emerges is, and remains, indicative of the whole character of this particular social system. The genesis
discloses more about a system than does any period of 'normalization'.
Normalization is the final product of genesis. The mark of genesis is the
substrate of normalization. Stalinism has remained the secret clue to
contemporary Soviet totalitarianism, and it is in this sense that
denizens of the Soviet world still live under the shadow of Stalin. All
attempts to abstract the present from this genesis and display the latter
as something gone and surpassed, fail to come to grips with the fundamental systemic features of the Soviet Union today. However, certain
distinct, genetic features have not sprung from totalitarianism *per se*,
rather from the particular process of totalization. Up until World War
Two, Stalinism had been the period in which the construction blocks
for the new society were produced and fitted together. Both the Führer
principle and waves of indiscriminate repression on a mass scale functioned as vehicles of totalization. Both became obsolete once the
systemic features of totalitarianism were sedimented. The Stalinist
'revolution from above' had transformed human attitudes, cultural
patterns, ways of thinking and acting to an extent required to ensure the
smooth reproduction of the system. A return to the Führer principle
and waves of indiscriminate repression is not a likely possibility,
though not because any systemic change to the regime, but because the
regime already exists in a sedimented form. However, there can be little
doubt that, were a legitimation crisis to emerge in the Soviet Union
(hardly likely in the foreseeable future), both the Führer principle and
waves of indiscriminate mass repression would be revived again, as a

result of the need for retotalization. The terroristic phase and form of totalitarianism has not been excluded from the systemic patterns as a result of its sedimentation. Terroristic totalitarianism has only become temporarily redundant, even counterproductive. In the event that the regime becomes confronted with prolonged and stubborn resistance, and in particular, armed resistance (as in Afghanistan), the machinery of wholesale terror would, again, be set in motion. Western analysts who have taken great pains to discover the evolutionary potentials, or even the manifest results of an essential, systemic reform of Soviet totalitarianism, are blinded by their own hopes. Needless to say, the substantial decrease, or disappearance, of waves of indiscriminate repression is an enormous relief to the subjects of totalitarian societies. Such sobering and gratifying events, however, should not be misread as evidence of 'social progress' or 'systemic change'. The system can only go under in a manner similar to which it emerged.

Arendt made the important distinction between totalitarian movements and totalitarian rule (governments). I would add a second distinction to the list, that between totalitarian rule and totalitarian society. This differentiation does not involve evaluation. From a human point of view totalitarian rule can be just as unbearable as a totalitarian society. Further, the distinction is relative. The tendency to totalize society is inherent in every totalitarian rule but not all kinds of totalitarian rule aim at complete totalization. Totalitarian rule can restrict its objective to the political and ideological totalization of society. Among the three distinct types of totalitarian rule which emerged in Europe after World War One, Fascism (Mussolinism) did not aim (at least not before the Salo Republic) at an overall totalization of society, whereas both Nazism and Bolshevism did. However, the 12 years of the thousand-year Reich, as Arendt put it, did not suffice to accomplish the totalization of society. The only totalitarian society in this sense then is the Soviet type of society. I would not say that it is the only possible form to come, and some are perhaps already in the making, but at any rate, it is the sole existent one which lends itself to comprehensive theoretical analysis.

The Soviet state was already totalitarian as early as 1921. What followed was the totalization of society by the totalitarian state. This was the unique achievement of the Stalinist 'revolution from above'. The end result was, and has remained, a completely new social system, and completely new attitudes which ensure the maintenance of the system.

Totalitarian rule itself has to be defined in such a way that the definition should encompass all kinds of totalitarian rule irrespective of whether or not a society has been completely totalized. I call a rule totalitarian if a party is the sovereign of the state (the source of all powers) and if this sovereign outlaws pluralism. Since the party is the source of all powers, it is, by definition, the source of legislative power. Legislation is nothing but the expression of the will of this sovereign (the party leadership). If the party wills something, this will is by definition law (whether or not it takes the form of a law), and, as a consequence, every contrary will is outlawed. Of course, pluralism subsists, although it is not legal. Whether a certain kind of pluralism is practically (never formally and legally) tolerated, depends on the will of the sovereign. Society is not completely totalized (although its rule already is), if the will of the sovereign is merely ideological and political in nature. Society is completely totalized if the will of the sovereign determines the whole socio-economic structure of the society in question, thereby outlawing not only political and ideological but also socio-economic alternatives. The attitudes which maintain totalitarian rule are political and ideological, and, further, psychological and moral ones, in conjunction with political action and ideological myths. The attitudes which serve to maintain a completed totalitarian society are, thus, all-encompassing. Arendt was unfortunately only too right when she described the ease with which attitudes can be reshaped into totalitarian ideological and political action patterns under specific social circumstances, though this insight also led her to the conclusion that Stalinist terror had been dysfunctional since 1934. In this, I believe, she was wrong. Since society had to be completely totalized in the Soviet Union (in accordance with the Bolshevik project), the sum total of the attitudes, and not just political and ideological ones, had to be re-shaped. This is why the 'Great Terror' was not at all 'unnecessary' or superfluous from the standpoint of the regime. Rather, it was precisely this period which accomplished the totalization of society. The 'Khrushchev intermezzo' was both an organic and inorganic period in Soviet history. It was organic for it opened the path to an oligarchic rule far more adequate to a sedimented totalitarian society than the auto-cratic charismatic rule of Stalin. At the same time it was inorganic, moreover, self-contradictory, for it turned against, if only marginally and inconsistently, a period which had created the very system within which autocratic rule could be abandoned.

Arendt seems, further, to underestimate the utilitarian motivations operating during periods of totalization. On one level it is difficult to see how a person's interests could be served in any theatre in which the secret police are the stage manager. Yet the interest basis of a totalitarian regime can be illustrated in two distinct ways. Firstly, if everyone is guilty of mass murder, everyone will have a vested interest in upholding the regime in whose name it was committed. Secondly, totalitarian rule implies in itself a change of elite, but the totalization of society is the very process in which a change of elite is effectuated on an unprecedented grand scale. This is how Stalin's rule is understood and even defended, especially by those who had benefitted from it personally and through their families, up until this day. The dissident Zinoviev is a good example here. His last interview (published in *Encounter*), an apology for Stalin coming from his otherwise resolute enemy, exposes without much ado that during the Great Terror, every corpse was a stepping stone for the careers of the living. Newcomers were hungry for position and power; the more the 'old guard' was wiped out, the better chance they stood to gain positions of power and move to the top. Arendt was obviously right in emphasizing that in a totally atomized society such as the Soviet Union under Stalin, class or group entity in any collective sense did not exist, or at least that it could not be properly articulated. However, this in itself never diminished the basis for interest motivation. The interests of millions of human 'atoms' had already been vested in the system during Stalin's lifetime, and thus it has remained ever since. Upward mobility, once made possible through brutal elite alterations, has disappeared with the advent of an ossified elite. I only have to add to this that in the Soviet satellite countries, where Stalinism proper had lasted only for a very short period, there was not time to transform human attitudes to the extent needed for the proper operation of a totalitarian society. The attitudes sufficient for political and ideological totalization were, unfortunately, not found wanting. But the moment the terror declined, legitimation crises set in, and no East European society has been able to be properly legitimized since. In fact, totalitarianism collapsed in Hungary, Czechoslovakia and Poland, and has, completely or partially, been restored solely by an occupying army and its proxies.

Soviet society as it now stands in the Soviet Union, conclusively corroborates Arendt's main thesis. It represents a distinct type of modern society. Totalitarianism has turned out to be the motive force and the intrinsic essence of a new kind of modernity. Without going into a detailed analysis of Soviet societies, and repeating my views I have argued at length elsewhere,[3] I mention only one of its outstanding features. N. Luhmann has pointed out, to my mind correctly, that in contradistinction to premodern, stratified societies, modern society is

---

[3] In *Dictatorship Over Needs*, Oxford: Basil Blackwell, 1983, Ferenc Fehér, György Markus and I have sought to give a comprehensive analysis of the dynamics of Soviet societies.

increasingly functionalist in character. Whereas in premodern societies the performance of specific functions was allocated to the position occupied by human groups on the scale of stratification, in modernity the reverse takes place: it is the performance of specific functions which allocates persons to specific social strata. Yet, and this has escaped Luhmann's attention, in the liberal–democratic type of modernity neither political nor social action evolves solely from, and crystallizes solely around, the performance of a function. In spite of an increasing tendency towards corporatism in certain Western-type democracies, both political parties and social movements recruit their constituencies along transfunctional issues. No constituency is constituted solely along functional lines. Thus the existence of civic liberties and the forms of political and social organizations and the kinds of action patterns ensuing therefrom, strongly counterbalance systemic constraints. Yet due to the complete lack of civic liberties and political and social pluralism, Soviet society, and it alone, has realized the functionalist tendencies embedded in modernity in full. The only action possible in the Soviet society is the performance of a function. Stratification is exclusively functional, and moreover, transfunctional action is outlawed. This means that in Soviet society, system integration and social integration merge into one. More precisely, in the absence of any normative basis of doctrines in support of the system has also become a systemic function, namely the function of the sovereign. Ideology, in the sense of an alternative interpretation of the doctrine, is outlawed. However, although the doctrine still cements the system as a point of reference and the source of legitimation, it has lost momentum since the sedimentation of the system. As Zaslavsky has pointed out, the word 'communism' has become empty, sometimes an object of derision, the overarching propaganda image, and the only point of reference for 'creeds', is the so-called 'Soviet way of life'.[4] Yet pluralism, though outlawed, still exists, in marginalized, privatized niches (for instance, religious devotion and practices). But such *intermundia* cannot counterbalance the sweeping preponderance of the system, at least not in the Soviet Union. This is why people not integrated into the system are viewed as mad and are readily transferred to mental asylums. In a world where there is no social integration, only system integration, such people must appear mad. In my view, the coalescence of system integration and social integration must eventually lead to a deficit in moral motivation and to neuroses on a mass scale which could

---

[4] Victor Zaslavsky, *The Neo-Stalinist State*, New York/Brighton: M. E. Sharpe/Harvester, 1982.

undermine the reproducibility of society. Lack of moral motivation is not identical with the irrational, shame-regulated morality which had dominated the period of totalization. The latter is now in retreat.

The other intrinsically modern feature of the Soviet system, not unconnected with the former, is its industrializing impetus. Soviet society is not only modern, it is also 'modernizing'. It is quite irrelevant in this respect how good or bad the performance of Soviet industry may be. Even if it is true that industrial production for household and private consumption cannot be compared to the performance of the military–industrial complex, it would be utterly ridiculous to term the greatest, or perhaps the second greatest, military power in the world an 'underdeveloped' society. If one type of modernity can be characterized by the triad 'capitalism, democracy, industrialization', the other type corresponds to the triad of 'functionalism, totalitarianism, industrialization'. Needless to say, I would not wish to suggest by this that there are no other types of societal organization, nor that there is any necessity in these combinations. Rather, I have only sought to specify the basic constituents of the Soviet model of modernity.

Terroristic types of totalitarianism may survive for a while (which is an unendurably long time for their victims) but, measured with yardstick of history, their longevity is generally limited. The permanence of a state of war always has limits. However, totalitarianism knows no temporal limits. Once sedimented and reproduced in accordance with functionalist patterns, a totalitarian society can continue to reproduce itself smoothly. Conflicts cannot be excluded but the equilibrium can be restored without excessive efforts. Contemporary Soviet totalitarianism, which has left its revolutionary birth-pangs behind, is an entirely conservative society, a legitimized and, at least for the time being, a well functioning one. Unfortunately, all hopes of a near collapse of this social structure seem as misguided as hopes for its eventual thoroughgoing social reform. This does not, of course, exclude changes within the framework of the existing structure, for no society can be completely static. Here, a few comments on dissidents, as the social locus of opposition within Soviet society, are called for. My point of reference is the dissident movement in the Soviet Union but my statements are, at least in part, relevant for other, East European, dissident groups and movements, excepting Solidarity.

In the Soviet Union, dissidence has become a vocation, an orientation which has absolutely nothing to do with the career paths followed by the caste or elite of 'professional revolutionaries'. 'Vocation' signifies the opposite of 'function'. The group of dissidents does not comprise a nucleus of any emergent anti-Soviet revolutionary movement; rather, it is the nucleus of 'society' as such. In a totalitarian world where only system integration is left, where action is nothing but the performance of a function, dissidence provides a niche for a social integration which is not system integration. This facilitates the performance of transfunctional actions of various kinds. Soviet society confirms the paradox that the outlawed sphere is the only one which can legitimately be called 'public'. Accordingly, if there are citizens left among subjects, they are dissidents by vocation. There is no need to speak about the content of the dissenting ideas, as they represent all possible colours of the rainbow. The main point is that the very existence of such movements provides a barrier, not against totalitarian ideas which may indeed set foot behind this barrier, but against a complete system integration. Nor are the different shades so terribly important in themselves, for several distinct versions of liberalism, democracy and authentically socialist discourse, all conducted within this outlawed public sphere, provide a counterbalance against the expansion of the political limbo which might prove fatal in the case of a sudden collapse of the regime and a resultant power vacuum. 'The flourishing of art' in which Hannah Arendt rested her hope, belongs to a bygone past, and its flowers now grow in a foreign soil. Totalitarianism was only shaken for a moment, if at all. However, a change in the attitude of a few is still discernible and, moreover, this changed attitude will continue to reproduce itself as long as it is not wiped out by brute force.

II

Colonizing imperialism is, according to Arendt, one of the major roots of, and preludes to, totalitarianism. Due to rapid decolonization after World War Two and to the growing national self-identity and nationalism of the middle classes in the vast region we refer to as the 'third world', 'race thinking', this poisonous fruit of imperialism, is in retreat. Needless to say, racism still holds one of the most powerful appeals to the social cluster which Arendt calls the 'mob', even though it had lost momentum among the 'masses'. Or, to put it more cautiously, racism has to be clad in presentable garments, political, religious or national, in order to mobilize a considerable proportion of the masses. Excepting South Africa, no publicly racist state has remained, notwithstanding the continued existence of several *de facto* racist societies. As a consequence, of the three original types of totalitarianism (Nazi, Bolshevik and Fascist), the Nazi type does seem to be inimitable. The ideology of the dominating race is unlikely to re-emerge, even more to spread. But simultaneously, a kind of covert racism has gained momentum within other types of totalitarianism. It has been often pointed out that anti-Semitism, conspicuously absent from Fascism and Bolshevism before World War Two, had rapidly increased in the Soviet Union in the last four decades, as has a strong anti-Russian and at the same time Russian racism (both are not simply identical with nationalism). Official anti-Semitism can partially be explained by a constant and renewing need for scapegoats. But there is an additional explanation. I mentioned earlier that with the sedimentation of the totalitarian system and the closure of the period of mass repression, the constant and unbroken flow of the process called a 'change of elite' had been thwarted, and the path leading to upwards mobility jammed. Racist scapegoating draws the attention of dissatisfied contenders of the 'disproportionately high' percentage of the members of certain nations or ethnic groups in lucrative positions. Ideology and factual truth can, of course, be miles apart. Despite the *numerus clausus* applied to Jews in all tertiary education institutions (and *numerus nullus* in case of sensitive government jobs) in the USSR, Russians, in particular, are made to believe that they remain on lower rungs of career ladders because of Jews. Similarly, Ukrainians firmly believe in the Russification' of all leading positions, while Russians claim that they are constantly discriminated against. In Sudan, racism makes its appearance in the guise of a religious ideology. The costumes may vary, but the costumes are constantly there, for which reason I believe that an undisguised, Nazi-type racism is very unlikely to re-emerge.

In contrast to Nazism, both the Bolshevik and Fascist types of totalitarianism have proved to be imitable, and both of them have gained momentum in the third world. The liberation of the colonies has brought very little liberty for the populace of this immense region of the world, and colonizing imperialism is far from being an innocent party in this outcome. It is too easy a line of defence to assert with ill-conceived self-righteousness that the totalitarian dictators in contemporary third world countries are of endogenous origin, some of them openly hostile to the West. Hannah Arendt's point holds true in this respect as well. Totalitarianism has nothing to do with traditional dictatorship, it is not the product of backwardness or underdevelopment, it is intrinsically modern, often the consequence of a deeply problematic development. Imperialist colonizers have expanded the world market on the one hand, and prompted modern industrialization on the other. However, instead of implanting the seeds of Western liberalism or democracy, with a very few exceptions they ruled the colonies with proto-totalitarian political practices. Now the chickens have come home to roost. Endogenous third world totalitarian rulers learnt the practice of power from Europe and not from their own traditions, and their power base is not the 'people deep down on the social hierarchy' but the power-hungry and greedy middle classes created by the capitalist world market and industrialization.

I do not wish to assert that all instances of dictatorship in the third world are totalitarian in character or even close to this pattern. There are traditional models of dictatorship among them, and not only in Latin America. In this region, as the Chilian scholar, Jorge Tapia-Valdez argues, a new kind of 'institutionalized militarism' has gained momentum, a phenomenon which can be identified in Asia as well. (Chile and Indonesia would be the major examples.) Institutionalized militarism is certainly not totalitarianism proper, but it creates certain typically totalitarian institutions and uses certain totalitarian practices. At the same time, in some third world countries traditional monarchies have often survived while in others, a certain kind of liberalism has taken root. However, to deny the gaining momentum of totalitarianism would be wishful thinking.

I have distinguished between 'Fascist' and 'Bolshevik' types of totalitarianism. Sometimes the two contest each other, while at other times they merge, even with great ease. Two reasons can be identified. Firstly, what Arendt called 'class thinking' is in decline in a way similar to, although not to the same extent as 'race thinking'. Nationalism (or pan-nationalism) is subsequently substituted for orthodox class thinking. Even endogenous 'third worldism' (and not its European and utterly inauthentic version) is a pan-nationalist thinking of a kind. Now, pan-nationalism was the ideological, organizing centre of (Mussolinist) Fascism, though, paradoxically, Lenin's doctrine of anti-imperialism likewise inspires a certain type of pan-nationalism. Secondly, the social basis of both kinds of totalitarianism is roughly identical (middle classes, the huge mass of university students, the mob), and the only difference is that of political affiliation. However, despite a possible merger, the distinction between Fascist and Bolshevik types of totalitarianism is fairly clear. In the case of Fascism, the rule (the government) is totalitarian, but society is only politically and ideologically totalized, and the totalizing ideology is nationalist or pan-nationalist. In the case of Bolshevism, the totalitarian ruler and the ruling party unleash a wholesale and complete totalization of society, and the ideology of totalization includes class thinking. The actual extent of repressions and the extent of terror felt by the populace are not dependent on the Bolshevik or Fascist character of the particular totalitarian regime, but on other factors. However, both Fascist and Bolshevik versions share to a certain extent what can be called 'the totalitarian imaginary'.

There is always something new under the sun. Third world totalitarianism has added two novel features to those of their European ancestors: anti-modernization on the one hand, and a religious ideology as an instrument of totalization on the other hand. The first anti-modernizing instance of totalitarianism was, surprisingly, a totalitarian movement within a totalitarian society: the Maoist cultural revolution. The second case was Kampuchea under Pol Pot and the third is Iran under Khomeiny. The first two instances were based on 'class thinking', elevated to a far more exclusive and pathologically exaggerated degree than usually evidenced among totalitarian societies, rules and movements in the third world. The third case emerged from a religious doctrine. Given that up until the cultural revolution, all totalitarian societies and states were in principle, industrializing and modernizing, this new phenomenon confronts us with a puzzle. I have already insisted in the wake of Arendt that totalitarianism is an intrinsically modern phenomenon. How can this assertion be valid if movements, practices and rules mobilizing the whole paraphernalia of totalitarianism, now turn against modernization? How can the thesis be upheld if an emerging totalitarian rule focuses on a pre-modern doctrine for, needless to say, the Shiite Moslem religious doctrine used as a tool of Khomeiny's terroristic totalization is a pre-modern type of imaginery, in contrast to 'nationalism', 'pan-nationalism', 'class' and 'race-thinking'. As far as modernization is concerned, the mystery is not so deep as it seems at first glance. Anti-industrialization has been a decisive trend in European ideological modernity right from the beginning. The romantic generation of intellectuals who jumped headlong into the radicalism of totalitarian movements in the second and third decades of our century had a very strong anti-modernizing bias. As Arendt has pointed out, they have embraced the new barbarians because they alone would be able to rescue 'us' (that is, the 'integral' or 'authentic' man) from Western civilization. It proved rather difficult for them to reconcile their longings with the actual modernizing fervour of totalitarianism, and, in fact, they often became deeply dissillusioned. The utterly misguided sympathetic reaction of certain Western radicals to the cultural revolution, to Pol Pot or the Khomeiny-dominated outcome of the Iranian revolution, their reluctance to face mass murder, pogroms and, in the case of Kampuchea, genuine genocide, can be accounted for, although not excused, by their adherence to a romantic anti-modernizing modernism. As for the movements and regimes themselves, and more important than the fact that Pol Pot studied in Paris and Mao called himself a student of Marx, is the undeniable fact that they understood themselves to be a conscious reaction to the Western (Soviet or American) industrializing and modernizing patterns and their concomitant 'decadent' features, while retaining totalitarian practices. (In Mao's case this was obviously a reaction to the Soviet type of industrialization, while in Pol Pot's and Khomeiny's cases to the American version.)

One puzzle still remains, that of the place of religious doctrine within such a modern compound. Up until now, 'synthetically made' modern myths of totalitarianism have claimed exclusivity, and have not seemed prepared to share the imaginaries of traditional religious myths. Yet Khomeiny's Iran is still comprehensible in Arendt's terms, for the Ayatollah's brand of Islam can be conceived as a new pan-religious movement, in addition one which, if organized on the basis of a totalitarian state, can far more easily totalize the whole of society than can any kind of nationalism or pan-nationalism. The latter are normally vehicles of politico-ideological totalization. They are, as such, vehicles, sufficient to shape the attitudes which are necessary to keep a political and ideological totalitarianism running, but they do not, and cannot alone provide the kind of doctrinal diet people must live on, for a considerable time, to change all their social attitudes, down to their most elementary everyday routines. Put bluntly, nationalism (pan-nationalism included) does not constitute a way of life moulded after the pattern of a new totalitarian society. Yet a religious doctrine interpreted by a charismatic totalitarian Führer could be as perfect a diet for the eventual change of all behavioural patterns as the 'class thinking' of Western origin had been in its Stalinist interpretation. Of course, it is a distinct possibility, even probability, that the Iranian brand of totalitarianism will fail before the time necessary for a complete totalization lapses. Arendt once made the reasonable guess that only countries of sufficiently large size can embark on the totalitarian venture with any chance of success. This prognosis turned out to be incorrect, and it will suffice here to point to the example of Albania. Totalitarian rule is not dependent either on size or on time but any complete and all-encompassing totalization of society does take time. Since the more diverse the political factors that have to be considered, the shakier all long-term political predictions turn out to be. I shall not venture into prognoses concerning the viability or non-viability of a religiously founded totalitarian system or the longevity of third world totalitarianism in general. I only stress that the phenomenon exists and it has to be understood by use of the same theoretical tools, analytic and historicist, which were once shaped by Hannah Arendt, calmly, objectively but never *sine ira et studio*.

III

While shifting their main thrust to the third world, totalitarian movements have abated in Western, Central and Southern Europe. Sporadically, one can still find totalitarian parties, but they do not command movements, but rather cater for specific interest groups and subclasses. The detotalization process of the most influential communist party of the Western world, the Italian, has been spectacular. Totalitarian psychology, mentality and ethos survive in marginal groups rather than in mass movements, in particular in the underworld of international terrorism and national right-wing Fascist terrorism. Masses no longer rally around charismatic Führers to seek salvation in a superhuman will. De Gaulle was a charismatic leader but not of the totalitarian kind. He was no Führer and following him was at least rationally motivated (because based on his actual rescuing of a nation); as a result, many people became disappointed in him simply because their interests had not been satisfied by him. These well-known facts only serve to buttress one of my initial statements: certain decisive factors enumerated by Arendt among those comprising the origins of totalitarianism can contribute to the emergence of social tendencies quite different from, occasionally diametrically opposed to, totalitarianism. Let me recall some of Arendt's tenets: a disillusionment with parliamentarism, including traditional political parties; the substitution of certain grand issues for the pursuit of well-defined collective (class, group) interests, the withering away of classes, and the emergence of a 'classless' society of a kind. In my view, these tendencies, far from having disappeared since World War Two, have rather gained momentum without giving rise to any new kind of neo-totalitarianism. What they have given rise to is a new type of social movement.

As far as disillusionment with parliamentarism is concerned, Arendt made one exception: Great Britain. In 1984, the exceptions are rather the historical newcomers to the parliamentary system: Spain and Greece and to some extent Italy, where all parties, except the neo-Fascist MSI, define themselves against the background of a fatal

Fascist past. (Formally, not even Stalinist Greek communism is an exception here.) The disillusionment with parliamentarism can be strongly detected in France, West Germany and Britain. In present-day France, no party, except the dwindling communist party has a tradition. In Britain, the emergence of the liberal and social democratic alliance, irrespective of how it might fare electorally, challenges the traditional two-party system, whereas the traditional background of conservatism has given ground under Thatcher to a more ideologically oriented than pragmatically circumscribed right-wing politics. In West Germany, the success of the Green Party has divided social democracy, whereas a new brand of nationalism has superimposed itself across party and class lines on merely interest-motivated objectives. Although Western societies have not become classless – least of all Britain, the traditional class society *par excellence* in Europe – and class affiliation still expresses itself in voting patterns, cross, i.e. ideologically motivated, issues have moved to the forefront of contestation. These issues are carried by social movements which increasingly dominate the scene of the European political theatre.

In times bygone, big demonstrations were organized by parties, and the biggest ones by totalitarian parties which still held sway over a social imaginary. However, the biggest demonstrations of the last decades have not been organized by parties at all. The sweeping movement of 1968 in France took the Communist Party by surprise; communists did not even understand how they might capitalize on the movement. Even if totalitarian fringe groups participated in the events, they were relegated to the margins. More recently, almost a million demonstrators marched on the streets of Paris in defence of private education. Although all rightist political parties (Le Pen's neo-Fascist party included) were conspicuously present, the demonstration was not organized or orchestrated by them. Similarly, certain totalitarian groups regularly participate in the enormous peace rallies in Germany and Great Britain, but they neither organize nor dominate them.

In pinpointing these new phenomena, I must stress that I am not engaged in gathering material for a refutation of Arendt's theory. At first glance rather, the contrary is the case. Arendt, herself a prodigy of a romantic generation, was far from happy with soulless parliamentary politicking. Rather, her ideal-type of democracy was shaped by the image of the ancient city-state, while later, the old American township and the conciliar system spawned by the Hungarian Revolution of 1956 suited both her theory and temperament far better. I am speaking in her spirit if, regarding recent changes in the European political theatre, I strike a cautiously optimistic chord: instead of the passivity of atomized masses, we see a rather active populace ready to fight out issues directly by circumventing the channels of representation. On the other hand, Arendt regarded mass movements *per se* with a not unfounded suspicion. Movements often fail to encourage discourse. If issues are carried by a crowd with one single voice, differences in opinion cannot be articulated and particular groups cannot stand for the complex network of their interests. What Arendt called 'the mass', is still the subject of mass movements, even if the mob is absent or relegated to the background. This is why optimism must be subdued, though not completely abandoned.

In conclusion, I should like, briefly, to touch upon certain misconceptions concerning the internal cohesion of totalitarianism. There is a widespread view that whereas traditional dictatorships frequently collapse from internal causes, totalitarianism, once established, never does. I have already mentioned Hungary, Czechoslovakia and Poland as conclusive evidence to the contrary. As long as totalitarian rules totalize society only ideologically and politically, the system can as easily collapse from internal causes as any traditional dictatorship. Moreover, as long as a particular society is not completely totalized (the totalization of attitudes included), the collapse of the regime from internal causes is equally possible. I would rather argue that it is precisely during the process of the complete totalization of society that a collapse like this is most likely to occur. The complete totalization of a society requires a very long period of time, during which anything can happen. (And anyhow, the Soviet type of totalitarianism is the only example of complete totalization; religiously based totalitarianism could perhaps be the second.) If nationalism is a strong imaginary institution in a totalitarian society, external threats decrease, rather than increase, the chances of collapse. Soviet totalitarianism was ultimately cemented in the Great Patriotic War. Taking into consideration both this and my firm conviction that the collapse of Soviet totalitarianism could not occur through any gradual change, but only by a predictably cruel revolution, I repeat that external threat decreases, rather than increases the chances of such a collapse. No ruling totalitarian oligarchy could be shaken by the fear of an external threat (to be what they are is simply a condition of existence for them); the populace would, rather, be pushed into rallying around the oligarchic leaders in defence of the imperial might or the mythologized 'national pride' of their country. Further, attempts at undermining the economy of a totalitarian society never weakens the totalitarian character of a Soviet type of society; they can only unleash waves of repression in them. If people starve to death, this is indeed their problem, and not a factor of, say, the government's 'electoral chances'. Although totalitarian oligarchies, as all governments, prefer to satisfy the elementary needs of their populations, they will not alter a single cog of their sham objectives, select new scapegoats or increase oppression instead. The Soviet leaders are no longer 'free' agents of an arbitrary policy, not even in the sense that Khrushchev had been. They are themselves caught in the web of systemic imperatives. They are unscrupulous and cynically lucid as to the *modus operandi* of their regime and its requirements. But they are no longer infernal, in the sense that Stalin (and his entourage) was evil incarnate. Nor have they any hidden wisdom on their side. Therefore, the never-ending attempts by Sovietologists to fathom the secrets of a possible future leader are but academic exercises.

I have drafted this paper as a new preface to the imaginary re-edition of *The Origins of Totalitarianism*. Some of Arendt's prognoses in 1966 proved wrong. I hope that some of my prognoses will equally prove wrong. It is with this hope that I can look forward to a further preface to *The Origins of Totalitarianism*, in the next millenium.

11

In the Bestarium –
A Contribution to the Cultural
Anthropology of 'Real Socialism'

Ferenc Fehér[1]

The culture of Venice can be read from the perspective of the Bellinis or the tragic grandeur of the last Tintoretto of the Scuola San Rocco, but, equally legitimately, from the perspective of the horrible dungeons of the doges. The first way of reading 'from above', practiced by the overwhelming majority of cultural historians, understands civilizations from the angle of their 'transcendence', from the 'celestial' efforts, the institutions and objectivations which transcend the 'normal' in-humanity of social contexts, from peaks which represent and relay the humanistic maximum of the culture under scrutiny. (Needless to say, 'inhumanity' and 'humanistic maximum' are modernizing terms, but I deliberately adopt here the position of modernity as the basis of my understanding.) The introduction of a 'reading from below' is the great deed of Foucault. Actually he does not use the term of 'bestiarium',[2] but the level at which he operates, the ensemble of the institutions that perpetrate and perpetuate inhumanity in a given civilization, the agglomerate of men bred by such customs and institutions, can be comprehensively called the 'bestiarium'. Every culture up until now has lived in a tension between 'transcendence' and 'bestiarium'. If it did not, it could only mean that the second factor homogenized society as a

---

[1] From *Praxis International*.

[2] I borrow the word from Heinrich Böll, who coined and applied it to the Soviet institutions for punishing and taming humans described in the memorable book of the Soviet dissident, Lew Kopelew. L. Kopelew, *Aufbewahren für alle Zeit*, Munich: Piper, 1975. Kopelew, a Jewish soldier of the Red Army, fought nearly till victory, and was imprisoned as a traitor for systematically defending German civilians in East Prussia against rape, plunder and murder by the soldiers of the Soviet Army.

whole, in other words, that we are confronted with the state of barbarism.

To provide this often used, rarely clarified, term with some significance, one has to break drastically with the traditions of enlightenment so clearly represented by Schiller. For Schiller there was, prior to all social regulations and sins instigated by the reign of social rules, the innocent savage. The barbarian offspring of a perverted civilization, emerged (or rather sank to the level of the savage) only later. The barbarian had lost the capacity of creating and observing social rules, and had therefore relapsed into a state of anarchy. His relapse was no longer a happy innocence prior to knowledge. It was a loss of knowledge of what is pertinent to our being human, the punishment of culture for our perversions. There is obviously a considerable difference between the states of having pure and yet uncontaminated innocence and loss of knowledge, but, in the Enlightenment conception, there is a common denominator to which both are reduced: their common absence of regulations. Even Marx, with his famous allusion to barbarism prevailing if both contestants, bourgeoisie and proletariat, destroy each other in a draw, must have had something similar in mind. But this was just an uncritical acceptance of the Enlightenment mythology on the part of an overwhelmingly critical heir: there is no lasting social structure without the reign of some rules, imposed or self-imposed.

Rationally speaking, barbarism can have two meanings. The first was supplied by Greek antiquity which regarded the city-state, its inhabitants (and, of course, everything for which the city-state stood culturally) as civilization and everything else (the alien) as non-civilization. The second meaning is derivative of a culture at the pinnacle of which stands the concept of humanism, however debased it may appear in the daily practice of this culture. But in both cases barbarism is not identical with a simple absence of regulations – it is something positive, culture seen as 'perverted' in the light of the central concept of post-Enlightenment civilization, but a cultural formation nonetheless, a social state with regulations of its own. In my terms, it is a social constellation in which the permanent tension between the bestiarium and transcendence has collapsed and where there are no longer effective institutions, accepted customs, or regular collective human efforts aimed at the transcendence of the prevailing inhumanity.

Even so sketchy a typology of the bestiarium in modernity (to which I restrict myself) has to analyse its appearance and its different extensions in three cultural formations: in traditional liberal capitalism, in Nazism, and in 'real socialism' (or as I am more inclined to call it: in the dictatorship over needs). My main concern here will be finding the *differentia specifica* of the latter. Foucault is the great historian of the bestiarium of liberal capitalism *qua* the oppressive rule of *raison analytique*, of its prisons, mental asylums, clinics, of its reifying rules and habits which, precisely in their capacity as a universal quantifier, turn everything living and organic into a cosmos of inanimate objects. Hateful as this cosmos appears viewed from the angle of its bestiarium, nonetheless it is not a state of barbarism. One can still see counter-tendencies, active and influential, in this society.[3]

There is, of course, a way of reading liberal capitalism as barbarism as well: through explaining Nazism, for me inadmissibly, as a simple continuation of the inherent principles of liberal capitalism. When Adorno and Horkheimer drew the map of the negative dialectics of enlightenment, they believed they had discovered in the original and triumphant forms of *raison analytique* the instrumental rationality of the 'final solution;. But this view is either a propagandistic and totalizing exaggeration or an expression of despair, perhaps even of capitulation in the face of an apparently invincible enemy rather than any kind of realistic assessment of the actual state of affairs.

With Fascism the situation, for obvious reasons, is just the contrary: it is the bestiarium, and that alone, which comes to the fore in all analyses. Even mentioning the fact that Fascism, undoubtedly a kind of barbarism, also represented a kind of culture, was sacrilegious in a morally healthier period in which no scholarly research was needed for the scrupulous conscience of eminent academics, such as Noam Chomsky, to prove the existence of gas chambers beyond reasonable doubt. But no understandable reticence must block the recognition that Nazi Fascism was a barbarian culture whose system of symbols shines through the horrendous scenes of extermination camps as well as the choreography of menacing mass rallies. It is the image of an aesthetic–necrophilic barbarism that emerges here, with the following main characteristic features. Firstly, it is rather a culture of pure and unadulterated irrationalism that a continuation of instrumental rationalism. Not only the repeated and deliberate ignoring of practical exigencies testify to this (for instance, the categoric dismissal of any kind of conci-

---

[3] Of course, a radically different view is presented by those colonies of liberal capitalism in which a traditional counter-culture did not prove effective enough to serve as the safeguard against the bestiarium unimpeded by liberal values. Sartre, in his famous preface to Fanon's *Wretched of the Earth*, justly shows a modern barbarism in full vigour in such colonies. But for a balanced view, it has to be stressed again that this statement applies to colonies only in which a traditional and strongly rooted culture could not act as check and balance, as a force of transcendence.

liatory political formulae which could have temporarily mobilized social groups on behalf of Nazism, or the use of vehicles of transport for the purposes of deportation when a desperate and harassed army most needed them). The ultimate proof is the all-embracing telos of Nazism: universal conquest, which can only conclude either in a collective suicide of the 'race' or in the irrelevance of the objective itself when the conquest becomes truly universal. The second distinctive feature is that the whole bestiarium, the camps, the round-ups, the rallies, the public punishments and awards, the funerals of the 'heroes' (think of Heydrich's funeral supervised and organized by the Führer himself in the best Bayreuth tradition), all follows a carefully planned, aesthetic design, a choreography which serves the purpose of mythical community. It is the race, not the individual, that demonstrates superiority here over all other races, and it demonstrates the strength of the race in part by its ruthless power, in part by its aesthetic superiority (and order). When it comes to the (mythologically conceived) interests of the race, the otherwise unrestrained Fascist individual is kept within strict boundaries. Despite certain inconsistencies of the regulations, the SS personnel, normally at large to do what they deemed fit with Jews, Slavs and members of other inferior races, were mostly strictly punished for the sexual use of these objects. The purity of race had to be observed and purity was threatened not only by children of 'mixed' racial features, but, in terms of a mythological culture, consistently by intercourse as well. Finally, it was an organistic–mythical culture, the pseudo-artistic forms of which resembled a certain kind of folklore opera and folklore fete. It was organized on organistic symbols such as blood, soil, magic animals (mostly eagles) and magic signs (the most important of which was the swastika). All these symbols either directly grew out of, or equally directly, referred to the bestiarium. In principle, the symbolic gestures and signs could have proved fertilizing for a future barbarian creation. But as a result of a number of factors (the short lifetime of Nazism, a part of which was already spent in war, and, deeper still, the conflict between the universal and narrowly national, the Nazi movement's final recoil from showing its genuine physiognomy at its most bestial in public, its option of masquerading in a shabby classicistic charade instead, etc.) the Nazi mythology could never produce any art *sui generis* of consequence. In fact, it only had one representative artist of its own: Leni Riefenstahl. A number of misanthropic great names, past their creative prime (Hamsun, Celine and others) only joined the movement for 'anthropological' and political, rather than artistic, reasons (not to mention the vulgar opportunists).

The bestiarium of 'real socialism', nowadays simply called Gulag

(but which, as we shall see, is far more extended and much more intricate than Gulag *sensu stricto*), can only be understood as the combination of several factors. The first of them derives from the main telos of
production in this society, from the increase of social wealth strictly
under the control of the ruling apparatus.[4]

The increase of social wealth as the maximization of total social
control implies general unfreedom, the wholesale transformation of
human subjects into quasi-natural objects who only count as
computable elements of an ever-expanding social control. This goes
together with the rigidly upheld lie of an enlightened humanism, the
propagandistic but compulsory cult of *The Magic Flute*. Above all, this
dual structure ends in the brutal indifference displayed in the process
and methods of suppression employed in the bestiarium of 'real
socialism'. All readers of reports from Kolima, Norilsk, Vorkuta and
other annihilation camps of Stalin, accustomed to the operatic *mis en
scène* of Auschwitz, an atmosphere which usually invites regisseurs
working with this 'material' to add Wagner to the scenes of the 'final
solution', are generally surprised by the everyday drabness of the
Gulag. Millions are thrown here into their inevitable but slow death
without much theatrical accompaniment. In the Gulag there is no
choreography of sadism, just brutal acts, no artistic pleasure and
collective fete of sending people to their death: that would be regarded
as bourgeois mannerism. There is no torture for torture's sake, only
torture and a pedantically prepared and rehearsed script of the show
trials when they are functionally necessary: torture for torture's sake
would contradict socialist humanism. There is not even the reward of
an unrestrained and self-indulgent bestiality for the warders who are,
even if, of course, at a different level, objects of total control themselves. An insensitive and impersonal mechanism is at work here. But
the total victory of functionalism transforms the originally existing
fundamentalist symbols (the red star, the red banner) into simple 'road
signs', pieces of an empty iconography. They are important as icons
simply through their presence: their destruction or simple removal is in
itself a proof of counterrevolution (as Kádár's government argued after
1956 in Hungary). But they are no longer cultic objects, targets of
quasi-religious or mystical devotion, as they had been for a short
period after the Russian revolution.

A second constituent of the Soviet bestiarium is the mob-like rudeness of its personnel, rudeness as a general atmosphere. The adjective

[4] This problem is explored in detail in F. Fehér, A. Heller, G. Markus, *Dictatorship Over
Needs*, Oxford: Blackwell, 1983.

has some importance here. All explanations of the system which adduce 'backwardness', not to speak of the Russian character, are either insufficient or turn into an outright slandering of a national community. On the one hand, 'backwardness' or 'primitiveness', with its unmistakable allusion to the roughness of peasant cultures, does not explain anything. Peasant cultures, even the toughest of them, usually contain elements, even institutions, of caring and protecting, sometimes of charity and commiseration, in other words, features which are excluded from the bestiarium for reasons of principle. On the other hand, explanations by reference to the 'Russian character' of oppression, apart from their unmistakably racist accent, cannot account for the universality of the bestiarium which is to be found in Czechoslovakia as well as in Korea. But crowds of humans pushed into the political dynamic of the system and organized by external compulsion and internal atomization, become mobs. They supply the suitable human material for an indifferently brutal oppression which is apparently freed of the ballast of conscience.

A further element is provided here by a false kind of atheism. Atheism combined with dis-enlightenment, with the destruction of the individual critical intellect as the authentic seat of moral authority, and, at the same time, with the loss of a morally relevant community leaves us penultimately with no binding norms of action. Dostoevsky's famous *aperçu*: 'if there is no God, everything is allows', applies precisely to this type of social constellation. In fact, apart from the short intermezzo of Khrushchev, who bore visibly some sort of personal grudge against religion, the process of construction of the Soviet bestiarium had only one, relatively short, period of an ideologically passionate atheism: the Leninist phase. After that atheism for the members of the apparatus was taken for granted. Faith was replaced by a cheap type of utilitarianism which has made the maxim 'everything is allowed' socially valid. As a just punishment for this, an ever-increasing number of dissidents turn now towards the most obscurantist types of traditional religions.

The final constitutent is the Jacobin element. It is a strange dialectic that many refined aspects of the Jacobin project serve as a foundation of the outright animal indifference of the bestiarium. The first of them is the legitimation of all inhuman acts in the name of the 'future generation' whose happiness is allegedly at stake. This is a good antidote against the vestiges of a personal conscience. The second is the collective moral slandering of the enemy: belonging to a non-accepted social group becomes here a sin which also has the useful side-effect of eliminating the remnants of Christian compassion. If being a class enemy is identical with being morally gravely reprehensible, there is understandably no room left for sympathy. Finally, the Jacobin project provides a pseudo-rational pretext for collective repression, in contrast to the racist–mythological ideology of Nazism, and pseudo-rationality adds to the self-assurance of those perpetrating collective repressions. All this distinguishes the Soviet bestiarium from the aesthetic and overtly irrational–mythological character of the Fascist bestiarium on the one hand, and from the atomizing–individualistic character of oppression and domination of *raison analytique* in liberal capitalism, on the other hand.

The extension of the bestiarium in 'real socialism' cannot be reasonably reduced to the scope of Gulag proper. The culture created by Stalin, attenuated but left fundamentally unaltered by his heirs and successors, is barbaric precisely in the sense that in it there is no strict line of demarcation between the bestial and the non-bestial. The confines of the former are certainly not identical with the walls of the concentration camps of the Gulag. There was very good reason for the visceral hatred against Solzhenytsin on the part of the founders and guardians of the collective ethos of the new barbarism. The great writer showed the whole of 'real socialism' as cancer-ridden, in other words, as striken by the plague of barbarism.[5]

The triumph of barbarism in 'real socialism' is a historically just punishment for the original sin of the terror with which the regime started its career and of which Stalin was a logical continuation. I will return to the main feature of the bestiarium: the imprisonment of the body by the soul. But since 'soul' (the dominant ideology) became a ruthless guardian of every subject and of all aspects of social life, all institutions, doctrines, habits, norms have lost their culture-creating validity precisely because they had originally a general humanistic claim. Therefore it is not accidental that the only cultural creation in this society has been coming for decades now only from dissidents who are writing about the bestiarium and whose outraged question is precisely this: what have you done to our people?

While the existence of the bestiarium *sensu stricto* is always an officially denied fact in 'real socialism' which can only be recognized retrospectively, it is, nevertheless, the secret organizing centre of

---

[5] I note here only, for those who read with bias, that the above statement does not imply that every Soviet citizen is a barbarian. Kopelew, in his *Aufbewahren für alle Zeit*, shows not only the martyrs of resistance against such barbarism, but also the many uninvolved who kept at least a distance from it as well. What creates the generally barbaric character of a society is the ruling ethos to which no countervailing ethics, habits, and institutions of 'transcendence' are counterposed.

society.[6] This is so primarily because people very often become beasts in a very genuine sense of the word only to avoid the inner circles of the bestiarium. Moreover, the Gulag, in its past and present forms, is an encyclopaedia and an open display of the hidden principles which keep the society of the dictatorship over needs running. Forced labour in the camps can serve here as a general explanatory model, despite the obvious differences between the workforce inside and outside the camps. (To mention only the most important one: inside the camps the workforce consists of slave workers in the original sense of the word, outside they are dependent workers, dependent to an extent that would not be tolerated by any wage earner in liberal capitalism, but they are not slaves.) The whole area of life activities of the slave labourer is controlled by the authorities. No collective (or corporative) organization is tolerated, nor are the rights of the individual recognized, above all not their right to leisure or to do work other than that prescribed. They are denied any collective representation of interests (or demands as well). Denying the right to leisure is very closely tied up with the telos of production in 'real socialism'. This is the simple but deeply-rooted creed of Major Godynnik, this exemplary specimen of Soviet barbarism, the present commander of the annihilation camp reserved for the handicapped in Dnepropetrovsk, in the Ukraine. In reply to the question of a convict: 'Why have you set up a camp for the handicapped if they are forced to work just like those who are in a good shape?' the commander of this Soviet Buchenwald answered without hypocrisy and to the point: 'You are the sad ballast of our society . . . rather than shooting you it is more worthwhile making you work to exploit some profit for society.'[7]

The bestiarium in 'real socialism' has a wide variety of techniques to transform human subjects into obedient objects of total social control. The first of them is mobilizing the endlessness of time against the finitude of the individual's life. This holds true primarily of the prisoner of Gulag, but also of the 'free' citizen of 'real socialism'. Hitler's regime

---

[6] After the 20th Congress, the camps surfaced in Khrushchev's very incomplete presentation. Up until then even mentioning them was a dangerous anti-state crime which was punished by being sent to the non-existent camps. At present, for Soviet authorities, no mental asylums designed for the treatment of dissenting minds exists, nor do, for that matter, mass camps of punishment and forced labour which embrace millions, common deliquents and political 'criminals' alike.

[7] The exchange has been reported by A. Zelyakov, 'handicapped second class', a man of exceptional courage who has smuggled out and signed his testimony, obviously destined only for posterity. It was published in *Bulletin de samizdat*, Brussels, 1981, I., pp. 2–4. Let me add once again: this memorable institution of Soviet 're-education' is a presently functioning camp, not a figment of recollection from Stalin's days.

lived, morally and psychologically, in a state of permanent *Blitzkrieg*. The training of the 'blond beast' could only be realized in continuous necrophilic actions of military destruction and mass extermination. Therefore the Nazi culture recognized no *durée*, only the timelessness of the great moments of action. This is why it not only demanded courage from its own adherents, it also provoked heroism as the only adequate response to its necrophilic destruction. But Stalin's goal of education, taming the individual into an obedient tool of maximized social control, required a completely different technology. It could only work if all the time necessary for the difficult task of internalizing fear and obedience was taken. Neglecting this fundamental structural (not moral) difference between the two types of destructive barbarism can lead to misjudgements of the first order, as it did with Solzhenytsin who is inadmissibly apologetic of the Vlasovites. The faulty logic and the even more erroneous moral judgement in this case stems not from an exuberance of Christian compassion (the latter is Kopelew's, not Solzhenytsin's attitude), nor from disregarding the fact that, whatever the original motivation, a considerable part of the Vlasovites became perpetrators or accomplices of mass murder. Ultimately, Solzhenytsin does not seem to grasp that the destruction of whole human groups in a frenzy of speed was not a by-product of Nazism but the cultural premise of its existence and 'educational' work. Hitler understood his own universe and its barbarous values much better than Eichmann who regarded the final solution as a strategic mistake of the Führer. As against this spirit of ongoing and compulsive destruction, taking sides with Stalin was a reasonable and morally legitimate decision even onthe part of those who knew what Stalin's barbarism represented, while taking sides with Hitler was an unpardonable sin. Where there is the endlessness of time, there is at least the abstract chance of escaping the worst.

But where time works for the warders, there is no need for the spectacular instrumentarium of destruction, gas chambers and crematoria. The target groups to be destroyed will be simply abandoned to nature, to the 'natural' process of decomposition and disintegration. Suffice to read the shattering recapitulation of the Kulak Holocaust by Solzhenytsin. Many millions were here, according to the writer: 13 million (or those of them who survived the trip, not a bit more humane than the one to Auschwitz) simply thrown out of the wagons and driven right into the conditions of the stone age in the arctic regions of the Soviet Union. All this happened without the minimum of tools necessary for simple survival, in other words, with maximum efficiency, but without the fanfares and backdrops, without the lightening speed of the SS mise en scène. Maximum efficiency of destruction is the key term here, for it is a deliberate Stalinist propaganda lie that the famine which the prisoners of the bestiarium suffered was no worse than the lot of the civilian population. Between 1937 and 1940, there was no famine in the Soviet Union, only the 'normal' short food supplies arriving on schedule, but all reports from the bestiarium testify without fail to a lethal combination of a systematically administered undernourishment and the overload of hard physical work, an exact match to the conditions of the Nazi camps. Or to mention another example: from among the nearly 200,000 German soldiers who surrendered at Stalingrad not many more than 6,000 returned home, which is certainly not the ratio of survival of the civilian Soviet population. This frightening statistic conceals (or rather uncovers) a brutal retaliation for the treatment of Soviet prisoners of war on the part of a government which neglected the elementary legal protection of its own soldiers and sent them to camps after the victory for 'treason' (i.e. for not dying voluntarily in a hopeless situation but surrendering). In all these cases, abandonment to natural destruction via famine played the prime role in the arsenal of mass extermination. Eminently 'materialist' considerations predominated in this policy. There was the shrewd calculation that a systematically weakened body will produce a listless and obedient mind, therefore the danger of camp mutinies will be minimal. Further, the Soviet 'criminologists' maintained that a systematically undernourished organism must harbour a mind perforce subservient to the unquestionable supreme authority. This is the educational value of systematic starvation. All reports arriving from Chinese, Korean and Vietnamese camps corroborate this 'enlightened' aspect of a shrewdly administered undernourishment.

Famine is just one instance of using the finitude of the body in the service of an alienating and imprisoning 'soul'. Another typical form has remained: denying prisoners of the bestiarium of anything but the most elementary forms of medical care, in other words, instead of torturing the body, abandoning it to self-torture. A further method was directly provided by nature: exposing the prisoner's body to the excesses of climate, heat or frost. But in all cases, it was a kind of bestial utilitarianism, never aesthetic sadism, as with the Nazis, that prevailed.

The personality yield was adequate. Aesthetic sadism produced necrophilic and playful beasts who, even at the lowest level of intelligence, transformed carnage into a kind of aesthetically organized game in which the victims were the involuntary protagonists of a choreography imposed upon them. No such playfulness or inventiveness was needed, and therefore tolerated, for the purposes of Stalin's utilitarianism. Both attitudes rejected chivalry or commiseration towards the victim, as both barbarian cultures were non-Christian, or even outright atheistic, if in different ways. But the compulsory norms of behaviour by which these values were replaced differed in each case. With the Nazis it was libertinage, with the Stalinists indifference heightened into a wholesale contempt for the very existence of the enemy.

A main feature in common between Stalinist barbarism and the oppression of *raison analytique*, as described by Foucault whose categories I shall use here, and a feature distinguishing both of them from Nazism, was remitting the body to the constant custody of soul. From Foucault's exhaustive analysis of prison, clinic, mental asylum and the like we know now how and why *raison analytique* used the body as the vehicle of oppression. A different case is presented by 'real socialism'. Here the universal telos is the principle of total social control, a self-abandonment of enlightenment, a return to the tutelage of authority, i.e. to complete disenlightenment. The several forms of punishment inflicted on the body are means to this universal telos.

But what is the exact content of the telos, of keeping the body in the soul's confinement? First of all, it is remarkable that there were formal sentences in Stalin's bestiarium at its most lunatic, when a sentence in itself meant absolutely nothing. Had the prisoner the luck to have served his or her time, s/he very often got a new automatically extended sentence. Moreover, in contrast to Nazi camps, there was in Gulag a regular spying on the prisoners' opinions (and not on their clandestine activities which were, of course, closely supervised by the Nazis as well). At the same time a most telling silence surrounded the duration of the time to be served in the case of certain groups (the kulaks for instance), an unmistakable indication of their premediated extermination. All this suggests a special strategy of imprisoning the body in the dungeons of a perverted soul. The hope of being liberated sometime, when they will have 'deserved' it, had to be aroused in the prisoners. Without such hopes the whole strategy would have been doomed to failure.

It was then a sign of grace if one was admitted into the 're-education process', into the process of 'voluntary' self-abandonment of one's Ego, of one's opinions, if one was allowed to participate in being fully absorbed by an alien and unchallengeable authority. If one was not, it simply meant that one had been selected for destruction, as with the kulaks, or as in the case of the victims of the Nazis who could not be 're-educated' because of their 'racial' inferiority. Re-education, this key category of disenlightenment, implies, in the main, a transfer of the seat of the individual's critical intellect to the unchallengeable authority.

Only when one has lost the capacity of thinking individually and, above all, critically, is one worthy of considerations of mercy which may or may not be conferred. It was precisely this re-educational work of dis-enlightenment which distinguished the Soviet bestiarium from the Nazi institutions: the latter only bothered about the opinions of alien races if they wanted to impose a special humiliation on the enemy before destroying them physically. It is not generally known how consistent this re-education was. Even the peak of Soviet mercifulness, Khrushchev's Great Amnesty, stipulated that only people could be released who signed a document in which they admitted their guilt. The few who insisted on their innocence were returned to the camps.

It is the particular type of culture of remitting the body in 'real social-ism' to the soul's custody that determines the ethos of oppression and the reactions ensuing from it on the poles of the warder and the victim as well. As to the warder's official culture so truthfully portrayed by 'socialist realism', we find a boring and philistine Victorianism. The protagonists of its works of art mostly do not have bodies, and certainly no erotic aura. Malyarov, the deputy State Attorney of the Soviet Union, one of the leaders of the present-day Gulag system, yells angrily at Sakharov during an interrogation with righteous indignation: 'Do you want the kind of filthy liberty which produced the disgusting pornography I saw with my own eyes on the streets of Stockholm?' Lesbianism and homosexuality are still regarded officially as hardly explicable 'deviations' (the latter is very heavily persecuted in Cuba). Kopelew mentions in his memoirs that the so-called front marriages (semi-legalized relations between front soldiers of both sexes who had families at home) only became recognized when Stalin's remark that while a man sleeping with another man was 'unnatural', a man sleeping with a woman was 'natural', started to circulate. (And no one dared let gossip stemming from Stalin circulate if it did not in fact stem from him.) Together with the usual double standards, the Victorianism of the warder resulted in a strange functionalism: unrestrained indulgence in, instead of functional use of, torture was generally not encouraged, nor is it now. No doubt, the daily practice of the bestiarium partly attracts, partly breeds, sadists, morally not at all better than the average Gestapo functionary. Some of them, for example the infernal Khmer Rouge security chief, Brother Deuch, are an exact match for their famous colleague, the Gestapo Müller who after the collapse of the Reich, as rumour from authoritative sources had it, served Soviet security for years. However, to use the language of Soviet ideological debates, the self-indulgent sadist was not typical.

Typical was rather, in every sickening detail, the official report in

1950 by Dr M.B., lieutenant-colonel of the AVH, the Hungarian secret police (which I later had the opportunity to read), how he tormented to death István Riesz, the former minister of justice, then a 65-year-old man. (Riesz was one of those leaders of the social democrats who helped to eliminate their own party and who in reward were imprisoned for many years, hanged or beaten to death by their communist allies.) Dr M.B. had a long party career behind him, a part of which was spent outside Hungary, in resistance to Fascism, according to the testimonies, in a courageous loyalty to his cause. He was a fine, educated man who spoke several languages well. In this atrocious barbarian it was certainly not primitiveness that stimulated action but perverted culture, the telos of subjecting everyone – if need be with the utmost violence – to the authorities of an unchallengeable social control. The regard which carefully scrutinizes the thing called István Riesz left to his discretion, is cold and objective as it appears in his report to his chief, the head of the AVH. Dr M.B. describes how, after having beaten up the old man several times, he still cannot see signs of 'softening' in him, at least not to a degree which would show readiness to sign any confession presented to him by the interrogator. Therefore, together with intensification of the 'physical punishment', he shifted his line of attack. He 'scolded him', as a child, for 'his dirtiness, for having wet his pants'. The detail is significant. It provides, especially as it became a generally used trick of interrogatory technique, a deep insight into the culture of 'real socialism'. The interrogator must be a puritan of morality and personal habits. (Dr M.B. is well known as a model family man in Budapest where he lives unharmed after a short imprisonment, a punishment adequate for shoplifting.) It is this physical and moral purity that provides the inquisitor's superiority over the victim. And never mind the double standards which are anyhow protected by the secrecy surrounding government matters. But Stalinist purity knows no moral, psychological or legally stipulated restrictions regarding handling and manhandling victims. The latter have to be pushed into a physically and psychologically humiliating position, their whole process of socialization has to be deliberately reversed in order to recognize the absolute authority of the inquisitor, as intimidated and physically mistreated children recognize that of a brutal father. Later Dr M.B. laconically communicated to his superior commander that he had beaten István Riesz to death and had him 'buried' in quicklime in order that no trace of him should remain. But even this last act does not seem to be the deed of an orgiastic dionysian, rather a coldly indifferent and utilitarian barbarism. Riesz was too stubborn, therefore he proved useless for purposes of a show trial. Anyhow, according to a political decision of the Party leadership during the process of interrogation, the 'case' was not going to be open; therefore it made no difference whatsoever in what way the defendant was taken care of. As long as Riesz seemed to be a useful chunk of raw material, his body remained in the prison of the soul, of the oppressive external telos and its ingenious methods. When he was no longer functionally needed, murdering him as a 'punishment' for his disobedience could be instructive for both prisoners and other warders. Dr M.B. stressed in his report that he often mentioned his 'severity' towards Riesz to his less experienced and perhaps more lenient colleagues. And in fact, such reports were carefully studied by the superior officers of the secret police, its 'lessons' were built into the manuals and the technology of taming and punishing.

A special chapter within the whole system of the bestiarium is provided by the mental asylums used during the last 20 years against the dissidents. But why is such a complex, burdensome and, at the same time, expensive institution of punishment used? And further: why weren't they used under Stalin, why did they only become fashionable during Khrushchev's last years, and used extensively under the 'peace-loving' and 'moderate' rule of President Brezhnev? The answer is that the mental asylums are symbolic institutions of punishment in a situation in which a certain degree of re-enlightenment has already taken place. It is not without relevance that one of the first political prisoners of the mental asylums was precisely General Grigorenko, a man of great integrity and intellectual capacities. Grigorenko started his critical campaign from the premises of Khrushchev's secret speech, the devastating critique of Stalin's unpreparedness for the German's attack with an incomparably higher level of competence than Khrushchev's impulsive criticisms, but he immediately went futher and criticized Khrushchev himself. That much enlightenment was no longer tolerable for the First Secretary, and he sent Grigorenko for his critical and autonomous mind to a mental asylum. The whole system has retained ever since its original symbolic meaning. The definition of madness in the Soviet bestiarium is dissenting thinking. The mental asylum is a public announcement of this definition and a social institution preserved only for the symbolic cases of independent thinking. In other words, the mental asylum is a Bastille of compulsory disenlightenment.

Of the two great rivals and parallel educators, Stalin proved by far the more successful and realistic one. Barbarism of his brand not only outlived the Hitlerite 'blond beast' and its spectacular *salto mortale*, Stalin's new man has also learned how to wear silk gloves on his fist and become respectable. But Kopelew's sharp eyes watched closely the moment in which Stalin's 'man of new type' started to uncover his genuine face to a wider audience. In the months preceding victory, then already a certainty, just as for a longer period afterwards, an element of uncertainty was detectable in Stalin's strategy. Strangely enough, at first he did not know what to do with his greatest triumph. He was vacillating, as it were, towards regarding the part of Germany captured by him as simply an enormous piece of loot and treating its population in the way he later treated many ethnic groups, the 'punished nations', of his own empire. Without doubt, that was at least one of his options. Barbarism, up till then inward-directed, was just picking up momentum to perform the same work on a tenfold scale to what had been done after the annexation of the Western Ukraine in 1939 when 2 to 3 million Poles and Ukrainians were deported to Siberia. Later, under the impact of different strategic considerations, Stalin reconsidered this option. But between January and May 1945, there was a delicate division of labour between the actual attitude of the army towards the German population and the official declarations. The latter emphasized unceasingly the Stalinist motto ('Hitlers come, Hitlers go, but the German people remain'); adequate, indeed very severe, orders were issued by the commanding officers. Occasionally some of the looters, rapists, and murderers were even executed (Stalin was never particularly fussy about the lives of his own soldiers). But in the main, the army personnel treated the inhabitants of East Prussia as likely candidates for a new forcible population transfer, for whose lives or goods they didn't have to account. The most tragic feature of this situation was not simply the general thirst for revenge of the soldiers even if this is far from being as normal as commentators are inclined to assume. A demand of revenge against a community without discrimination is normal only in a barbaric culture in which hate aroused artificially by every means of propaganda (for instance by the vile racist pamphlet of Ehrenburg against the 'Kraut') reigns supreme, and in which various sorts of collective retributions are daily occurrences. One fact, however, remains undisputed. There were so many victims in Russian, Belorussian and Ukrainian families that the feeling of revenge was understandable, even if it was far from natural, if we have in mind an at least somewhat humanized nature. A far more disgusting feature was the hidden complicity of the Soviet Supreme Command in all these acts of plundering and violence. While the authorities were issuing the most vigorous bans on such crimes, at the same time they authorized the personnel to send home enormous amounts of goods from Germany. Kopelew, a convinced socialist for whom such deeds could never become 'normal' was outraged. What else, he asks, if not an indirect encouragement of all sorts of barbarism, could this sudden lenience mean? And finally, only one little step below the surface of humanistic declarations, bans and orders lurked the undisputed and triumphant ideology of open barbarism, challenging which was a serious crime in itself. (And eventually Kopelew paid with 11 years in concentration camps for having questioned it.) He clearly observed the new type of barbarian, the yield of Stalin's scrupulous training, in the person of his commanding officer, Sabashtanskij. After a series of clashes because of Kopelew's inadmissible liberalism towards the German populace, Sabashtanskij, finally, in a fit of rage, sums up his philosophy in the following way: '... the soldier must hate the enemy like pestilence, he must have the wish to annihilate him to his very roots. And in order for the soldier to maintain his combat readiness, to know why he jumps out of trenches, why he is crawling through minefields in enemy fire, he must also know: he came to Germany and everything is his – all the belongings of the Germans, the women, everything! Do what you will! Hit them so hard that even their grandchildren and great grandchildren will tremble!' And when Kopelew asks the logical question: 'Does this mean that the soldier is allowed to murder women and children?' the true adept of the Stalin school shows his radicalism: 'what is this all about children, you idiot? These are only exceptional cases. Not every soldier will murder children. We both certainly will not. But if you are already mentioning this let those, who do it in a state of frenzy, kill little Krauts until they have got fed up with it ... Brother, this is war, not theory and not literature. Of course, there must be everything in the books: morality, humanism, internationalism. All this is beautiful and theoretically correct. but now first of all let us set all of Germany to fire, after that, you can write correct and beautiful books on humanism and internationalism.'[8]

The outburst of this radical and consistent cultural philosopher deserves a somewhat more detailed analysis. First of all Sabashtanskij, as all theoretically conscious barbarians, is a 'naturalist'. In his anthropology, it is a natural propensity of human beings to fight as beasts, led only by rapacious instincts, therefore it is precisely these instincts that have to be cultivated and enhanced. It no more occurs to him than to his idol, the master strategist, that, had the infantry been better covered by artillery fire and air support than was usual under the Generalissimo's Spartan way of warfare, less bestial instincts would have been necessary. Beyond this, however, his plaidoyer for unpunished

---

[8] L. Kopelew, *Aufbewahren für alle Zeit* (Munich, 1975), p. 96.

plundering, rape and even infanticide is just a straightforward expression of cultural pattern in which hate plays the leading role: hatred against the kulaks or the Trotzkyites, or hatred of Germans as such. For Sabashtanskij it is also 'natural' that the soldier can only be motivated and rewarded by the licence of robbing and brutalizing a population which simply became the property of the soldier. In this context of a consciously declared new slavery, it is consistent not to regard infanticide as a crime.[9] Finally, without intentional frivolousness, but with cynical realism, Sabashtanskij accurately understands the role of ideology as an empty icon and a simple decoration for the Soviet bestiarium. His words do not mean that the books about humanism and internationalism are superfluous. On the contrary, they are most important as a facade after the work of destruction had been done, only they have no bearing whatsoever on our deeds. And if someone still believes that this is an exceptional case of a subordinate and primitive man, one should read *Night Frost in Prague* by Zdenek Mlynář recounts how, during the signature of the August 1968 'agreement' between the Czechoslovak and Soviet leadership, an agreement which was foisted upon Dubček in the best Sabashtanskij manner, the top barbarian, Brezhnev bursts out in a rage. He rationalizes the Soviet interventions not with ideological arguments but with Sabashtanskij's reasons. The borders of the Soviet Union are the borders of Czechoslovakia, he yells, it is a conquest of war, and so it will remain for all time.[10]

There is a most telling interrelationship between the barbarous habits and the aggressive claim of health in this culture. The official propaganda of 'real socialism' is constantly boasting about health as a distinctive feature of its culture as against morbid liberal capitalism decadence. As a matter of fact, focusing on health and therapy is indeed a novelty in Western society, where, at the *fin de siècle*, illness

---

[9] The following relevant objection can be made here. The communities which invented the very concept of 'barbarian' and 'barbarism' committed several acts not a bit better than those described by Kopelew on mass scale. In fact, the destruction of Carthage was one of the most spectacular (and one of the first well-documented) cases of genocide. However, the Greek, Roman, etc. cultures were familiar with the distinction between the barbarian and the citizen (where the latter stood for individual refinement and culture), but not yet with the socially valid concept and allegedly binding norm of universal humanism.

[10] Z. Mlynář, *Night Frost in Prague*, London: C. Hurst and Co., 1980. And, of course, the refined Moscow literary theorist who will assure you that he despises Brezhnev – he only identifies with him if he were ready to launch a pre-emptive nuclear strike against the Chinese (because they are the yellow peril? or to cure them from their 'dogmatism'?) – is not a bit better than the First Secretary for whom he feels contempt with such good reasons.

was a sign of sublimity, of being special and refined. Liberal welfare capitalism, turned into 'therapeutic society' with a cult of health as a large-scale industry, is a much later development. On the one hand, it was a reaction to the strange and destructive symbiosis of a relatively enhanced life security (which provided time and energies for the average man to bother about sublime types of suffering) and an unmitigated and publicly proclaimed egoism which still dominates the scene. On the other hand, it ensued from the 'cancerously growing' industrial production (working for peacetime consumption and armament alike) which has 'contaminated' nature and man in it. In both cases, the cult of health was centred on objectivations: industry, dominant social patterns of behaviour and the like.

Nothing like this has ever appeared in the generalized bestiarium of 'real socialism'. On the one hand, in this agglomerate of brutal and internally uninhibited egoists, the ideology of egoism was never permitted to make a public appearance. On the other hand, there was not even a short period of relative security in it (except for privileged layers of the post-Stalin intelligentsia in complicity with the ruling group), a security which would have allowed for a cult of neurosis. Life has constantly been too hard on people in this area of the world to cultivate sublime neuroses. And finally, increased productivity has constantly remained a leading principle of this society, a principle of health, vigour and optimism which tolerated no criticism and no competition.

In order to distinguish 'real socialism', which is a neurotic society beyond a seemingly balanced surface, from the hysterical culture of Nazi barbarism and from Western liberal capitalism which is equally neurotic but in a different way, the following features have to be taken into consideration. (It is neurotic because in 'real socialism' everyone is potentially guilty, and potential guilt can be actualized at any time.) The Soviet bestiarium imposes a false ideology of collectivism and cheerful optimism on every citizen which is no longer internalized even by a minority but which has no accepted public competition. This is the major feature distinguishing it from the dominant neurosis and widespread pessimism of the Western world. Superficially, collectivism is a feature in common with Fascist culture and its ideology of race, but the differences in the interpretation of collectivity and the very tangible results of such differences of interpretation as far as the status of individual is concerned (race is ideally a community of individual heroes) makes the two cultures fundamentally different. However, there is one characteristic feature in common in both types of barbarism. Not only do both of them locate the main cause of 'social pathology' in liberal capitalism (both are health-centred), even if they interpret the contaminating effect of this culture in different terms. More fundamentally, both are organicist in this respect, Bolshevism otherwise functionalist–mechanistic as well. Both discover illness in the body. Fascism finds in it the alien body (this is why it can and must be destroyed), Bolshevism in the body of 'its own' subject which, therefore, has to be incarcerated and re-educated.

Despite all its horrors, the thirties were obviously still a decade of great hope and expectation for at least a certain type of radical. It was in this spirit that George Lukács said, in reply to the complaints of Johannes Becher, the expressionist poet, himself an organic part of the apparatus but in secret revolt against the barbarism of the period: no new culture of Renaissance could be born out of the ancient and decadent Rome. The Visigoths were needed in order to have Giotto and Masaccio. Now, apart from the aestheticist inhumanity of such a philosophy of history, one statement of fact can be made now: the Visigoths have come, the Giottos and Masaccios have not. Admittedly there was a time-lag of approximately 800 years between Alarich and Giotto with which only 70 years of Soviet history can be compared. But given the rhythm of events in modernity and the total absence of morally or culturally encouraging signs from the depths of oppression, is there any reason still to wait for the arrival of Giottos and Masaccios from the new bestiarium?

Index